RED CROSS
INTERNATIONAL
and the Strategy of Peace

"Our world now, as never before in its history, needs a spirit, an idea, which can hasten the inevitable day when all men lift the cry of *Tutti fratelli!* ("All are brothers!"). As never before, it needs this great human idea on whose behalf, as has been recalled, men have never taken life, but have been inspired to give of themselves, to *save* life."

Justice Emil Sandström
Chairman of the League of
Red Cross Societies (1958)

The headquarters of the International Red Cross, in immediate left foreground, looks down the hill-side to the magnificent mile-long frontage of the United Nations European Office, on the outskirts of Geneva, and across Lac Léman to the perpetual snows of Mont Blanc, Europe's highest peak.

RED CROSS INTERNATIONAL

and the Strategy of Peace

by

JAMES AVERY JOYCE

With over one hundred illustrations

London

HODDER & STOUGHTON

Copyright © 1959 by James Avery Joyce

MADE AND PRINTED IN GREAT BRITAIN FOR
HODDER AND STOUGHTON LIMITED, LONDON
BY C. TINLING AND CO. LIMITED, LIVERPOOL,
LONDON AND PRESCOT

Contents

Illustrations

COMITÉ INTERNATIONAL
DE LA
CROIX-ROUGE

SOCIÉTÉ
DU
CROISSANT-ROUGE TURC
COMITÉ CENTRAL

جمعیت شیر و خورشید سرخ ایران

هیئت مرکزی کل

Introduction

FEW authors want to divulge their secrets so early in a book. That is why some introductions should be printed at the end—to confirm the reader in the conclusions the author hopes the reader will arrive at, rather than to warn him beforehand what to expect.

This confession must be made at once because, in this case, the author himself made a vital discovery—though he had always suspected it—while working over this hundred years of Red Cross history; a discovery he feels he must, right from the start, share with his reader.

Outwardly, these few chapters trace, step by step, the development of a tremendously worth-while experiment in humanitarian co-operation. To most people, "Red Cross" means numerous committees and conferences, rules and regulations, badges and blood-banks, canteens and covered wagons, nurses and stretcher-bearers, and thousands upon thousands of dedicated field-workers, spread across the five continents. A more real-life adventure of global altruism could hardly be imagined. And it is a drama which has been discussed, depicted, and described, in one form or another, many, many times.

But that is by no means all. If it were, another book about the Red Cross would not be so urgently needed.

Inwardly, this book is about an idea—an entirely revolutionary idea which has been growing stronger and stronger, always profoundly disturbing to the contemporary conscience; an idea which, today, just one hundred years after Henri Dunant set it afloat, has swung back in a full circle to its starting point and suddenly confronts the human race with the greatest challenge of all time.

It is *this* aspect of the Red Cross which has been almost completely ignored, in spite of the immense literature which the movement has given rise to—until the Space Age has burst upon us and caught us unprepared to live in it.

The first chapter, beginning with Dunant's own conception of the Red Cross, in 1859, should also, like this introduction, be read last. For it is only today, with space-ships opening a new heaven above Man's head and atomic weapons opening a new hell beneath his feet, that the inner meaning of Dunant's original approach to the Red Cross idea has become plain for everyone on earth to see.

In the minds of the vast majority of the millions of the earth's ordinary citizens who vaguely "know" about the Red Cross and who admire it for the wonderful things it has done for all humanity, the Red Cross exists, first and foremost—to put it quite bluntly—to make warfare more bearable, more acceptable, more "humane".

Of course, everybody knows, too, that the magnificent record of the Red Cross in peacetime to relieve human suffering—a record which will not be under-estimated in these pages—has fully equalled its wartime performance. Yet, when all is said and done, it is war, the brutal, ugly fact of *war*, which has given the Red Cross its status, its *raison d'être*, its frame of reference.

But Dunant never saw things that way. That is why this book, centred on the discovery—or re-discovery—of what Dunant himself was really after, differs from so much that has been said and written—some of it beautifully and movingly—about the Red Cross.

It was once remarked of another of Geneva's great citizens, Jean-Jacques Rousseau, that he made his private ideals a world programme. It can now be asserted of Henri Dunant that, unless his private ideals *become* a world programme—and that pretty soon—there will be no world left.

It may, indeed, come as a sharp surprise to many people to learn that the founder of the Red Cross himself never regarded his chief mission in life as one of mitigating the horrors of war, of lessening its suffering, or of limiting its evil. But the uncomfortable truth which can no longer be hidden is that it was not a *palliative* to war that Dunant was seeking, but an *end* to war.

Our first chapter will reveal Dunant in this new light. As Max Huber, for many years Executive President of the International Red Cross Committee and one of its intellectual giants, expressed this primary issue with unmistakable candour, as long ago as 1928, on the occasion of the centenary of Dunant's birth:

Henri Dunant himself saw clearly that the task of the Red Cross would always be a dual one: succour for the victims of war, and repudiation of war itself.

It is that unseverable dichotomy which confronts the whole international organisation at this moment. It has always been there, of course, at the heart of things; but, today, it cannot be by-passed.

"The underlying principle set forth in the Geneva Convention—the sacred principle of the Red Cross, which had its origin on the battlefield of Solferino and later spread to all corners of the world—is diametrically opposed to the very idea of war." These words were spoken far back in 1889 by Mgr. Freppel, the Bishop of Angers, speaking at the Madeleine, Paris, to a distinguished audience of the French Society for the Relief of Wounded Soldiers. "It is quite possible," the learned prelate continued, "that the work which you have undertaken with a view to alleviating the suffering caused by bloodshed will end, if not by preventing warfare, at least by making it more rare. By dint of continually calling the attention of nations to the deplorable consequences of these terrible calamities, you may perhaps succeed in defeating the ends of those who might be bold enough to assume such awful responsibilities before God and mankind. You are starting a pacific movement which sooner or later will win the day," Mgr. Freppel concluded (our italics), "*and the height of your success will without doubt be attained when the world is made to realise that your services are no longer required.*"

★　　★　　★

So much for the beginning. The final chapter of this book, reporting the epoch-making debates which took place at its most recent world conference in 1957, finds the Red Cross, at the end of its Century of Mercy, face to face with just these primary ideals of its founder. Three score governments and over 70 National Societies then met at New Delhi to discuss amending the Red Cross law, and discovered that they were at the focal point of the world's inescapable choice—the abolition of war or the abolition of man.

This fundamental dilemma raises an immediate difficulty for the present book. The Red Cross, by its very nature, is, and must remain, "above politics". If the Red Cross had been the sport of political influences within states, or the instrument of power-politics between

3

states, a story of this kind could never have been written at all. The consistent and unchallenged neutrality of the Red Cross—abundantly illustrated in these pages—has been the guarantee of its integrity, the criterion of its development, and the condition of its survival.

Max Huber himself has been among the first to insist on the "non-involvement" (to use a more recent term) of the Red Cross in international politics—even the politics of war prevention. In an important article on "The Red Cross and the Prevention of War", published at the beginning of the Second World War, this incomparable Swiss jurist openly recognised what he described as the paradox of the Red Cross: "paradox because its original activity, relief work with wounded and sick soldiers in the field, rests upon two contradictory ideas, strangely combined—war, the utter denial of human brotherhood; and charity, which knows no foe."

Nevertheless, it is because of this continuing paradox that the amazing growth of the Red Cross and its untarnished prestige have been due, time and time again, to its direct intervention in "politics". For example, the Red Cross could never have undertaken its inspired work for millions of prisoners-of-war had it not defied contemporary criticism and moved, over half a century ago, from a strictly humanitarian path into the tumultuous political arena. Could anything be more "political" than to challenge what is called "military necessity" —a dogma that has probably cloaked more crimes against humanity than any other?

Thus it is, today. What the New Delhi Conference brought to the surface, in 1957, was the fact that the Red Cross could not ignore or evade the politics of the H-Bomb.

How could it? "*It is no longer possible to believe,*" says Prof. J. Robert Oppenheimer (who helped to make the Bomb), "*that the human race could survive an atomic war.*"

"If the whole 170 million Americans had air-raid shelters," Mr. Val Peterson, U.S. Civil Defence Administrator (1953-57), has stated, "at least 50 per cent of them would die in a surprise enemy attack. In the final analysis, there is no such thing as a nation being prepared for a thermo-nuclear war." Another American defence authority, General Gavin, Chief of U.S. Army Research and Development, has said as bluntly: "Current planning estimates run on the order of several hundred million deaths; that would be either way, depending on which way the wind blew." Such categorical statements can be matched, over and over again, by expert and conservative opinion in every country today.

The Research Development Corporation in the United States issued in the summer of 1958 its dramatic "Report on the Study of Non-Military Defence", which predicted 90 million deaths (over half the population), if there were a nuclear war with Russia at the present stage of "defence", but a scaling down of this hypothetical figure to only 25 million, if the United States were to spend *thirty times* its current civil defence budget over the next decade! Commenting on this macabre fantasy—or is it reality?—the Defence Correspondent of the London *Times* concluded: "The irony of the thermo-nuclear age is that the prospect of being able to save even tens of millions of lives, as suggested in the Report, is not enough to make any difference, because other millions must still perish."

That may possibly be one reason why the world's Press—which lives on disasters and thrives on conflicts—found it so embarrassingly difficult to report either intelligibly or adequately the most significant conference the Red Cross has ever held. The New Delhi draft proposals on the application of Red Cross principles to the conduct of nuclear warfare, have come, therefore, not as the consoling conclusion to a hundred years of triumphant achievement, but as the shattering awakening to a vast new crusade of terrible urgency— perhaps mankind's last.

That was just where Dunant began his campaign. Dunant was far ahead of his generation; far ahead of the generals and politicians, the diplomats and lawyers, to whom he had to sell his great idea. They grasped the shell, but did not notice the kernel. His nineteenth-century contemporaries never understood him; and he died a disappointed and heart-broken man.

That is why Dunant belongs to us—if we can keep up with him.

Said Martin Gumpert, in *Dunant: The Story of the Red Cross* (Oxford University Press, New York, 1938), one of the most refreshing portraits of him ever penned: "For him, Europe's insurmountable boundaries did not exist. Internationalism was his constant goal." Dunant thus recorded his own life-long conviction in his Memoirs: "To inspire in all a horror of the spirit of vengeance, of hatred and destruction, is to force backwards the terrible scourge of war, and perhaps even make it impossible."

It is only today, therefore, confronted with the imminent reality of atomic extinction, that we can assess Dunant's strongest motivation at its true worth and appraise his lasting place in history—if there is to be any more history.

★   ★   ★

We are still, however, at the beginning of this book.

The main chapters attempt to bring out, not only the development of Red Cross principles and their gradual embodiment in international law, but the astounding range and variety of Red Cross activities on behalf of suffering mankind. It is a story fraught with deep pathos, individual tragedy, and man's incredible inhumanity to man; yet one strangely illumined with the light of noble deeds; a story of the unexpected triumph of mercy over violence, of magnanimity over hatred, of life over death.

Unfortunately, in coming closer to our own times, a narrative of this kind cannot be told frankly and directly without running risks of "taking sides". The very nature of the subject-matter—peace and war—renders a non-committal attitude towards contemporary events difficult, if not impossible. As our later chapters will reveal, even the National Red Cross Societies—and certainly the Governments— have often clashed and divided on these basic issues, in spite of the best endeavours of national leaders of the movement, gener- ally speaking, to keep the International Red Cross "above the battle".

But this book has not been written for or on behalf of any section of this world-wide movement or of any National Society, and definitely not for any Government. It has been written purposely for the sovereign citizen, who, as a sentient human being, is ultimately responsible for the sort of world we live in.

In fact, the author has aimed, however imperfectly, in dealing with strictly Red Cross affairs, to emulate the independence of attitude of the International Red Cross itself in its impartial approach to the bitter controversies and violent conflicts of our own times—of which the Cold War is the most glaring, but by no means the only example. Furthermore, in a Postscript, he has gone right outside Red Cross domestic affairs, as such, and endeavoured to show how, in the present context, this great humanitarian force, with its *hundred-and-a-quarter*

6

million members, might enter its second century as the most powerful agency for peace mankind has ever known.

★   ★   ★

After an adult lifetime of writing and lecturing on international affairs across three Continents, the present writer has few illusions that even his most studied efforts to hold the balance straight on any given issue of Red Cross policy will escape criticism from this quarter or the other. Nor does he imagine that his personal diagnosis of the war problem, which forms the continuing background of these chapters, and his consequent interpretation of a new strategy of peace, will meet with the approval of everyone who reads these pages. But, at least, the controversial sections of the book—and there are doubtless many—arise directly from the subject-matter, and the author cannot be blamed for that. He feels that he owes it to his readers to share with them the courage of his convictions in answering their tacit question: "If not *this*, then *what*?"

Yet he also owes it to his readers to explain a little more specifically how he has tried to give fairly the Red Cross angle on a number of disputed current issues. Two or three recent examples must suffice, for the moment. The "inside story" of the Red Cross difficulties in Korea, touched on in Chapter VIII, requires a ruthless exposure of Russian tactics in attempting to block the world organisation from making an on-the-spot investigation into their own "germ warfare" allegations, as well as of American intransigence in prolonging this ill-conceived and inconclusive struggle. But, when we come to consider the indiscriminate character of nuclear weapons, in Chapter IX, it is Russia's turn enthusiastically to welcome Red Cross initiative, and we find the West having a sudden attack of cold feet. Again, during the Hungarian revolt, we notice that the Red Cross was the *only* international rescue organisation to get through the closed frontiers in 1956 and perform miracles in saving the lives of the rebels; but, in one Hungarian town, the Red Cross Delegate (a Swiss) stood out against the execution of a number of members of the political police by the insurgents; facing a group of angry, bitter young men, he declared that, under the terms of the Geneva Convention, members of the enemy forces captured with arms in their hands *could not be shot without legal trial and sentence*. Furthermore, in following the activities of the Red Cross in Algeria, it is the duty of an independent writer as faithfully as he can to set out, against each other, the deplorable record of the French army's atrocities, on the one side, and the equally shocking record of the rebels, on the other side.

The Red Cross can never shut its eyes to the facts. Nor shall we in this book.

Dunant's later memoirs are studded with translucent gems of insight, culled from a lifetime spent in the company of poets and philosophers, which must have shone like stars in the darkness and loneliness of his long, self-imposed exile. One such passage, which he more than once quoted from the writings of his compatriot and contemporary, the gentle Frederic Amiel, has a fitting place in this Introduction:

> The number of individuals who have a longing to see the Truth is extraordinarily small. What dominates men is fear of Truth, at least of the Truth that is contrary to their purpose.

It would have been a superhuman task to include in this hundred-year outline even a fraction of so variegated a record of universal action. The main problem has been, not what to put in, but what to leave out. These brief chapters must be taken, then, as tiny samples of this measureless store of global achievement. Not one of the thousands of Red Cross personnel all over the world, but could relate—from individual and memorable experience—deeply touching instances of what the Red Cross has done, in war or peace, to succour and save men and women and children of all races, colours, and creeds.

Moreover, it is the *international* Red Cross which forms the focal point of these pages; and this general term has been somewhat loosely employed throughout the book to distinguish International Red Cross activities, over and above those of the 80 or more National Societies.

Even as these words were being written, a Swiss acquaintance re-marked to the writer: "How well I remember my Red Cross days here during the worst period of the war, while the German bombers and yours were nightly droning over our Alps, passing and repassing on their horrible missions—how we finally managed to collect those heavy curling stones from sports clubs all around Geneva so as to have them transported hundreds of miles, over the German frontier, to those home-sick Scottish officers in that P.O.W. camp—though I always suspected that they really asked us for them in fun, not believing for one moment that the Red Cross could rise to the occasion!"

*　　*　　*

Since this book aims to be what publishers term a "popular" account of the Red Cross movement and not a work of scholarship, the author has reduced his source references to a bare minimum. He has resolutely refused to insert, except where normal courtesy requires, those impressive but wearisome footnotes which would measure his great indebtedness to the many writers who have preceded him in this field, and to those acknowledged authorities in many countries who have made the achievements of the Red Cross so widely known by their painstaking research or by the skill of their pens.

Mountains of documents—in the five main European languages, and in many others quite unknown to the author—have been surveyed with a growing sense of awe. While, behind all these, further ranges of reports, magazines, and other periodic literature, produced unceasingly by most of the 80-odd national societies, stretch beyond the reach of human vision.

For many years, the writer has come frequently to Geneva, either as student, journalist, or official. Every time he does so he discerns a new snowy peak on the horizon, which he never noticed before. His present marginal comment on the Red Cross can perhaps be likened to one of those characteristic Swiss scenes, showing row after row of distant peaks, glistening over each other's shoulders, and collectively described: "PANORAMA—SEEN FROM GENEVA".

To make up somewhat for this deliberate suppression of source references, a short book-list on Red Cross activities, as such, has been included in the Appendix, containing some suggestions of further reading material usually available either publicly or through one of the international committees or the National Red Cross Societies. In any case, the reader will find that his National Society, or, sometimes, its regional or local branches, will possess library or other local facilities to help him in exploring these questions further. Two or three such books, which the author believes to be the best in their respective fields, are so indicated in the list. To these the reader is recommended to turn in order to supplement the present record, especially concerning the primarily national activities of the American and British

Red Cross Societies, which are dealt with only incidentally in the following chapters.

The material facts, however, on which the present book has been based have been taken almost entirely from the official records available to the author in Geneva. Where his citations or quotations rest on translations from original documents or other foreign sources, as they frequently do, he asks to be excused for sometimes having given a free rather than a strict rendering.

The assistance which the author has received from both the International Red Cross Committee in Geneva and the League of Red Cross Societies should be as obvious as it has been boundless.

The generosity with which busy leaders of the international movement have put advice, documents, photographs, and their valuable time at the disposal of the author is beyond his power to praise. Several of the photographs and other illustrations—which have been so arranged as to make a continuous story in themselves—have been assembled from Red Cross collections in half a dozen different countries, and many of them are published for the first time.

He is specially grateful to Mr. Wilfrid J. Phillips, former Director of General Affairs and now Under-Secretary General of the League of Red Cross Societies, and to Mr. Ralph C. Dudrow, Jnr., its Director of Information, who, in fact, first suggested to the author that he should attempt a book on Red Cross history. But it need hardly be added that these and other officials of the League are in no manner responsible for the treatment which their most valuable suggestions and material have received at the author's hands.

Like other writers who have, from time to time, explored the rich treasures of the University Library at Geneva, which houses the most significant of the early correspondence and manuscripts of the International Red Cross, the present author is all too gratefully aware that its Curator, M. Bernard Gagnebin, has no rival in the study of Red Cross origins. Conversations with Monsieur Gagnebin, while this book was being written, not only confirmed the author in the distinctive interpretation he has given to Dunant's philosophy and career, but convinced him that a truly authoritative work on the life and work of Henri Dunant has yet to be written, and that, here in Geneva, is the one individual who is pre-eminently qualified to write it.

The author has, above all, been greatly honoured by the wise counsel accorded him by several prominent members of the International

Committee of the Red Cross and by the staff—all Swiss—of its Geneva headquarters, who have assisted and encouraged him in many practical ways, but who must obviously remain anonymous, except where he has quoted from their published writings.

It must, finally, be re-emphasised that nobody but the author can be held to be committed in any way whatsoever to any of the statements or opinions expressed herein. Hard facts, extracted from official records, and expert advice, however well-informed, could never, by themselves, produce a book which, like the present one, envisages the history, achievements, and possible future of the International Red Cross within its total world context as an indispensable force in the strategy of peace.

Geneva, Switzerland
1st October, 1958.

CHAPTER ONE

Henri Dunant—The Haunted Man

A S dawn broke on 24th June, 1859, Henri Dunant walked into the heart of the battle for which everyone in Europe was waiting. Pressing on day and night from Switzerland, his homeland, so as not to be late, he travelled by whatever vehicle was to hand. He could hear the cannon thundering in the distance as he came nearer to Solferino, in Northern Italy, where one of the bloodiest battles of the century was just beginning.

Bridges had been blown up, so he waded a stream. On the other side, he found an old wagon, to carry him closer to the battlefield. He had got there in time. Then the full horror of the scene burst upon him. It was crazy, unbelievable—yet it was *real*.

More than 300,000 men faced each other, stretched along a ten-mile front. The Austrians marched in closed ranks, with the eagles of the Imperial House flying over their battle array. Shining in the morning sun, galloping towards them, came the French lancers and cuirassiers and dragoons, with uniforms of all colours. Drums rolling, trumpets sounding, muskets cracking, cannons pounding from the outskirts— what a gallant picture for a children's history book!

White puffs of smoke from the bursting shells, dust-clouds from the tramping feet and kicking hoofs—was this big game of soldiers being put on the stage for the Swiss gentleman's benefit? What was *he* doing there, anyway?

Then thousands of men threw themselves at each other like wild beasts—and mangled each other. The Austrians had been marching all night; they carried no rations and a double dose of rum substituted for breakfast that day. The French had just had time to swallow a few mouthfuls of bad coffee, as day dawned, and they were immediately thrown into the fight. Hunger and thirst drive men mad and these creatures had only one hope of life left—to KILL.

13

"The Battle of Solferino", as seen by a contemporary painter in 1859.

The heat grew as the sun rose higher. Many of them threw their heavy knapsacks away, and even the food they needed so badly. For the two armies were locked together. Horses' hoofs and wheels of gun-carriages crushed those who escaped the bayonets and the bullets.

The dead now lay thick upon the ground. Grenades and bombs completed the human wreckage. Down in the plain, the wind began to stir up a mass of dust which very soon completely covered the roads, while dense clouds of smoke darkened the air and blinded the men. Positions were taken, lost, and retaken many times over. In every direction men were falling in thousands, mutilated, dis-embowelled, riddled with shot or struck down, mortally wounded, by projectiles of every description.

All was chaos, and the blazing sun rose higher. Every farmhouse became a fort; blood flowed down each mound and sandheap. When ammunition ran out, men fought with knives and fists. The Austrians fired from houses and churches, as the French stormed again and again the higher ground—but in vain.

Then, at noon, the summer storm swept down upon them—the worst in living memory. The heavens burst, as though aghast at all this slaughter. Lightning shot through the sudden darkness, thunder crashed above the shouting and the cannons' roar. By now, villages and woods were burning; wounded and dying men, tattered and crying, lay on smoking heaps. The Last Day of Judgment had arrived. Hell continued to engulf its victims.

As the lifting storm raged across the countryside, fear-struck faces of peasants began to appear from holes and cellars and broken walls. The battle was coming to an end.

Fifteen hours of unspeakable carnage. For *what? Someone* had won. But how many had lost—and lost everything?

Then Dunant, who had travelled all this way with intent to meet personally with the French Emperor, but in fact to watch the clash of the two armies, took a hand. What could *one* man do—amidst such confusion and horror? Very little indeed. But the memory of that terrible sight was to haunt him for the rest of his days.

The casualties in this one-day battle amounted in killed and wounded on both sides to three field-marshals, nine generals, 1,566 officers of all ranks (630 Austrians and 936 on the side of the Allies) and about 40,000 men and non-commissioned officers. But two months later, this appalling list for the three armies engaged was *doubled* by 40,000 more deaths from fever and disease—and neglect.

The causes, the cruelties, and the accomplishments of the Battle of Solferino are now remembered by few. But, for a hundred years,

Henri Dunant at the age of 35.

what this Swiss business-man *did* about it has brought life and hope
to unnumbered millions. Nor does it matter, now, how much of the
fighting he witnessed with his own eyes, or whether (as some accounts
tell) he surveyed the slaughter from his carriage on a distant hill-top.
"I have never claimed that I was a spectator of the battle," said Dunant,
himself, many years later in life, "for such battles can never be *seen*,
but only the din of them *heard*. What I did see were the horrors of
Solferino."

THE MAN IN WHITE

Meantime, Dunant acted at once. His carriage or wagon, with the
peasants helping, was quickly put to use. Groups of soldiers and
peasants, volunteers, began to sort out the dead from the wounded.
Sometimes no one noticed which was in which heap. Graves were
quickly dug, to clear the ground before nightfall. But the wounded
and broken men: what was to happen to them?

Both sides had brought a few doctors with them—but some of these
had been marched off as prisoners. Hospital tents had been set up as the
battle got worse, and some of the wounded had been dragged into
them. But many of these mercy spots had been swept away by the
rush of the battle. Who cared for a hospital tent, anyway? Who
could even recognise it?

The sufferings of the Austrians, whose position seemed to be the
most grievous, prompted Dunant to ask in his account of the battle:
"Though the army, in its retreat, picked up all the wounded men it
could carry in military wagons and requisitioned carts, how many
unfortunate men were left behind, lying helpless on the naked ground
in their own blood? . . . How many silent tears were shed that
miserable night when all false pride, all human decency even, was
forgotten?"

The little city of Castiglione, near by, was soon jammed with over
6,000 of the badly wounded. Oxcarts and mules were got together,
somehow, to bring in the battered men. Across the valley the little
church and the cloisters, as well as the local barracks, were being filled
by these unhappy survivors. There was only, at best, straw to put
them on. What was to be done with them now? And the rest groaning
outside—thousands of them, helpless, hopeless, dying?

"In some quarters," wrote Dunant later, "there was no water, and
the thirst was so terrible that officers and men alike fell to drinking

from muddy pools whose water was foul and filled with curdled blood." A Tyrolean lying near him kept calling for water, but there was no water to give him. "The next morning," Dunant recalled, "they found him dead, with his mouth full of earth and foam on his lips. His swollen face was green and black, and he had been writhing in fearful convulsions; the nails on his clenched hands were twisted backwards."

Dunant turned from the helpless anguish outside and was immediately in the thick of the brave improvisation amidst the stench and confusion within the little church at Castiglione. He—a foreigner and without official authorisation—began to organise the situation all around him. His white summer suit, now ruffled and bespattered, marked him out as a "gentleman". His commands rang out among the peasants and women, who began to collect together to do what they could. He inspired immediate confidence. Everyone around him worked like fury. Boys fetched buckets and went searching for food and begging bowls of soup from the farmhouses. Women brought sponges, soap, tobacco, linen, sugar and lemons.

In time, civilian doctors were brought in from the country around. Before darkness came, hundreds of men under Dunant's care had been put on straw pallets and arranged in rows within the little church, so

"The Man in White" improvises aid for the wounded, after the battle, assisted by a handful of Italian women. (Scene from the film The Man in White.)

that the few doctors could go along the lines of helpless men by candle-light, doing all they could to relieve their torments.

What moved Dunant so forcibly as he toiled among these helpless men was the fact that the majority of the wounded died in terrible agony through sheer want of attention. In many cases, slight wounds which, if dressed in time, would have healed very quickly, resulted in death from septic infection. Dunant describes the men's wounds as covered with flies: "The tunic, shirt, flesh and blood formed an indescribable mass, alive with vermin. A number of the men shuddered to think they were being devoured by these vermin, which they thought were emerging from their bodies, but which in reality were the result of the fly-infested atmosphere."

For three days and nights Dunant toiled without sleep or rest amidst this nightmare of pain and squalor. He was drenched in blood, the screams of the badly wounded ringing all the time in his ears. Then, exhausted, he dragged himself to his wagon and ordered a local driver to take him to the headquarters of the French army—to ask for immediate aid.

As the broken conveyance jogged over the rough Italian countryside through the night, Dunant had his vision. This was his Damascus road. Dunant knew then what he must do with his life, with his world. He must act—somehow—to stop what he had seen at Solferino from ever happening again. But how, how could he, an almost unknown private citizen, combat so much horror, so much pain, so much loss of life?

We shall witness, in the following chapter, how resolutely he set about answering that question. We shall test, in the chapters that follow, how much depended on that answer, on that vision, on that one man. For the moment, we follow "the man in white" on the first stage of a life-long quest which was to take him to all the capitals of Europe to enlist the services of the great and the powerful in a cause which was to adopt as its creed: *"Above all Nations—is Humanity."*

AN IDEA WHOSE DAY HAD ARRIVED

Dunant's hurried visit to the French Emperor, who was still with his forces in the plains of Lombardy, turned out to be most important because it resulted in the deep personal interest which Napoleon III took in Dunant's plans, leading later to the creation of the Red Cross organisation in France. Thanks to Dunant's plea, the Emperor issued on 1st July, 1859, the following proclamation: "Doctors and surgeons

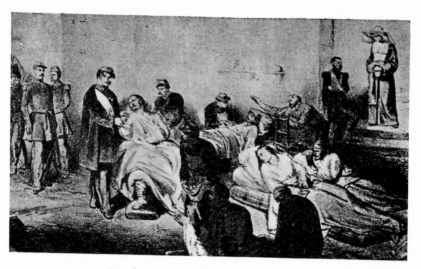

Napoleon III visits the wounded at Solferino.

attached to the Austrian armies and captured while attending to the wounded shall be unconditionally released; those who have been attending to men wounded at the battle of Solferino and lying in the hospital at Castiglione shall, at their request, be permitted to return to Austria."

Thus was taken the first *official* act towards recognising one of the basic principles of the Red Cross—within a week of the battle.

Dunant then returned to Geneva, where he hesitated for some time, as he says, "before deciding to write a brief account of the heart-rending scenes it had been my misfortune to witness". Nor was it his intention "to initiate the public into the terrible trials and cruel suffering" he had seen on the battlefield of Solferino. Nevertheless, he began to write his *Souvenir de Solférino*. During the twelve months he spent on this work, he tells us that he felt he was "under the influence of some all-powerful presence and guided by the hand of God".

A Memory of Solferino was published (in French) in November, 1862. Dunant's chief object in writing it, he maintained, was to promote "the adoption by all civilised nations of an international and sacred principle which would be assured and placed on record by a convention to be concluded between the Governments. This would serve as a safeguard for all official and unofficial persons engaged in nursing war victims." An examination of the specific proposals in

Dunant's book for setting up "in time of peace and quiet *relief societies* for the purpose of having care given to the wounded in wartime by zealous, devoted, and thoroughly qualified volunteers", we must postpone to the next chapter.

The book aroused enormous discussion and concern, though, to begin with, only a small edition was printed. The day following its publication, Victor Hugo wrote to Dunant: "You are arming humanity and serving the cause of freedom. I pay the highest tribute to your noble efforts." Gustave Moynier, the President of the Geneva Public Welfare Society—who was later to play such a vital rôle in the organisation of the Red Cross—stated: "After reading Dunant's *Souvenir de Solférino*, I hastened to call on the author to offer him my congratulations." The French scholar, Saint Marc Girardin, commended the book in the leading European literary review, *Journal des Débats*, as follows: "I hope that this book will be widely read, especially by those who are in favour of warfare, who seek to show its advantages and who speak of it in glowing terms." From all parts of Europe, from the wise and the learned, praise of Dunant's book and moral support for his ideas began to flow in.

Among the letters which Dunant received was one which at once arrested his attention, because it came—indirectly, it is true—from none other than that celebrated Englishwoman, Miss Florence Nightingale. It appears that Florence Nightingale, who was herself then very sick, had been among the first to read his book, and had discussed it with her brother-in-law, Sir Harry Verney. Her letter-writing being at that time confined to urgent official matters, Sir Harry wrote on Miss Nightingale's behalf to a certain Mademoiselle Gasson, a close friend of Dunant's, explaining Miss Nightingale's views.

No doubt this was a tactful and considerate way of conveying to Dunant—to whom, of course, the letter was immediately shown—some of Miss Nightingale's misgivings about his proposal for establishing, in time of peace, voluntary relief societies for operation in time of war. Although the distinguished lady accepted entirely Dunant's horrible description of Solferino as a "faithful picture of reality" and also approved his general purpose in writing the book, she nevertheless saw three main objections to his proposal—at least, from the point of view of her own country. These objections were: firstly, volunteer societies would, in practice, be taking over the job of the Government, which alone was in a position properly to fulfil such a task; secondly, in England, a wartime organisation had already been set up by the military authorities, after much effort and trouble; and, thirdly, an all-round hospital service had been created in England, which appeared to form an adequate basis for wartime expansion.

Dunant was somewhat taken aback by this response, coming from someone whose authority he regarded so highly and whose example he admired so profoundly. But his reaction was swift and forthright. He was much farther along the road than Florence Nightingale—with all her first-hand experience. And he knew it! The British organisation, excellent though it was, had done nothing to prevent the tragedy of Solferino. National organisations alone could never do that. "What I want," he exclaimed, "is a general mobilisation of all the charities of the world! I want an organisation which will be confined neither to England nor to any other country, but which will automatically go into action in every conflict—anywhere."

Never has the purpose and the function of the *international* Red Cross been put more cogently or succinctly—as we shall confirm, again and again, in the following pages. Dunant, the European visionary, had seen a light on the horizon which had been hidden from Miss Nightingale's more pragmatic English mind. Miss Nightingale saw the stricken soldier at her feet; Henri Dunant saw suffering mankind—everywhere.

"*Vision of Florence Nightingale.*"
(*After Sir John Stede.*)

Londres le 4 Sept. /72

Veuillez bien agréer, Monsieur, l'expression de ma très sincère reconnaissance pour l'envoi de la lecture que vous avez donnée à Londres sous la présidence de Lord Elcho. Permettez moi en même temps de vous féliciter de la réussite de votre noble Œuvre — œuvre vraiment de Dieu et de la ...

maladies continuelles dont je suis accablée m'empêchent, Monsieur, bien à regret de faire plus que vous offrir l'expression de ma profonde admiration.

Florence Nightingale.

Monsieur Henry Dunant.

Part of a letter from Florence Nightingale to Henri Dunant.

From that moment, by correspondence and (it would seem) personal visit, Dunant continued to consult with "the Lady of the Lamp", who had lighted so much of the way for his own feet to tread to a more distant goal. "I would first remark," he said in a speech to an English audience, some years later, "that I was inspired with the idea of this work by the admirable devotion rendered by Miss Nightingale to the English army in the Crimea. Her noble spirit, her generous heart, called forth the gratitude of the whole of England; but her lofty mission, from a patriotic point of view, has had results far greater than are generally supposed and surpassing even the imagination of the self-sacrificing heroine herself." It was the "results far greater than are generally supposed" which were the well-spring of Dunant's constant endeavour and which carried him to a higher level of achievement than a "lofty mission" which, as yet, had not translated local patriotism into universal terms.

He then turned, in the same speech, to the subject of the Geneva Convention and made a declaration which, surprising though it may sound to some ears, revealed so much of the man's humility and never-failing courtesy:

> To the many who pay their homage to Miss Nightingale, though a very humble person of a small country, Switzerland, I yet want to add my tribute of praise and admiration. As the founder of the Red Cross and the originator of the diplomatic Convention of

Geneva, I feel emboldened to pay my homage. *To Miss Nightingale I give all the honour of this humane Convention.* It was her work in the Crimea that inspired me to go to Italy during the war of 1859, to share the horrors of war, to relieve the helplessness of the unfortunate victims of the great struggle of June 24, to soothe the physical and moral distress, and the anguish of so many poor men, who had come from all parts of France and Austria to fall victims to their duty, far from their native country, and to water the poetic land of Italy with their blood.

Before we pass on, however, to recount the series of events by which—and so quickly—Dunant's dream took practical shape in the first Geneva Convention, we must try to answer a basic question: What sort of a man was he?

"The activities of the Red Cross have become so familiar to all," wrote a representative of the organisation recently, "that one can hardly realise the revolutionary character of its first efforts, or the courage displayed by those who founded the movement. When we realise that it was proposed to do nothing less than introduce rules of

Florence Nightingale in a Crimean field-hospital. (After a contemporary drawing.)

23

humanity to govern warfare—an activity in which the most un-compromising realism was regarded as essential and the slightest concession to sentiment was construed as weakness—we must admit that, when the Red Cross launched its first efforts, its chances of success seemed extremely remote."

To the character of the man who took that singular initiative, therefore, we must look for some, at least, of the elements of this surprising success.

WHO WAS THIS MAN?

"I gradually came into contact with misfortune and poverty in gloomy and squalid streets," wrote Henri Dunant at the age of 18. "In hovels, which at times were more like stables, I saw men entirely destitute of any worldly belongings and bowed down under a burden of unspeakable suffering, who knew neither love nor kindness. . . . I then realised for the first time that one man alone is powerless to act in the face of such misfortune and that no relief, however small, can be brought to him unless the whole world joins hands in the fight against such dire poverty."

Born in Geneva on 8th May, 1828, Henri came of an ancient and well-to-do Genevese family. Both his father, Jean-Jacques Dunant, a member of the Council of Representatives, and his mother gave much of their time and money to a charitable institution for the care of orphans. Young Henri spent, therefore, the first years of his life in surroundings which inspired him to relieve the sufferings of his fellow men. His favourite subjects of study—languages, literature, ethnography, archaeology, and the history of nations and religions—equipped him to see the world as a whole.

On the threshold of his manhood he came under the influence of three outstanding women who, although active in different spheres, were none the less primarily devoted to the relief of human suffering. The first was Mrs. Beecher Stowe, the author of *Uncle Tom's Cabin*, a book which played so great a part in bringing about the abolition of slavery in the United States. The second was Florence Nightingale, whose devoted service to the wounded during the Crimean War of 1854 Dunant acknowledged so frankly to be the direct inspiration of his life's major achievement—as we have already noted in this chapter. The third was Mrs. Elizabeth Fry, who did so much during the first half of the nineteenth century for prison reform, both in her native country and in Europe. Later on, he was to come into contact with another powerful personality, Mrs. Clara Barton, founder of the American Red Cross—who, also, will have her due place in these pages. Dunant clearly recognised these formative forces in his own life when he wrote: "The influence of women is an essential factor in the welfare of humanity, and it will become more valuable as time proceeds."

As a citizen of Geneva, he came under the influence of Christian doctrine and of Rousseau's social philosophy. He saw clearly the necessity for universal fraternity and the rule of law, if peace were to prevail. He rejected the rôle of military force in international affairs, and regarded war as a primary evil. He condemned, in speech and writing, the folly of erecting barriers between peoples—psychological or political. To him, a "Cold War", deliberately and systematically sustained between civilised nations, would be inconceivable—an intellectual and moral absurdity to be rejected by common sense and Christian ethics alike. He even wrote a book on the subject of slavery in Moslem countries and related it to the race problem in the United States, comparing these more savage modern examples of racialism with the ancient and more "civilised" system of bondage amongst the Hebrews.

He had always been a confirmed pacifist—but a most consistent and practical one. If he appeared to have devoted his chief attention, after his experience at Solferino, to the direct consequences of war, it was because he realised that there was an immediate job to be done, which was nevertheless a positive step towards his more remote ideal of permanent peace. He dealt first with the most urgent—the negative —side of his programme. But his programme never rested there; though most writers on Dunant have paid too little heed to the positive side of his programme. He sought, throughout his life, a constructive *alternative* to war.

In 1872, for instance, we find him at Plymouth, England, presenting a plan to the Congress of the National Association for the Promotion of Social Science, for (in his own words) "the creation in a town, to be determined later, of a standing committee for diplomatic mediation, which would hold annual sessions and on which every nation would be officially represented. At the request of nations on the verge of war, this committee could be transformed into a court of arbitration whose duty it would be to prevent such war."

This idea was by no means a new one, but it puts Dunant amongst those who, through the ages, have devoted their lives to advocating peaceful alternatives to war and the establishment of the rule of law among nations. The practice of international arbitration grew slowly but steadily during the latter half of the nineteenth century, *pari passu* with the international Red Cross organisation, and led directly to the First Hague Conference in 1899—which formed a notable landmark in the history of both movements. It is not without significance that the room in Geneva's Town Hall where the First Geneva Convention was actually signed was renamed "The Alabama Room" a few years afterwards, to commemorate the most important act of arbitration between two sovereign states up to that time. To Dunant, the Red Cross was the beginning, and only the beginning, of a world-wide crusade against war. To this important and frequently neglected side of Dunant's life we shall devote the rest of this chapter.

WORLD CITIZEN IN ACTION

This short sketch of Dunant's career is far from being a biography. We are merely attempting to look, by means of a few of his public activities and his writings, into Dunant's own mind and personality in order to discover something of those dynamic forces which moved him to great ends and made his life-work so lasting a contribution to human progress.

The key to his intellectual strength, his unflagging zeal for great causes, and his invincible idealism—often in the face of cynical opposition and shattering disappointment—must be sought in his world outlook. He belonged, intellectually and spiritually, to the broad human future, though he had to struggle against the narrow prejudices and selfish parochialisms of his day. He was a natural world citizen. In *his* world, everybody counted for one. For him, "democracy" did not stop at the frontiers of his own country, but at the ends of the earth. To Dunant, local or national "patriotism" could only be adequately expressed and fulfilled in loyalty to mankind. *Because* he was a Genevese, a Swiss, and a European, he was a member, also, of the human race. To him, a man—wherever he was born or wherever he lived—was not primarily a Frenchman or a German, a Russian or a Chinese, but (as Robert Burns knew so well) "a man for a' that!"

"His approach to every problem was universal," writes a Swiss scholar, "whether it was protection of the sick and wounded or

26

prisoners-of-war, the limitation of maritime warfare, the abolition of slavery, the economic development of the Near East, disarmament, or international arbitration."★

When quite a child, he was horrified at the spectacle of convicts in chains unloading a ship in a Mediterranean port, and he swore to stir up public opinion on their behalf. When he was a little older, he began to visit Geneva's prison, where he later gave lectures on social and religious topics to the prisoners. At the age of 21, he formed a local group of young men interested in religion and social welfare. To Dunant "religion" and "social welfare" were interchangeable terms. In a short time, their "Thursday meetings" became a Young Men's Christian Association.

But why should not this Association become a *world* movement? So he corresponded with similar associations in France, Holland, Germany and America, and then proceeded to tour Europe, forming new groups on the way. In 1855 he sent them all a circular, calling for an international organisation. Religious faith, for Dunant, meant Christianity, not a Church—and Christianity meant universality. Thus, the World Alliance of Y.M.C.A.'s was established. Its headquarters is still in Geneva.

Again, following the immense success of his Geneva Convention (and following, also, the unhappy collapse of the Algerian farming scheme, which he entirely neglected for the greater task) we find him, in 1866, in the company of a former carbonari, developing the idea of an International World Library. This Library was to publish the most important books of every civilisation. It was to be available in every country, so that every town and village could provide every individual with the means of acquiring knowledge of the wider world and of learning to understand better his fellow-citizens on this planet.

Of course, this ambitious project was too much ahead of its time. With national war budgets always on the increase, it never had a chance to acquire the necessary funds. Nations get what they *pay* for. They pay for war; they *get* war—not world understanding and peace. Nevertheless, UNESCO today, with its magnificent façade in the heart of Paris, looking down on many a mouldering monument of

★ The author gratefully acknowledges his debt to an unpublished study made by M. Bernard Gagnebin, Curator of the University of Geneva Library, for some of the following incidents in Dunant's career.

forgotten military splendour, has inscribed Dunant's basic purpose of a World Library in the opening sentence of its constitution: *"Since Wars begin in the minds of men, it is in the minds of men that the Defences of Peace must be constructed."*

One more example of Dunant's universal-mindedness is evident in a little booklet which he wrote, entitled *Rebirth of the Near East.* In it he advocated the formation of a powerful international corporation, with an independent budget, supported by both public and private investments, which would secure land concessions in Palestine from the Sultan (who was always hard up), and sell them again for purposes of organised colonisation. Roads, railways, and bridges were to be constructed; desert lands irrigated; and new towns built. Dunant's forward-looking Middle East "doctrine" had as its underlying purpose the peaceful liberation of the Holy Land and the international economic development of the backward Arab lands, instead of military intervention and economic exploitation from the outside. His plan should be carefully re-read today.

This further dream of Dunant's becomes almost uncanny in its realism when one turns over the pages of the current reports of what are now the United Nations Specialised Agencies, as well as the projects for "SUNFED" (the Special U.N. Fund for Economic Development), and, especially, the ever-growing documentation on the actual achievements of U.N. Technical Assistance programmes in Near Eastern countries. Dunant foresaw—thanks to his many visits across the Mediterranean and his business and personal contacts in Moslem lands—the establishment of an autonomous Arab Federation, stretching across North Africa and the whole Middle East; but one which would live in close harmony with a prosperous and powerful Jewish state.

Enough has been said to demonstrate the practical bent of mind which always accompanied Dunant's faith in Man's expanding future. We now turn—remembering the dual *motif* which ran constantly through his life—to examine at closer quarters his revulsion to war itself.

WAR—THE ENEMY

The strength of his convictions on war was all the more pronounced in view of his unfailing courtesy towards men of the military profession. All through his life, he was the trusted friend and close confidant of generals and marshals and military experts in many countries. Never once do we find him wanting in his regard and respect for the man-at-arms, *as a person*. His life-long collaboration with the leading professional soldiers of Europe was, as everybody knows, the operative basis of his most enduring achievement. His utter devotion to the common soldier—to whose idealism, bravery, and self-sacrifice almost every page of Dunant's great book bears witness—made him the symbol of human fraternity. It was the common soldiers who called him "The Man in White".

Yet he was unequivocally outspoken about the nature and conduct of war, or, as he so tersely summed it up: "Those splendid horrors which men call glory." Reviewing, in painful memory, the terrible aftermath of the Solferino "victory"—which he unhesitatingly termed "a European disaster"—he asks: "Where now is the love of glory, where the martial ardour, which was a thousand times heightened by the proud and melodious accent of military bands and the warlike tones of resounding trumpets—which were but sharpened by the whistling of bullets, the thunder of bombs, and the metallic roaring of rockets and shells bursting and exploding, in those hours when enthusiasm, when the attraction of danger and fierce, thoughtless excitement, put out of men's minds all thoughts of their latter end?"

Nor had he any illusions about the inglorious future of war. In the last paragraph of the famous book from which we have frequently quoted, we read his grim prophecy: *"If the new and frightful weapons of destruction, which are now at the disposal of the nations, seem destined to abridge the duration of future wars, it appears likely, on the other hand, that future battles will only become more and more murderous."*

But he comes nearest to the ugly realities of our own times, when he tells us, in two pregnant passages: "New and terrible methods of destruction are invented daily, with perseverance worthy of a better object, and the inventors of these instruments of destruction are applauded and encouraged in most of the great European states, which are engaged in an armaments race . . ." and, again, "Men have reached the point of killing without hating each other, and the highest glory, the first of all arts, is mutual extermination." All this was written in 1862.

Can any reasonable person doubt where Dunant would stand on the "nuclear" question were he alive today, when (to quote the Rt. Hon. Philip Noel-Baker, former Minister of State and leading British authority on disarmament, in his monumental work, *The Arms Race*) "competition in modern weapons has become a mortal peril to mankind, the horror and urgency of which no language can express"?

In that little church at Castiglione, administering to those broken and dying men, tradition has it that to Dunant's lips came, unconsciously, certain key passages from the writings of the great philosophers which his studious mind had often pondered and which he was later to quote, again and again, in his own writings and speeches. Here are some of them:

'There is greater glory in eliminating war by the words of peace, than in exterminating enemies by arms.' (*Saint Augustine*)

'That destructive fury called war turns into wild beasts men who were born to live as brothers.' (*Voltaire*)

'War is the greatest of earthly crimes. War is the most evil of all human follies and nothing can be more uncivilised than the profession of killing men. It is an apprenticeship for universal homicide; it is the last refuge of barbarism, a crime that nothing can legitimise.' (*Condorcet*)

'If isolated murder is rightly condemned by the world conscience, how much more should we condemn that vast and terrible organisation of homicide which we call war?' (*Frederick Passy*)

"REVERENCE FOR LIFE"

Dunant's uncompromising opposition to war runs through all he says and does. When he speaks of "the moral sense of the importance of human life" as being the spiritual foundation of the Red Cross, we clearly hear the sentiments of Frederick Passy, the Swiss pacifist with whom, years later, he was to share the *first* Nobel Peace Prize: "If life is sacred to every man, it is sacred also to every nation."

Thus, Henri Dunant opened the way for a later Nobel Peace Prizewinner, Albert Schweitzer, whose master principle, "Reverence for Life", directly entails, not the alleviation of war, but the abolition of war. Dunant then, like Schweitzer today, looked on war as neither a political inevitability nor a military necessity, but as a preventable anachronism and man-made catastrophe.

Between them, in point of time, Alfred Nobel, international armaments purveyor and uncrowned dynamite king of the nineteenth century, reaching the end of his earthly life, saw too late the evil

Dr. Albert Schweitzer, theologian, musician, philosopher, missionary-surgeon in French Equatorial Africa, and Nobel Peace Prize winner.

fallacy on which he had built his own career and by which he had gained his blood-soaked millions, and he sought to expiate his error by rewarding and encouraging future Heroes of Peace. So the living Albert Schweitzer, from the world rostrum which Nobel's profits from death had provided, sent around the earth in 1957 an "Appeal to Conscience", carried over the leading national radio-networks (with certain notable exceptions), a clarion call to all mankind to abandon, without conditions, its nuclear weapons, echoing so much that Dunant tried to say—almost exactly one century before—to a generation as obsessed with the "glory" of war as our own generation might seem nowadays to be obsessed with the perverted ethics of "massive retaliation".

To the mind of a Schweitzer, the use of nuclear arms or similar weapons of mass destruction is not, and can never be, a question of strategic expediency, even in a partly-divided world, but a moral transgression against the sacredness of human life, which no military need can justify, no exalted ideology can defend, and no political institution can legalise—as this is a matter for God alone.

The obvious parallel between Dunant, toiling amidst the wounded at Castiglione, and Schweitzer, tending the sick at Lambaréné, though tempting to pursue, would take us beyond the confines of this book. But, in each case, the simplicity of genius gave to Dunant, as it has given to Schweitzer, an insight into the causation of war and the making of a durable peace, which would appear to have escaped those political leaders today whose reiterated protestations of peace—always on their own nation's terms, of course—sound so much alike that hardly anybody believes them any more. When practice is everywhere seen to be the direct opposite of precept, faith in the spoken word vanishes, and the rule of force parades in the tattered shreds of the rule of law.

Perhaps the greatest thing Dunant ever said was the simplest. For it contained everything else. And his *actions* confirmed its truth. He was answering the natural doubt which arose in the minds of some of the courageous Italian peasants who had ventured on that awful night into the reeking charnel-house at Castiglione, to help him as best they could among the bleeding remnants of the battlefield. "But he's an enemy!" exclaimed one of the trembling women, bending over the shattered frame of an Austrian invader—an aggressor and a would-be conqueror. Dunant put his hand for a moment on her shoulder, and, looking into her eyes, said gently: "The enemy—is a man!"

Watching Dunant (to use his own words) "showing the same kindness to all these men whose origins were so different," the phrase soon went round the frightened women: *Tutti fratelli! Tutti fratelli!* "They are all brothers! They are all brothers!" What the politicians and the strategists, the arms manufacturers and the Press magnates, had forgotten, before the battle, the common people had remembered—after the battle. The enemy is a *MAN*.

That was where the Red Cross began. That is where War will end.

CHAPTER TWO

The Heart of Europe

❧

"EVEN in Paris or London," wrote John Ruskin, "it will be noticed if a jewel is made at Geneva."

What is this quality that has made the City of Geneva the heart of Europe? As Geneva will occupy a big place in the Red Cross story, we may as well pause and try to answer that question now.

When Henri Dunant, who had many friends in high places in Paris, was about to go there and launch his campaign, following the remarkable impact which his book had made on intelligent opinion in all parts of Europe, he was persuaded to stay in Geneva awhile and begin his mission there. "But Paris is the centre of the universe," he protested, "and if my project catches on there, that will be a guarantee of its wider success!"

But his friends—the practised advocate, Gustave Moynier, chief among them—prevailed on him to stay. "Don't forget," said Moynier, "it was a Genevese, Jean-Jacques Rousseau, who began the Revolution of 1789!"

So Dunant stayed. Thus, it was in Geneva that the Red Cross had its birth, and it has been ever since from Geneva that the Red Cross has spread its mantle of compassion wider and wider to the far ends of the earth.

Could any world-based movement—fostering the rights, the dignity, the sanctity of the individual—have begun under more promising auspices? Geneva has so long stood—like its surrounding peaks—for so many high achievements of the human spirit that its example has become the touchstone of political historians and social scientists alike.

But in three special ways, Geneva laid a sure foundation for the Red Cross, and has ever since given it an abiding habitation. Here—if anywhere on this earth—was a symbol of Independence, a centre of

Reform, and a guarantee of Neutrality. These basic elements formed, from the start, the very fabric of Dunant's grand design.

Without independence, the Red Cross could never have developed the unique techniques which have given it its strength. The reform of human attitudes towards war—a reform which has still barely begun—has taken the Red Cross into every dark corner of that untamed jungle where men are still occupied in destroying men. And neutrality has been so much the condition of its existence that even a decade of Cold War "diplomacy" has failed to shake its integrity. We do well, therefore, to ponder this intimate link between the City and the Cause, for a feckless world has yet to acknowledge the great debt it owes to Geneva.

No visitor to the City can be unmoved by the ample evidence in its public monuments, in the names of its quays, its squares, its streets, of Geneva's centuries-long tradition of independence. No resident can have failed to observe that, time and time again, the Canton *and Republic* of Geneva asserts this hard-won independence even against the Swiss Federal Government, conduct which few other Cantons would dare to copy. The bitter struggle against the powerful House of Savoy terminated only when the last invading Savoyard was ignominiously thrown down from the famous Wall of the Escalade, on the night of 12th December, 1602, under the unexpected impact of a bowl of Mother Royaume's scalding stew.

Just below the site of the Escalade, looking across the quiet lawns to

The Reformation Monument at Geneva.

34

The headquarters of the International Committee of the Red Cross crowns the hill above the U.N. European headquarters, over the Lake.

the ancient University whose Library today houses the ever-growing archives of the Red Cross, is yet another famous wall. The Reformation Wall, built in 1909, is in every sense monumental—the four towering figures of Calvin, Farel, de Bèze and John Knox reminding the dwarf-like humans who gaze up at them today that Calvin's City has always been an international city and that the reforms to which it has never ceased to give birth have been universal in their scope and effect.

When the League of Nations, in the early twenties of this century, held its first Annual Assemblies in the *Salle de la Réformation*, it continued a tradition which today has made the (almost) mile-long façade of the *Palais des Nations*—the European Office of the United Nations—the headquarters, *par excellence*, of the modern reformer.

From the high windows of the majestic *Palais* on the wooded slopes of Ariana, one looks up the hill-side to the dignified white frontage of the headquarters of the International Committee of the Red Cross, clear-cut against the Jura sky-line. With all Geneva at its feet, this beautiful mansion commands a view over blue lake and snow-capped mountains which can hardly be matched in all Europe.

The Red Cross was almost the first of the world-wide organisations to choose Geneva for their home. Shortly before the war, the over-sized Hotel National—renamed the *Palais Wilson*, after President Woodrow Wilson, architect of the League of Nations—became the combined headquarters of no less than 200 international non-governmental organisations of every kind and variety. Today, it houses the 50-year-old International Bureau of Education, the century-old International Telecommunications Union and (overflowing the Annexe across the road) the more recent Intergovernmental Committee on European Migration, and a dozen other active organs of the expanding world community; new buildings are constantly going up within and around the City to accommodate the scientific and technical, the social and religious organisations which look to Geneva as their natural headquarters—from the ever-spreading installations of "CERN" (Europe's gigantic atomic energy centre) to the more modest offices of the World Brotherhood Movement and the Women's International League for Peace and Freedom.

One mammoth world conference follows on the heels of another. Within the last two or three years, Geneva has brought together, for example, the "Big Four", with their attendant retinue of experts and personnel (when the heads of state met each other for the first time since the war); the Atomic Scientists (when 5,000 delegates and observers came together in 1955 and, again, 7,000 in 1958); the Law of the Sea (when 83 nations gathered for the first time in history to begin to plan the wide oceans in the interests of all); and a succession of less spectacular technical and professional conferences which have covered the major activities and occupations of the human race. Even the monthly list of these periodical gatherings now runs sometimes to over two score.

Around the *Palais des Nations* itself, the permanent organs of the coming World Government already operate, smoothly and efficiently. The summer session of the United Nations Economic and Social Council, which meets every year in Geneva and which brings hundreds of departmental ministers and their specialist staffs together—with its periphery of regional and functional commissions—is fast becoming a World Economic Parliament which no national government can afford to ignore. While the World Health Organisation, the World Meteorological Organisation, the International Labour Organisation (mankind's budding parliament of labour, which reached a record of 900 top governmental, employer, and trade union delegates at its last annual session), and a host of other international executive bodies and voluntary agencies, carry out, *as a matter of course*, the earth's most essential common services—without which modern man would have slipped back long ago to barbarism. The bare recording of their titles and functions would fill many pages of this book.

Much has been written in the Press, in recent times, about what is called "The Spirit of Geneva". But, usually, the newspaper reader is left in total ignorance as to what this spirit really is—except, perhaps, as representing the temporary effervescence of the latest cross-currents in the turgid stream of power-politics, which is the major concern of the editorial mind. How much does the average victim of the screeching headlines, tormented by the alarms and excursions which are his daily portion, really know about the positive works of peace, the constructive tasks of humanity, which quietly proceed, all the year round, from a thousand growing-points of world co-operation in this City of Reform?

The World Health Organisation—so closely related to the Red Cross—has placed the following striking definition in the forefront of its Constitution: *"Health is a state of complete physical, mental and social well-being, and not merely the absence of disease."* If today's peace-loving statesmen were to substitute "peace" for "health" and "war" for "disease", they would arrive nearer a solution of the war problem than all the "defence" experts have managed to bring them, up to the present precarious breathing spell.

This is the fundamental and revolutionary reform which Geneva, by its example, is trying to teach the whole world today. "The Spirit of Geneva" surely means that humanity's protection against war lies, not in piling up bigger and more terrible disease germs, but in building up the "complete physical, mental, and social well-being" of the world community. Geneva has done more to practise this life-giving truth than any other city on this planet.

Finally, the very name "Geneva Convention" has become synony-mous with neutrality. But Swiss "perpetual" neutrality, which has been directly associated with a hundred years of Red Cross activity, has given more to mankind than a legal doctrine. We shall have to return to this vital principle after examining the nature of the Geneva Conventions in the next chapter. For the moment, then, we need only remind our-selves that, through two devastating World Wars, tens of thousands of Red Cross administrators, organisers, and personnel working in Geneva—the big majority of them Swiss by nationality—held unfalter-ingly in their hands the reins of sanity in a world of belligerent nations

37

bent on mutual destruction. We go on, therefore, to ask the question: What would it have been like for the numberless millions in all lands, whose fears and sufferings, whose loneliness and deprivation, the Red Cross assuaged and alleviated amidst the madness of war—had it not been for the *neutrality* of the Swiss and the *sanctity* of Geneva?

THE FIVE WISE MEN

So it was Geneva which, inevitably, became the cradle and home of the Red Cross.

Looking back over those early years, one is astonished by the speed with which the organisation took shape. "The history of international treaties," Max Huber has said, "has no parallel for the rapidity with which the idea of Dunant and his friends became incarnated in the Geneva Convention." Only an outline of that swift progress can be attempted here. Of one thing we can be certain. The delays and frustrations inherent in the political environment and the social fabric of mid-nineteenth-century Paris or London, would have defied the organising genius of even the dynamic Dunant. The far-sighted and astute Moynier was right in counselling Geneva.

Just the instrument Dunant needed was readily to hand in his native city. This was the Geneva Public Welfare Society—with Moynier as President—which immediately placed its services at Dunant's disposal. This Society was composed of old Genevese, belonging to the most cultured families of the town, and it was known as much for its good works as for its learning. On 9th February, 1863, the Society appointed a Committee to examine the question of "attaching a voluntary medical corps to armies in the field". This Committee soon became known as the "Committee of Five". It consisted of General G. H. Dufour, former Commander-in-Chief of the Swiss armed forces, who was elected President; Gustave Moynier, Genevese lawyer; Théodore Maunoir and Louis Appia, both well-known medical doctors; and Henri Dunant himself. On 17th February, the first meeting of the Committee was held. "This programme," explained Dunant, in presenting his plan, "includes the improvement of military hospitals, the universal adoption of new ideas on the treatment of wounded and sick soldiers, and the creation of a museum for the display of life-saving appliances, which would also be of use in civil life."

The immediate objective of his programme, however, was the establishment of voluntary "medical services" in each country for the relief

of the wounded in time of war. At the same time, Dunant foresaw that
the future Red Cross Societies would also be called upon to act in times
of peace. "These Committees," he insisted, "should be permanently
established and their activities inspired by a real spirit of international
charity; they should facilitate the despatch of various forms of relief,
overcome difficulties as regards customs, prevent waste of every description," and much else. In fact, he already had their duties clearly
worked out in detail.

It might be noted, in passing, that Dunant enlarged on this idea of a
permanent organisation in a book he published a year later, when he
stipulated that "Special Relief Committees" should be kept in readiness,
for *any* eventuality that might arise—such as epidemics, fires, floods, and
famines—and should consist of "groups of thoughtful and devoted
persons, as well as trained and organised military corps, capable of
rendering immediate assistance to the victims of such disasters. The
Committees shall prepare and organise rescue work, recruit willing
helpers and centralise the numerous offers of assistance received in such
circumstances, but which through lack of previous organisation are not
always put to the best advantage." Thus, Dunant's own experience,
gained so painfully at Solferino, was now taking the shape of a concrete
scheme for submission to the governments.

*General G. H. Dufour, the first Presi-
dent of the International Committee of
the Red Cross.*

39

The discussions of the "Committee of Five" were fast becoming a matter of public interest. The *Souvenir de Solférino* was translated into the principal European languages and sent to leading personalities in the different countries. The Press everywhere—in Switzerland, England, France and Germany—published long and, generally, favourable articles on Dunant's ideas.

THE FIGHT FOR NEUTRALITY

Meanwhile, Dunant, still believing that political forces in Paris would greatly contribute to the success of his plans, paid a visit to that city and he was received by quite a number of important persons. He next travelled to Berlin, to attend the Berlin Statistical Congress, where one of the questions on the agenda was the examination of "comparative statistics regarding health and death-rates amongst civilians and soldiers".

This may not appear to have been a particularly exciting event, but in Berlin Dunant met a Dr. Basting, who was representing the Dutch Government and who turned out to be a person of energy and zeal similar to his own. These two kindred spirits immediately struck up a friendship and submitted a joint proposal to the Congress for establishing the *neutrality* of army medical services—the very germ of the Red Cross idea. Their proposal was eagerly debated and, in the end, approved by the experienced body of savants and public officials who had come from many countries to the Congress. In the event, the Berlin Congress unanimously voiced the hope that "all Governments would recognise the *neutrality* of the wounded, as well as of military and civil volunteer surgeons and auxiliary medical personnel".

Often, on later occasions, was Dunant to fight strenuously for this cardinal principle of *neutrality*. Moynier would, at first, have nothing of it; but Dunant's zeal finally won the day. The terms "neutral" and "neutrality" appear several times in the first Geneva Convention of the following year as evidence of Dunant's persistence—for the very thought of neutrality was as repugnant to certain minds then as it is today. There seems, indeed, to be a definite emotional flaw in those temperaments, frequently to be found among political leaders, which are only at peace when they are taking sides. The psychological kink which tends to divide the surrounding world perpetually into the "ins" and the "outs", forms the basis of most social conflict, unless held in check by some wider loyalty. It is difficult to convince those who can see things only as either black or white that there is generally a third "side" involved in their mutual antagonisms—the human race. Dunant was more concerned with the human race than with who was going to win any "next" war. He was the first to realise, in modern times, that "neutrality" need not be a negative attitude—the indecision of the physical coward; but a *positive* attitude—the resolve of the morally courageous to preserve at all costs, at least within a limited area, what was once called the Truce of God. If he had lost on this point, it is hardly possible to conceive of any Red Cross movement at all.

For a more fortuitous reason, too, history might have been differently written—on account of what was, literally, an ill-wind—but for Dunant's alacrity at meeting the unexpected. He tells us in his memoirs that, on the day the Congress was to take up their proposal on "neutralisation", Dr. Basting and he took a carriage to go to the meeting. Dr. Basting had translated into German the discourse he had prepared and the learned doctor was to deliver it on his behalf. Dunant continues the account: "We crossed the River Spree in a high wind. The windows of the doors of our droshky were open on both sides. All of a sudden the papers that were to be read at the meeting, and which we had carefully spread out on the opposite seat, were blown right out of the vehicle and began whirling over the bridge we were crossing. We hastily jumped out of the moving carriage and ran after our scattered manuscript, about to fall into the river. Finally, we were lucky enough to reclaim all the precious papers which had been in such danger."

While in Germany, Dunant seized the opportunity of explaining his plans to influential members of the reigning families and to leading politicians. Thus, both in France and Germany he won his first converts outside Switzerland. Yet—as we shall observe later in this chapter— barely a decade had passed before Dunant's scheme, as well as his personal services as mediator, were put to full test in the Franco-Prussian War.

Before he left Geneva, the "Committee of Five" had decided to summon an international conference at Geneva on 26th October, 1863, "for the purpose of putting M. Dunant's suggestions into operation ... and, if necessary, to recommend the appropriate measures for their execution". All European Governments were invited to send representatives. But, without waiting to get the approval of the Geneva Committee, Dunant—still in Berlin—issued a circular of his own setting forth the conclusions of the Berlin Congress endorsing his new proposal on neutrality. In the name of the Committee in Geneva, he actually requested the Governments invited to the Congress to come to an agreement on the neutrality of the personnel of the army medical services and to grant facilities in wartime to relief organisations for conveying supplies to invaded areas.

Dunant was, not unnaturally, severely taken to task for acting without previously consulting his colleagues in Geneva. His precipitate conduct certainly did not ease his relations with Gustave Moynier, who was himself a forceful and independent personality, and who, ten years later, was destined to supersede Dunant as the leading public figure in Red Cross affairs. But Dunant contended, rightly or wrongly, that there was no time to be lost, as the Conference was to meet on 26th October. In his enthusiasm, he never imagined that his colleagues would not appreciate and approve the course he had taken. Thanks to the prestige of his name, however, his audacious act largely contributed to the success of the Conference. (One wonders how many headstrong generals have won great victories by such brash methods; though, in Dunant's case, there were no human casualties left on the battlefield.)

Before returning to Geneva, Dunant paid visits to Vienna and other European cities, where he was everywhere received enthusiastically. He left Vienna with the promise that Austria would be officially represented at the Conference. Regardless of personal expense and unflagging in his energy, he proceeded to Munich, Darmstadt, Stuttgart and Karlsruhe, receiving in each town similar promises—which were all kept. There is a record that Dunant expended nearly 50,000 Swiss francs on these tireless journeys and his innumerable letters—a considerable sum, even in these days, and worth a great deal more then! His enforced retirement from public life after 1867 was not unconnected with this prodigal expenditure of his private means, while he had them.

"But for the personal campaign undertaken and the repeated appeals made other than by the printed circular," he wrote long afterwards, "it is extremely improbable that any official Government representatives would have attended the first Geneva Conference; and it would have failed in its object." Historians of the movement have since confirmed that this was no immodest claim. Dunant *made* the Conference succeed.

THE FIRST GENEVA CONVENTION

The International Conference was held at the Athenaeum in Geneva from 26th to 29th October, 1863. Representatives from seventeen states

The 1863 Conference, which proposed the First Geneva Convention; Dunant, Dufour and Moynier are seated on the dais.

attended, including Great Britain, and voted resolutions recommending the creation in all countries of voluntary committees for the relief of the wounded. As this Conference was an unofficial one, it requested the early convening of a diplomatic congress to settle questions of international law raised by the problem of "neutralising" the wounded.

In accordance with these 1863 resolutions, committees were formed in almost every country in Europe, and the Geneva Committee was transformed into an International Committee, with General Dufour as President, Gustave Moynier as Vice-President, and Henri Dunant as Secretary. Of Gustave Moynier more will be said hereafter, but what of General Dufour, formerly Chief of the Swiss armed forces? To say that he was of the noblest of a noble line of Swiss national leaders would be no exaggeration; but who could measure how much the Red Cross owes to a General who, in the middle of the nineteenth century, with its never-ending succession of ruthless and ferocious wars, could yet issue commands such as the following to his troops?

> Be always moderate in the struggle, do not lower yourselves to excesses which can only embitter a population that we are seeking to win through mildness.... When the enemy is beaten, care for his wounded as if they were ours; show them all the consideration that is owing to misfortune. Disarm the prisoners, but do no harm

to them and do not curse them—let them return to their homes if they promise to discard their uniforms and not to take up arms again. When the enemy is guilty of atrocities, take care that we can be reproached with nothing of that kind. Under no circumstances, reprisals—they only damage our cause. . . . Under your protection I place the women, the children, the old people and the priests. Whoever lays his hand on a harmless person is dishonourable and has soiled his country's flag. The prisoners, and above all, the wounded, deserve your greatest care.

The new Committee wasted little time in sending a questionnaire to all European Governments, asking them whether they would agree (1) to give their support to any Relief Committee set up in their own country; (2) to accept the principle of the neutralisation in wartime of field-hospitals and military hospitals and of army medical personnel; and (3) to adopt a distinctive emblem, such as a white flag bearing a red cross. This last proposal—attributed to General Dufour himself—was a stroke of genius, both in its boldness and its simplicity. What could more graphically speak for this universal mission of salvation, than a cross; or for its impartial operation, than the flag of the permanently neutral Swiss—but with colours reversed?

The purpose of the questionnaire was to prepare the ground for the coming diplomatic Conference. It is perhaps necessary to explain, at this stage, that, although the Red Cross movement has held many scores of international conferences for one purpose or another, it has only been at what are known as "diplomatic" conferences, that is to say conferences of government representatives, that Red Cross *law* can be laid down in the form of Conventions. In order, then, that this first official conference should be a success, it was necessary that the Governments should take the Geneva proposals seriously and that their replies should be forthcoming without delay.

So Henri Dunant again set out on his travels, full of confidence in a method of procedure which had led to success on previous occasions. In Paris he renewed his relations with the Emperor's entourage, and once more aroused the interest of his numerous friends. Napoleon III notified Dunant that "he heartily approved the objects of the Conference" and added that he desired to support the movement by encouraging the creation of the Relief Committee which Dunant was endeavouring to establish in Paris, and readily authorised him to make full use of the declarations he had made in this respect. Furthermore, Napoleon later advised Dunant that, on his next visit to Paris, he would put him in touch with the Minister of Foreign Affairs, with a view to the examination of his proposals regarding the neutrality of field-hospitals, military hospitals, the wounded, and the army medical service.

This was a good start on the diplomatic level. By the following April, Dunant had received assurance from the French Minister of Foreign Affairs that France was prepared to give her support, provided the Swiss Federal Council issued the invitation to the Powers to attend the Congress. It was agreed that Geneva should be the seat of the coming event, and that the United States, Brazil and Mexico should be added to the list of principal European Powers. It is believed, however, that it was chiefly due to a personal letter which Dunant wrote to President Lincoln, that the United States was officially represented—by an observer only—at the International Conference of 1864.

The Conference opened on 8th August, 1864, at the Town Hall, Geneva, and sixteen countries were represented by 26 delegates or observers. Fifteen countries reported they had followed the recommendations of the unofficial Conference held the previous year, and had already set up Relief Committees for wounded combatants in their own countries.

The success of the diplomatic Conference, which produced the First Geneva Convention, undoubtedly owed most to the remarkable ability displayed by Dunant himself in assembling, just one year after the Geneva resolution had been voted, the leading plenipotentiaries of Europe and America. Specialists in organising international conferences will be among the first to admire this extraordinary achievement, carried out in days when travel and communications were so much slower than they are today. Moreover, the sixteen countries who had gathered from every part of the world reached a broad agreement on a scheme of purely humanitarian character almost in the terms initiated by this intrepid citizen of Geneva. M. Bernard Gagnebin, who probably has greater knowledge of the historical facts behind this event than any other living person, has described it as "a miracle due to the energy and will of a man inspired by some superhuman influence".

Like all miracles, the eventual agreement was extremely simple—once it was achieved. It would be difficult to imagine a more direct or business-like document, and much credit must be given to Moynier's

Signature ceremony of the First Geneva Convention in the Alabama Room of Geneva's Town Hall, 22nd August, 1864. (From the painting by Armand Dumaresq.)

brilliant legal mind for its draftsmanship. Its basic provisions were as follows:

First, all establishments and hospitals for the treatment of wounded and sick soldiers and their personnel, must be immune from capture and from acts of destruction.

Secondly, this protection also covers voluntary aid performed by civilians in favour of the wounded.

Thirdly, sick and wounded soldiers must be received and treated without regard to the side on which they have fought.

Fourthly, a heraldic emblem—the red cross on a white field—should be employed for distinguishing hospitals, ambulances, transports of wounded, and the personnel protected under the agreement.

On 22nd August, 1864, the representatives affixed their signatures to this "Convention for the Welfare of Soldiers Wounded in Action". Thus, after only five years, Dunant saw the realisation of the vision which had come to him that lonely night on the road which had led him from the cold despair of Castiglione to the warm heart of Europe—Geneva.

In the year of its signing, the Convention was ratified by Belgium, Denmark, France, Italy, the Netherlands, Sweden, Norway, Spain and Switzerland. By 1867 all the Great Powers had followed suit, with the exception of the United States, which adhered fifteen years later—thanks, largely, to the vigorous campaigning of Clara Barton. Since then, practically all the world's governments have become signatories of either the original Convention or of the several revised Conventions, which will form the subject of the next chapter. Since, however, the First Convention contains the essence of the later ones—and it is also a short and non-technical document—the complete text, together with the list of ratifications, is reproduced as Appendix A of this book.

Being, in the true sense of the term, a *peace* treaty, and not a legalised subterfuge for future war preparations, the Geneva Convention did not share the fate of the thousands of so-called "peace" treaties which have paved mankind's bloody and tear-stained path all down the intervening years. It remains today intact in its usefulness, its integrity, and its

The Red Cross endeavours to alleviate suffering in time of peace: anti-malaria campaign in Italy in 1900.

47

humanity—though vastly improved upon—a model and prototype of what a genuine international treaty should be.

Why should this be? Perhaps Max Huber's characteristic comment on the First Geneva Convention will supply part of the answer. "Sceptics may disparage the noble idea of aiding one's enemy like one's own," he asserted; but "this fundamental principle of the Geneva Convention and the Red Cross sprang from no cold computation of selfish interests, but from the pure humanitarian urge of consciences grown vitally aware that, above the hatred and dissensions of the world, each man remains his brother's keeper."

BAPTISM OF FIRE

No sooner was the Convention signed than it went into action. This is by no means surprising, seeing that Europe—the cradle of the advanced Christian culture which is now called the "West"—hardly enjoyed a single year of peace between 1864 and the outbreak of the First World War in 1914. In fact, most of these interim wars in Europe over-lapped with each other—not to discount the all-too-easily-forgotten "colonial" wars, which extended European civilisation to heathen lands and thus laid the foundation for yet more conflicts in the present century, now that the same lands are attempting to reverse the process. So the

The Franco-Prussian War, 1870-1: wounded Germans and Frenchmen are separated by a narrow street, but united by the Red Cross ambulance service.

Red Cross was always, somewhere, undergoing its baptism of fire.

The reorganised International Committee at once offered its services to lessen the suffering in all the major conflicts and many minor ones and civil disturbances, from the Prussian Wars of 1864, 1866 and 1870, against Denmark, Austria and France, onwards. The first International Agency for Relief of the Wounded was created by the International Committee when the Franco-Prussian War broke out in 1870. It was established at a near-by neutral point, Basle, Switzerland, and it carried out a pioneer relief supply scheme across the frontiers; while in Geneva the exchange of lists of prisoners-of-war and their correspondence began to assume a major part of Red Cross duties.

To complete this bare historical outline, before reverting to Red Cross action during the Franco-Prussian conflict, it should be noted, first, that the Committee organised another International Relief Agency in 1877, on the outbreak of hostilities in the Balkans. Trieste, Italy, was then chosen as the Agency's headquarters, again just beyond the fighting zone. This practice continued in later years.

Then, in 1899, the Boer War broke out and lasted over two years. The International Committee went at once to the assistance of the victims of the conflict, although the British Red Cross movement had been valiantly at work from the beginning of the War. At Lourenço Marques the Committee organised, jointly with the Portuguese Red Cross, an International Agency which not only took care of the prisoners-of-war, but also co-ordinated the relief supplies and the work of the National Red Cross Societies and other bodies who were co-operating.

When, in 1912, war again came to the Balkans, the Committee opened its International Relief Agency in Belgrade, Serbia, with a still more elaborate programme of assistance to all the belligerent countries. Thus, by 1914, the Red Cross had established a broad pattern of wartime relief operations. (We shall go on to examine this method of working in greater detail in relation to the First World War, in Chapter IV.)

It was during the Franco-Prussian War of 1870-71, that Dunant distinguished himself and showed by his personal intervention how flexible was the scope of the first Geneva Convention, if applied by determined men and women to new situations as they arose. For instance, when the Prussian troops were nearing Paris, he suggested to the Empress Eugénie that she should propose to Prussia that certain non-military towns—such as Versailles, Fontainebleau, and St. Cloud

E

—should be neutralised and used for the evacuation and care of the wounded. "Thus they would find themselves sheltered from the storms of combat," Dunant argued.

In September 1870, he was received by the French Minister of Foreign Affairs whom he reminded of the terms of the Geneva Convention, to which both France and Germany were parties. Extracts from the Geneva Convention were thereupon published in the French *Official Gazette*, and white flags, bearing a Red Cross, were put on hospital buildings in Paris. Dunant helped to shape the early course of the French Society for the Relief of the Wounded. All through that terrible winter, the Society distributed dressing kits and parchment identity discs to the soldiers in the fortresses and to the waiting guard around Paris. In December, Dunant himself set up a "Warm Clothing Commission", which was to bring comfort to many needy soldiers.

Always looking ahead, Dunant anticipated the fall of Paris and prepared a plan for the evacuation of women, children, and old persons. He negotiated in person with the Prince of Saxony, and proposed that tents and huts should be set up in the Paris suburbs, between Saint-Denis and Compiègne, for the evacuees, who would subsequently be sent away to safety into the country. That everything did not go according to plan, however, is clear from the records. Like all major

Under the white flag of the Red Cross, Henri Dunant seeks protection for evacuated civilians crossing the Seine during the Franco-Prussian War. (Scene from the film **Man to Men**.)

wars, this one soon got out of hand and finished, for the defeated, in a bloody revolution. One Red Cross historian, Belinda Peacey, in her movingly vivid account, *The True Book About the Red Cross* (Frederick Muller, London, 1958), depicts some of the final scenes in these terms:

> On the evening of May 24th, an ancient prophecy that Paris would be burnt by its citizens was fulfilled. The Seine gleamed and flickered with the reflection of the Hotel de Ville, the Tuileries and other famous buildings set alight with petrol. . . . Dunant was powerless. His efforts to bring about an armistice between the Versaillais and Communards had failed; his appeals on behalf of the hostages were ignored. The Red Cross no longer had any power to restrain the savagery and terror which seized the desperate mob. Anyone was likely to be denounced as a spy and led before the firing squad; more especially a foreigner. Like that of many others, Dunant's only hope if he wished to survive was to take refuge in hiding.

It should be observed, however, that the creation of "neutralised" towns or security-zones, as well as the distribution of identity discs to soldiers, was later to receive international sanction. In fact, all these brilliant innovations of Dunant were ultimately included in the 1929 and 1949 Geneva Conventions. Similarly, Dunant proposed that prisoners-of-war should be guaranteed adequate shelter, food and clothing for the duration of their captivity, that they should be allowed to correspond regularly with their families, and that they should be repatriated as soon as possible. These proposals were discussed at the First Hague Conference in 1899, and were finally recognised in 1929 and later included in the Geneva Conventions.

THE CONQUEST OF VIOLENCE

Let us glance back, for a moment, at Africa. It was during the early years of the present century, when the white empires of Christian Europe—British, French, German, Belgian, Dutch, Spanish, and Portuguese—were still competing so fervently to share the black man's grievous burden, all across the "empty" continent, and while, at the same time, the messengers of the Gospel of Peace were struggling through impenetrable jungles and infected swamps to reach the heathen soul with the Sermon on the Mount, that a certain poor and persecuted "coloured" man passed through his own baptism of fire.

In 1906, Mohandas Karamchand Gandhi, then 37 years old, was a leader of the Indian community in South Africa. Already a redoubtable champion of the Rights of Man, we find him serving as a humble stretcher-bearer and medical orderly with the Indian Ambulance Corps of the Red Cross in what was euphemistically called the Zulu "rebellion". Like Dunant before him, Gandhi, from a deep inward conviction, as well as from actual experience on the battlefield, knew that the Christian warning, "He that takes the sword shall perish by the sword," had to be regarded as a rule of life, which no individual and no nation could evade or, in the end, defy.

By the time the Mahatma was martyred for his beliefs, on 30th January, 1948, he had seen the power of non-violence—first put into operation under his guidance on African soil—not only prise away this Indian keystone from Britain's world-flung empire, but, with the same stone, construct a new kind of bridge of uncommitted, or "neutral", peoples. Within ten years of his death, this neutral area was being recognised by ever more millions of ordinary people as a more sensible force for peace and human freedom than the continual threats flung out at each other by the spokesmen of the two opposed nuclear blocs. The East had unexpectedly come to the rescue of the West, caught in the fission-fusion dilemma of its own precarious balance of terror.

In 1906, M. K. Gandhi, 37 years old, served as a stretcher-bearer with the Indian Ambulance Corps during the Zulu Rebellion. (From a pencil drawing by Lt.-Col. S. M. Basu.)

During the Boer War, 1899-1902, the British Red Cross co-operated closely with the International.

This "new look" in world politics may well startle the newspaper-fed public, but it should come as no surprise to the International Red Cross, following what was said at the New Delhi Conference in 1957. When Gandhi's spiritual heir, Pandit Nehru, welcomed to India's capital city the delegates from 71 National Red Cross Societies—then representing over a million members—and an equal number of governments, he told his guests that the healing of the mind was more important than the cure of the body, that the *prevention* of war came before the mitigation of war's physical suffering, and that this was the chief function of the Red Cross today. Yet this "new approach", as Nehru termed it, was just where—over 50 years ago—Gandhi entered upon his Red Cross duties in Darkest Africa; and where—40 years before that—Dunant launched the Red Cross movement itself in neutral Geneva.

POSTERITY'S REWARD

But what of Dunant himself, as the Red Cross grew in strength and in popular esteem? We have already hinted that, in devoting himself entirely to the realisation of his ideals, Dunant neglected his business

The Red Cross was already in action in Africa during the Ashanti War of 1874.

affairs. In 1867 the financial enterprise which he had earlier established in Algeria, to exploit a concession, collapsed into bankruptcy. Not to associate his personal misfortunes with the movement he had done most to found, he resigned as secretary of the International Committee on 25th August of that year. This sad episode need not further detain us, as it is outside our purpose. "With a heart so easily touched, so easily stirred, one does not become a successful speculator in millions," says Martin Gumpert, in his masterful biography: "Dunant lapsed into the contemptible ranks of those who make plans and have constructive ideas, but who lack the ruthlessness and selfishness to turn them into money."

Dunant then left Geneva, almost penniless, and was forgotten by many—though he occasionally travelled to a European capital to lecture in support of the Red Cross, only to return inauspiciously to his mountain seclusion. "I had learned what poverty meant for others," he wrote, "but now it has overtaken me." Thus it was that, during much of the latter part of his life, the man who had done so much for mankind suffered the neglect and ingratitude of his fellows.

Dunant had retired to the little town of Heiden, on the banks of Lake

Constance. Here he lived, quietly reading and writing for the best part of 23 years, until his existence was brought dramatically to the attention of the world through a challenging article written by a Swiss journalist, George Baumberger, in a Stuttgart newspaper.

"He welcomed me with the most exquisite courtesy," wrote the enterprising journalist. "This man of nearly 70 years is a magnificent figure with a nobly-formed head, expressive features, a rosy, almost transparent complexion, silver hair and beard. His whole appearance has something patriarchal and venerable about it, and yet something that marks him as a man of the world in every line and gesture. His simple brown dressing-gown, from the sleeves of which gleamed snow white cuffs, and his little cap are unable to hide the man's noble origin and the distinction of his bearing."

Now, honours and subscriptions began to flow in from all sides. Henri Dunant was "rediscovered" by a fickle world, to share, a few years later, as we have seen, the first Nobel Peace Prize with his compatriot, Frederick Passy. He at once gave away his share of the Prize money—keeping not a cent for himself. He lived, however, to enjoy the universal renown which was so much overdue, until his death at Heiden on 31st October, 1910, at the age of 82.

When, shortly before his death, he was asked what value he thought

Field units of the Finnish Red Cross in the Russo-Turkish War of 1877 included these horse-drawn ambulances for the transport of the sick and wounded.

Henri Dunant, in 1908, on the occasion of his 80th birthday.

posterity would place on his world-famed Geneva Convention, a light came into his eyes and he replied: "All Europe has united to study the means of putting a curb on the brutalities of war, and to create instead a striving to vie with each other—nations, peoples, and races—in dedication to humanity, whatever their origin, colour, or tongue."

Is this truly the value that posterity has placed upon the work of Dunant? Or has Dunant's real work only just begun?

CHAPTER THREE

What are the "Geneva Conventions"?

꧁꧂

IT is now necessary to come to grips with what is, perhaps, the most difficult, though at the same time the most important part of our subject. We must attempt, at this point, an all-round picture of the *laws* of the International Red Cross—which are often referred to as the "Geneva Conventions", though they include much more.

Later chapters will carry forward to our own days the story of *how* these Conventions have been—or not been—put into practice in war and peace. The purpose of this chapter, therefore, is to outline in the simplest possible terms the often complicated legal requirements which, over many years, have been brought together and, to a large extent, embodied in four distinct, but closely related, Conventions.

The author has stressed elsewhere that there are dangers in over-simplifying legal questions.★ It must be admitted straight away that the *application* of the provisions of the Geneva Conventions is often far from easy and gives rise to many differing interpretations—quite apart from the notorious occasions when governments or individuals deliberately break them. That is always the case with rules of law, which seek to be exact and to foresee and provide for every possible eventuality—but often fall down in the event.

After that warning, we must proceed as best we can. For one reason, these particular Conventions touch very closely the lives and welfare of millions of our fellows, who are by no means lawyers; and they must be constantly applied by tens of thousands of lay persons— politicians and civil servants, commanders of armies and private soldiers in the field, nurses and ambulance drivers, and so on. A non-

★ See J. Avery Joyce: *Justice at Work* (especially Ch. I on "CAN THE LAW BE SIMPLIFIED?") Pan-Books (London), 3rd Edition, 1957.

technical discussion, such as this, should assist towards a clearer understanding of what these important Conventions mean for the ordinary
people of the world, whom they affect most.

Let it also be said that, around these Conventions, there has grown up
a considerable range of handbooks and reference books, issued by the
National Red Cross Societies, and numerous authoritative publications
of the International Committee and similar bodies, as well as weighty
tomes and detailed field instructions issued by War Departments for
use by their armed forces. But, as far as the present writer has been
able to discover, this impressive collection neglects almost entirely
the needs of the average reader looking for a bird's-eye view of the
whole subject; and who cannot be expected to peruse hundreds of pages
of legal language to get it. (The short *Reading List* on pages 258-9
includes one or two explanatory booklets for Red Cross workers which
go some way to remedy this lack.)

One difficulty of trying to trace, step by step, the growth of these
rules is that a great variety of international conferences and committees
have been at work revising the original Ten Articles of 1864. For
example, at many of the meetings of the International Committee,
over the years, its members have put forward one proposal after another
to improve the Conventions; and recurrent diplomatic conferences
have often given an official stamp to these endeavours on behalf of the
Governments. Then, outside the Red Cross movement proper, historic conferences were held at the Hague in 1899 and 1907, dealing with
many aspects of the Laws of War. Some of the most important of
their decisions were incorporated, later, in the Red Cross Conventions.

These developments led up to the 1949 Diplomatic Conference,
which resulted in much of Red Cross law being put under one cover,
as it were—but in four parts. Four separate revised Conventions
emerged on what today is called "world humanitarian law". Hence,
when people speak of the "Geneva Conventions", they refer to these
four international treaties, which came into legal effect on 21st October,
1950, and which now bind practically all the countries of the world.
(*See* Appendix B for brief outline of the four Conventions and list of
the countries ratifying.)

The *First Convention*, for improving the lot of the wounded in armies
in the field, was signed, as we have seen, by twelve Governments in
1864. Within about twenty years it became almost universal by the
accession of practically all the other governments. This original Con-

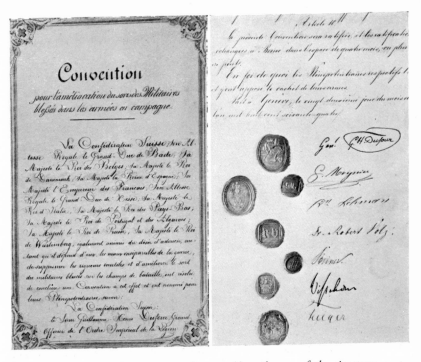

The *"First Geneva Convention"*: preamble and some of the signatures.
English translation of the full text is given in Appendix *"A"* (page 247).

vention was amended and considerably extended in 1906, 1929 and, finally, 1949. It laid down, in short, that wounded or sick combatants must be collected and cared for, that ambulances and military hospitals should be recognised as neutral and, as such, respected by the belligerents as long as they accommodated wounded and sick, and, finally, that hospital and ambulance personnel should be considered as enjoying the same neutral status.

But it will be noticed that this Convention dealt only with *soldiers*. In the course of 85 years of applying it—through two World Wars and countless smaller ones—this Convention was revised in two significant ways: first, it was considerably enlarged, and, secondly, another Convention was added to it, following almost the same lines, but concerned with *sailors*. So we now have two separate Conventions, both dated 1949, dealing with war on land and on sea, respectively, and based on the same principles. From now on we can examine these two Conventions together, before going on to numbers 3 and 4.

One preliminary fact must, however, be noted at once, as it affects Conventions Nos. 3 and 4 as well. The first chapter of each of these Conventions is identical, being repeated word for word in all four. These "General Rules", common to the four Conventions, are extremely important, and we shall look at them first. This is, in essence, what they lay down:

> Once armed conflict between states breaks out, the Conventions shall be applicable *in all circumstances*. In case of civil war or internal strife, certain humanitarian principles must always be observed. The taking of hostages, execution without regular trial, torture, and all cruel and degrading treatment are *prohibited at all times*. Reprisals on persons protected by the Conventions are forbidden. No one can renounce or be forced to renounce the protection accorded him by the Conventions. Finally, protected persons must at all times be able to have resort to a Protecting Power (i.e. the neutral State responsible for safeguarding their interests) and to the International Committee of the Red Cross.

From the above brief summary, let us select for special comment one rule which is of particular interest at the present time. It appears as Article 3 in all the Conventions and concerns "civil war or internal strife".

THE RIGHTS OF REBELS

Article 3 of the Geneva Conventions lays down that, in case of armed rebellion or civil strife within a country, states which are parties to the Convention must treat with humanity persons taking no active part in the actual fighting. This includes combatants who are put out of action through injury or sickness, or who have laid down their arms or are captured. They must be treated exactly as if they were prisoners *of war*. "The wounded and sick shall be collected and cared for," reads the Convention. Nor must there be any discrimination as to race, colour, religion, sex, or otherwise in dealing with captured rebels or civilians; and the following acts against them are always prohibited by international law: violence to life, murder, mutilation, cruelty and torture, the taking of hostages, humiliating or degrading treatment, extra-judicial trials or executions. (The treatment meted out in 1958 to those victims of the "cold war" who were leaders of the Hungarian revolt in 1956 is evidence of the kind of respect which some governments are prepared to accord this Convention; but Hungary, which ratified the Convention in 1954, is by no means the only law-breaker in this respect.)

This Article is perhaps the most striking example of legal evolution. It stretches the old Conventions—going back to 1864, and all of them concerned with war between states—to cover *civil* war, as well as other conflicts which cannot be classed as *international* war. It was not easy, in fact, to draw up provisions which would apply to civil war, without treading on the tender toes of various governments. The idea of extending the Conventions to cover domestic conflicts was at first considered to be legally impossible and quite incompatible with state sovereignty. Much blood had to be shed in another World War and drastic changes made in official thinking about International Law, before this idea could even begin to be accepted by nationalistically-minded Governments. But common sense—and humanity— won in the end.

With so many rebellions now proceeding in different parts of the world—in all of which the Red Cross is bearing an exemplary part— it would seem useful to devote several paragraphs to showing how some of the difficulties were overcome and how "humanitarian law" has gradually prevailed over the law of the jungle.

Early Red Cross ambulance in Schleswig-Holstein (1864).

The Geneva Conventions, it was rightly said, can bind only Governments. Hence, an *illegal* rebel group may never be recognised as a "sovereign" Power by any of the signatory States, so it could not be bound by the Convention. Other critics feared that a Government obliged to apply the Convention to a civil war would find its hands tied in suppressing the rebellion. They also thought that the Conventions would strengthen the position of a group of insurgents, by "legalising" them as belligerents. Then, too, they asked: who has to decide whether a conflict is or is not "international", in the sense understood by the Convention? Should the legal Government itself be judge of the nature of the conflict, or should this decision be left to some international body? Furthermore, where social unrest continues over a period, it is often difficult to say at what moment it becomes "civil war". For the Convention to apply, is it sufficient for a small group of rebels to give itself the title of a rival Government?

These misgivings were obviously not without foundation. It was all the more remarkable, therefore, that the Geneva Conference of 1949 was able to agree upon a text which, without making *all* the provisions of the Geneva Conventions obligatory in civil war, at least imposes on all parties engaged the duty of respecting basic Red Cross principles. Thus, Article 3 has the great merit of saving human lives and of reducing uncertainties on both sides.

On the one hand, the rebel party will be prompted to respect the Geneva Conventions, if only to show that they are *not criminals*, but are fighting as ordinary soldiers in a cause which they believe just. While, as far as the legal Government is concerned, there is no reason why the application of these agreements should constitute an obstacle to the legal suppression of rebellion. Article 3 in no way restricts the right of a Government to prosecute and condemn rebels, in conformity with its domestic laws. But if a Government applies the elementary principles of humanity to its thieves and murderers, giving them food and protection, should it have difficulty in applying to insurgents— even if it considers them common criminals—the same minimum legal safeguards, as provided in the Article? Great care was taken, therefore, in the last paragraph of this Article, to specify that "the application of the preceding provisions shall not affect the legal status of the Parties to the conflict". Thus, insurgents are prevented from benefitting from the fact that they respect the Convention merely to secure recognition as a belligerent Power.

An early American Red Cross ambulance station.

One further point is especially germane to these times of internal upheaval. Such conflicts may eventually take on the dimensions of international war, especially when Big Powers, for reasons of their own power-politics, take it upon themselves to send their armed forces into other people's countries, under one pretext or another, to suppress rebellions they don't like, or under the hoary pretence of "keeping order" for the world at large. The position of the civil population—particularly the sick and wounded, prisoners-of-war and internees—may be left in a precarious state, between the Devil and the Deep Blue Sea. This is partly because the bare "principles" laid down in the Conventions are not sufficiently detailed. So it then becomes essential to make speedy and clear-cut regulations for their treatment and relief. A clause was therefore inserted which states: "An impartial, humanitarian body, such as the International Committee of the Red Cross, may offer its services to the Parties to the conflict." The result is that, since 1949, the Red Cross can act legally within a "mixed" situation, which some people call "war" and others call "rebellion". In any case, it will be more difficult to maintain, in future, as was sometimes done in the part, that any offer of help by the International Committee is an interference in domestic affairs.

Relief for rebels and civilians alike is thus made possible at shorter notice, and, above all, on a more comprehensive scale than was, for example, the case in the Spanish Civil War of 1936. In Chapter VIII, commenting on some of the "limited" wars of recent years, we shall review instances of this new branch of humanitarian law in operation. While, in Chapter IX, on the dire prospect of "unlimited" war, we shall have to deal with the infinitely graver question of the unpredictable effects of nuclear war on civilians. Still to be covered is the treatment meted out to those individuals who, in Geneva, are sometimes referred to as "the prisoners-of-war of the Cold War". Neither the Hague Conventions, governing the laws and usages of warfare between nations, nor the United Nations Declaration of Human Rights, nor the Geneva Conventions, satisfactorily cover these last two fields of conflict. Much remains to be achieved, therefore, in this ever-expanding no-man's-land of "humanitarian law".

SOLDIERS' AND SAILORS' CHARTER

We are now in a position to resume our survey of the main provisions of Conventions 1 and 2. In identical terms they lay down that the wounded and sick of the armed forces and the shipwrecked must be respected and protected, *in all circumstances*. There must be no violence to their persons and they must be aided and cared for. Belligerents must, in fact, treat the wounded, sick, or shipwrecked members of enemy forces taken prisoner as they do their own. The dead must be collected and their bodies protected against robbery. Bodies must be identified before burial and death confirmed, if possible by medical examination.

Medical and religious personnel are likewise to be "protected". Such personnel must wear an armlet with a red cross, and carry an identity card; but they *may bear arms* for their own defence and that of the wounded. If medical and religious personnel fall into enemy hands, they are to be allowed to continue their duties towards the wounded and sick, while personnel whose retention is not indispensable must be repatriated. Those retained are not to be considered as prisoners-of-war and should have wide facilities for their work.

As regards medical units, these cover all buildings or permanent installations (hospitals, stores, etc.) and mobile units (ambulances, field hospitals, tents, open-air installations, etc.) used *exclusively* in collecting and caring for the wounded and the sick. They must not be attacked or damaged, or prevented from operating even if, for the moment, they do not contain either wounded or sick. The same rule applies to medical vehicles, ambulances, lorries and trucks, hospital ships, life-boats, medical aircraft, and so on. Similarly, medical equipment (stretchers, medical and surgical appliances and instruments, medical supplies and dressings) must never be destroyed, but must be left at the disposal of the medical personnel.

Finally, the emblem of the red cross on a white ground, as the symbol of aid to the wounded and sick, must be used to designate buildings, staff, and material entitled to protection. It must not be otherwise employed, but must at all times be "scrupulously respected". In the case of some Middle and Near East countries, the red crescent can be used in place of the red cross, and in Iran (Persia) the red lion and sun can be used. (It is not known, however, at the time of writing, whether the professional planners of the "next" war, who are urging vast public appropriations for establishing nuclear missile bases on the Moon, or on inter-planetary space-stations, have included in their specifications arrangements for ensuring that the enemy's medical units, here on Earth, are "scrupulously respected".)

From among this wide sweep of humanitarian law there are three sets of provisions which, even in a broad picture of this kind, need to be stressed; and, in the chapters which follow (especially in Chapters IV and VI, covering the two World Wars) further sections of these Conventions will be examined in action.

In the first place, the chapter in both Conventions dealing with the wounded and sick has probably proved to be the most valuable of all. In fact, the Conventions may be said to rest upon it, since it contains the essentials of the idea first championed by the founders of the Red Cross: namely, that the person of the soldier (or sailor) who has been wounded or who is sick, and who, in consequence, gives up his arms, or is placed *hors de combat*, is inviolable. He must be tended with the same care, whether he be friend or foe. (Need it be added that the combatant who continues to fight, despite his wounds, is not entitled to this protection?) The 1864 Convention confined itself to stating this principle, in its unadorned simplicity: "The military wounded and sick shall be collected and cared for, to whatever nation they may belong." But the 1949 Convention decided to make the rule more precise in two respects: first, certain ways in which the Powers may not discriminate against the wounded and sick they hold are specified, and, secondly, the present rule enumerates, as examples, a series of particularly grave attacks against the life and person of the wounded.

It was necessary to introduce these stricter prohibitions as a result of the bitter experience of the First World War.

Concerning the status of the wounded and sick, a distinction of vital importance must be made. If an individual not entitled to prisoner-of-war status should commit hostile acts and be captured, he would be considered as a *franc-tireur* and liable to treatment as such. Hence, the Conventions give a good deal of space to defining "status"; but, as this concerns one of the most difficult branches of International Law, we need not pursue it here.

Two new provisions, however, open fresh ground and bring us closer to the theme of this book. They deal with the search for casualties and for the dead, their removal, and the recording and forwarding of information about them. While the 1929 Convention imposed the obligation only "after each encounter", the new paragraph actually begins with the words: "At all times, and particularly after an engagement." This wording was thought to be better adapted to the conditions of modern war, as there are now rarely pitched battles, but an uninterrupted series of engagements, which make the search for the wounded and their removal infinitely more difficult than before. Moreover, a valuable idea was embodied in the 1949 text that the wounded must be given at once the emergency treatment (ligatures, injections, etc.) they may require. Many lives have been saved by such immediate care. This also implies, of course, a greater degree of training and efficiency of front-line personnel in the Medical Services. (By 1949, it should be noted, the full meaning of Hiroshima and Nagasaki—where the last war ended—had not made its impact on Red Cross law; but the "draft rules", to be studied in Chapter IX, are more realistic.)

The Article which opens by stating that the "Parties to the conflict shall record as soon as possible in respect of each wounded, sick, or dead person of the adverse Party falling into their hands, any particulars which may assist in his identification," lays down a procedure which has proved such a blessing to mankind—thanks to the co-ordinating function of the International Committee—that its general purpose need not be described further. What is above all important is that the first information should be sent *at once* to the home Government of the wounded or dead. The rest, which can follow later, when the wounded have joined the other prisoners, comes under such headings as: army or personal serial number, first name or other names, date

67

Burial of British aviator by German sailors at Heligoland in November 1939.

of birth, particulars on identity-card or disc, date and place of capture or death, particulars concerning wounds or illness or cause of death, and so on.

Such information can usually all be obtained without interrogating the wounded or sick, but this is not the case when it is required of other prisoners-of-war. This shows the importance of the identity-card—originating in Dunant's parchment discs during the Franco-Prussian War—especially in case of death, or where the bearer is seriously wounded and unconscious. Incidentally, under this provision the prisoner may refuse, if he is questioned, to supply more than his name, rank, date of birth, and serial number, to avoid giving the Detaining Power any information of military importance. These details must be forwarded by the persons who have collected them to an "Information Bureau" which the belligerent is required to open; the said Bureau sending the data both to the Protecting Power and to the Red Cross Prisoners-of-War Agency, which will, in turn, inform the country concerned.

As regards the dead, a similar procedure is to be followed. Actually, the 1949 clauses codify the practice adopted by several belligerents and by the Central Prisoners-of-War Agency during the Second World War. Everything concerning the deceased must be transmitted to the adverse Party through (1) the Information Bureau, and (2) the Protecting Power or the Central Agency. Then follows a list of the objects which, if found on the dead, should be forwarded with the death certificate, such as one half of the double identity disc, last will or other documents, money, articles of intrinsic or sentimental value, and unidentified articles.

In passing, it should be mentioned that "unidentified articles" are probably more important than at first appears. It often happened during the last war—especially in the case of aircraft—that no trace was left after an explosion except some stray objects, usually of metal, scattered around. Such objects would mean nothing to the enemy, but, if sent to the home country, would often permit identification. Sometimes, even one such object would be the only proof of the total disappearance of an entire aircrew. (Again, it might be doubted whether even this beneficent provision could operate so effectively in future—after a nuclear attack!)

Finally, the dead must have proper burial and—a new notion which does not occur in the earlier Conventions—"if possible, according to the rites of the religion to which they belonged". This is not an obligation, as certain religions prescribe rites that may be impossible to observe, such as the sacrifice of an animal or the use of certain rare ceremonial substances. Another consideration—also introduced in 1949—is that,

---

(Space reserved for the name of the country and military authority issuing this card)

IDENTITY CARD

for members of medical and religious personnel attached to the armed forces

Surname...

First names..

Date of birth ....

Rank ....

Army Number..

The bearer of this card is protected by the Geneva Convention for the Amelioration of the Condition of the Wounded and Sick in Armed Forces in the Field of August 12, 1949, in his capacity as

....

Date of issue   Number of Card

....

69

in addition to being decently maintained and marked, so that they might always be found, the graves should, if possible, be "grouped according to the nationality of the deceased".

NEUTRALITY ON THE BATTLEFIELD

In the second place, those parts of the Convention devoted to the position of medical and Red Cross units and their establishments and vehicles are, at one and the same time, a lawyer's dream—from the point of view of their careful draftsmanship; but also a layman's guide-book—from the point of view of the wide range of first aid and relief activities they envisage in the midst of war.

Fixed establishments (buildings used as hospitals or depots for material) and mobile units (field-hospitals and ambulances, particularly) must belong, in the same way as medical personnel, to the official Medical Service or to the Red Cross Society, and be *exclusively* devoted to the care of the wounded and sick of the forces. There can be no question of claiming protection for military units occasionally detailed for medical duty. The protection to which these fixed establishments and mobile units are entitled shall cease only in one case: if they are used to commit "acts harmful to the enemy". Such harmful acts would, for example, include the use of a hospital as a shelter for able-bodied combatants, as an ammunition dump, or as a military observation post. For it is evident that such establishments and units must observe, with regard to the enemy, the *neutrality* they claim for their own benefit and which the Convention accords to them. They are considered as completely apart from war operations and must refrain conscientiously from any intervention, direct or indirect, in military operations.

This was the point for which Dunant so strenuously fought—and won—in the 1864 Convention.

"Acts harmful to the enemy" have always been a matter of acrimonious war-time debate, and the dividing line has often been a thin one—even in "conventional" warfare. For instance, the actual presence of a medical unit might hinder tactical operations, as might also the illumination it would need by night; and an X-Ray apparatus could disturb the sending or reception of wireless messages from a military post, or the working of a radar unit. And so on. But there is a limit to defining the indefinable.

In conferring protection on "medical personnel", however, Conventions 1 and 2 are on firmer ground. The categories listed include not only medical personnel of the armed forces, but Chaplains attached to the armed forces, duly recognised personnel of National Red Cross Societies and of other Voluntary Aid Societies, and the staff of Relief Societies of neutral countries, who are authorised to assist belligerents. It is gratifying that the Conventions, by granting National Red Cross Societies a recognised status in International Law, have placed them on a firmer foundation than in the past. This is largely due to the reputation they have won all down the years on battlefields throughout the world.

But, although National Red Cross Societies are the chief aids to the official Medical Services, they are not the only ones. A number of other recognised Societies give services of a similar nature, such as the Knights of Malta and the Order of St. John of Jerusalem. The Red Cross does not, therefore, possess a monopoly of voluntary relief to the wounded, thereby refusing in advance all other co-operation. Hence, the 1949 Convention grants the personnel of Red Cross and "other Voluntary Aid Societies" the same legal status as the permanent medical personnel and affords them the same immunities, provided the Red Cross or other Society has been recognised by the Government of its home country. This must not be confused, however, with the recognition conferred by the International Committee itself upon each new Society which becomes a member of the International Red Cross—a topic to which we return in Chapter V.

PROTECTING THE MERCY SHIPS

In the third place, the position given to "hospital ships" (elaborately defined in the Second Convention) is most instructive. Hospital ships are vessels that have been built or equipped solely with a view to assisting the wounded, sick and shipwrecked, and for their care and transport. It is stipulated, moreover, that merchant vessels, which have been transformed into hospital ships, cannot be put to any other use *throughout the duration of hostilities*. These ships are thus absolutely devoted to their special purpose, and, because of this, they can be granted complete immunity without risk of abuse. Such ships and their lifeboats must be respected and protected, whatever their size or displacement. That is Red Cross Law. Hence, a careful procedure is laid down for their registration and notification to the enemy.

Here, again, provision is made for the humanitarian assistance of neutrals at sea. National Red Cross Societies and other recognised

Relief Societies, or even private citizens of *neutral* countries may assist the Medical Services of one of the belligerents by making a hospital ship available, provided the consent of the neutral Government and the belligerent himself is obtained. The idea of extending protection to craft utilised by private individuals was abandoned because, in the absence of adequate control, it would leave the way open to private owners calling their craft "lifeboats", in order to safeguard them in time of war. The utilisation of such craft by the State, however, or by Red Cross Societies would seem to afford the necessary guarantees under the Convention.

One other essential point can be noted before leaving the Second Convention, and that is the marking of hospital ships. The inadequacy of the system of markings adopted for hospital ships under the Hague rules of 1907—before military aviation existed—had long been recognised. Under the outmoded Hague Convention, the outside surfaces of the ship were painted white with a green or red band, and it bore the Red Cross flag. From 1937, however, the experts recommended placing large red crosses on a white ground on the hulls and bridges of hospital ships, and, during the last War, the belligerents did adopt this mode of identification. There is clear evidence, in fact, in the Red Cross records that *the lack of an effective system of marking*, which would identify a ship at long range, was the cause of *most* of the attacks against hospital ships—in spite of the propaganda to the contrary, which is part and parcel of every "war effort" on the civilian front.

So the marking of hospital ships, whether they belong to a State or

Hospital ship with proper markings under the Red Cross rules.

a Relief Society, has been made uniform. All external surfaces of the vessel must be white, and the use of green or red bands is abandoned. One or more crosses, painted dark red, and as large as possible, must be displayed on each side of the hull and on the horizontal surfaces, so as to ensure maximum visibility from air and sea. In addition, hospital ships must continue to fly the white flag with a red cross. At night, too, and in time of reduced visibility, such ships must take measures to render their painting and the distinctive signs apparent.

(It is not known, however, whether this more efficient method of identifying mercy ships was put to scientific proof, and, if so, with what positive results, when a considerable assemblage of "guinea-pig" craft—painted with various chemicals and "manned" by dumb animals dressed in "protective" clothing—were exposed to the effects of the atomic tests in the Pacific; but perhaps the general public is not expected to enquire what becomes of the Red Cross Conventions under such realistic conditions?)

WHY RATIFY?

When the Second World War broke out, neither Russia nor Japan had *ratified* the Prisoners-of-War Convention which existed at that date. This may explain—to some extent—why British and American servicemen, who fell into Japanese hands from 1941-1945, did not get anything like the protection which P.O.W.s in other sectors of the war were accorded. Certainly, the Japanese authorities made it clear that they considered themselves under no obligation to treat their prisoners with humanity, nor did the Germans in regard to the civilian internees in their concentration camps.

This business of ratifying international Conventions becomes more important for every human being on this planet as the years go by. For a Convention is reciprocal, that is to say, a nation gets *from* it what it gives *to* it. But every delay or neglect to legalise a Convention on the part of one nation, especially a powerful nation, weakens the rule of law among all nations. International life, on this interdependent earth, can only proceed on the basis of mutually agreed treaties, of which the Geneva Conventions are an excellent example, as they deal with humanitarian law.

If we are to be realistic, therefore, we cannot, in a survey of this kind, pass over in silence the manner in which modern governments tend to practise, in foreign affairs, standards of conduct totally different from those which their statesmen extol at international conferences. It is, indeed, lamentable how many governments, who pride themselves on their respect for the law within their national frontiers, refuse to ratify solemn international agreements which have been drawn up in the interests of their own people, as much as in the interests of the world community. The "defence of peace" is an empty and dangerous phrase, unless it means strengthening the rule of law in the world—*at all points*—for, in the last resort, world war means the absence or the breakdown of world law.

So alarming is this constant undermining of international order, and so ignorant is public opinion concerning the grosser lapses of its own government—for whom, ultimately, public opinion is, or should be, responsible—that, sometimes, a national catastrophe is needed to bring the defaulting government face to face with its world responsibilities. The same governments who rush blindly into complicated war situations find themselves bogged down with legalistic excuses whenever a scheme of peaceful procedure is proposed in the common interest. Moreover, by trying to "keep our hands free", beforehand, a government encourages international anarchy as much as by breaking its pledged word afterwards. It is the existence of this chronic lawlessness which is the root *cause* of war between sovereign states, whatever may be the local occasions which precipitate wars.

Let us be specific. The United Kingdom had not ratified a single one of the four new Geneva Conventions we are now studying—though great efforts had been made, since 1949, within the country, by public-spirited men and women and, from without the country, by the whole International Red Cross movement, to induce the British Government to do so—until the 1956 Suez Crisis dragged the issue forcibly before the British public. Sons and fathers, brothers and sweethearts were directly affected! Only then did a decisive House of Lords vote—in June 1957—compel the Government to act.

The Chairman of the British Red Cross (Earl Woolton), in that memorable Upper House debate, spoke the simple truth when he declared that national honour had been damaged by this default, and that the Geneva Conventions Bill had been delayed far too long. "We must not fall into the invidious position that we were in, in Korea and Egypt," he said, "when we had to announce that we would abide by the terms of the Conventions, although Parliament had not had time to ratify them." Hence, with the two exceptions of Sudan, a "new"

*In December, 1958, on behalf of the British Red Cross, Lord Woolton (right)
received the Austrian Red Cross Gold Medal of Merit for the Society's work
with Hungarian refugees in Austria.*

nation, and the tiny Dominican Republic, this Great Power becomes the
last (up to the moment this book is written) of the 70 Governments to
ratify these crucial agreements, protecting the lives and fortunes of
people everywhere.

In the very same year, when this belated step forward was taken, the
British Government suddenly announced its intention to limit drastic-
ally the jurisdiction of the International Court of Justice over its
disputes with other nations, thus insisting on its "right" to be judge,
jury, and executioner in its own cause—a step backwards to the Dark
Ages.

This astonishing example, is, unfortunately, typical of what is happening everywhere in the world because of public apathy and national-
istic self-centredness, stimulated by Press campaigns fomenting war
hysteria and vast armament programmes, and encouraged by spiritual
blindness in high places—just the elements which, in a milder form,
confronted Dunant in his day. For "where there is no vision, the people
perish".

Does it matter, to take another instance, whether the Genocide
Convention—closely related to the Red Cross Conventions—is ratified

75

or not? This important Convention marks a big development of "world humanitarian law" and prohibits, as "crimes against humanity", the mass-slaughter of human groups, "in whole or in part". The Convention was enthusiastically signed on behalf of practically all the nations as a basic principle of International Law—it actually affirms this fact in its Preamble—and, following unanimous approval by the United Nations Assembly, it came into effect on 12th January, 1951. It has subsequently been ratified by most of the civilised world—including all the Communist countries—*except* by the United Kingdom and the United States.

When it is realised that enlightened people are desperately seeking to build up a valid international code as the superstructure of a new moral order in the world, it must be admitted that the so-called "West" has a record, since the war, which leaves much to be desired. As a result, the initiative frequently passes over to the Communist countries to appear as defenders of "human rights"! The United States, for instance, has neglected or refused to ratify all but seven—and that many years ago—of the hundred or more International Labour Conventions which mean so much to the social welfare and living standards of the world's labouring masses. Worse still, to the detriment of all champions of freedom and democracy, the United States Government has given notice to the United Nations that, should the Draft Convention on Human Rights be eventually signed by other U.N. members, the United States cannot see its way to *ratify* it.

Professor Quincy Wright, doyen of American lawyers—whose great work, *A Study of War*, should be a handbook in every politician's study—sadly links Russia with the United States when he writes:

> The refusal of Soviet states to accept the Universal Declaration of Human Rights, promulgated by the General Assembly in 1948, and to permit investigations or report on the protection of human rights in their territories, and the refusal of the United States to ratify the Genocide Convention (which the Soviet Government *has* ratified) or to consider the ratification of Human Rights Covenants, are evidences of the waning since 1947 of enthusiasm for the universal protection of human rights.

It is, indeed, serious for the world's peoples when the Big Powers—especially of the West—are reluctant to defend and extend the reign of law. For, then, other nations—weaker, maybe, or less "principled"—

are encouraged to take what remains of the law into their own hands. This irresponsible attitude is the pre-conditioning of war. No amount of military "strength" can substitute for justice between nations; and justice must not only be done, but be seen to be done. To draw up elaborate rules as to how human beings are to be treated in time of war, while refusing to tread the road which all mankind must travel together towards World Law, is hypocritical, if not futile.

WAR'S FORGOTTEN MEN

In taking up, now, the more mundane task of describing the Third Geneva Convention, dealing with Prisoners-of-War, we realise how important are some of the innovations and improvements it introduced, and how essential it was to have ratified it promptly. Professor Leopold Boissier, the distinguished Swiss jurist who is President of the International Committee, had this to say about the Third Convention:

> When reading this Convention, one is struck by the amazing amount of detail it contains. This is because experience has shown that the prisoner, during his captivity, is exposed to all kinds of preventable suffering. That is why the Convention deals with every aspect of a prisoner's life behind the barbed wire, from the day of his capture right up to the day of his release. In these 142 Articles nothing has been forgotten which will enable the prisoners to lead a healthy and decent life.

One of its first Articles lists the categories of persons entitled to the benefit of the Convention. Some of these were not included in the previous Conventions. Particularly important are *partisans*, i.e. members of organised resistance movements in occupied territory. These, for the future, are given the same standing as militias and volunteer corps, and they must fulfil the same conditions. Also included are members of regular armed forces who profess allegiance to a Government not recognised by the Detaining Power. Other categories are specified, such as persons who accompany the armed forces without actually forming part of them. This category is of particular interest to Red Cross workers, as it includes units responsible for the well-being of troops. To be entitled to P.O.W. status, persons who accompany the armed forces should, of course, have obtained authorisation to do so and be supplied with an identity card.

Looking at the Convention as a whole, its terms make certain, once and for all, that a prisoner-of-war is not, by virtue of his captivity, a *criminal*, and so must not be held in close confinement. Nor must the fact of his capture be kept secret, but it should be made known at the earliest possible moment to the outside world, in particular to his next-of-kin and to the Power on which he depends. The rules for ensuring this are elaborate and detailed, and we can comment here on only a few.

It goes almost without saying that prisoners-of-war are entitled, in all circumstances, to humane treatment and to "respect for their persons and their honour". They must all be treated alike; privileged treatment may be accorded only on grounds of health, sex, age, military rank, or professional qualifications. If questioned, P.O.W.s are *bound* to give their name and age, rank and army number, but they may not be compelled to give other information. They are entitled to retain their effects and articles of personal use. The enemy may impound military equipment, except articles of clothing and feeding utensils. Sums of money and valuables must not be taken from them except against receipt, and must be handed back at the time of release. In general, they will be subject to the discipline and military code of the capturing State (called the Detaining Power), and, for security reasons, their liberty may be restricted. Yet they may not be imprisoned unless for breaches of the law, and, before sentence, they must be given the chance to state their case.

The rest of the provisions are, by now, fairly widely known; but a sketch of them may be useful at this point—and, not least, stress laid on the fact that the text of the Convention must be posted up in each P.O.W. camp, so that prisoners may at all times ascertain their rights and duties.

The Detaining Power must supply prisoners-of-war with *adequate* food and clothing, provide them with quarters not inferior to those of its own troops, and give them the medical care their state of health demands. With the exception of officers, P.O.W.s may be obliged to work. But they are to receive pay, working conditions being equal to those of nationals of the Detaining Power. They must not, however, be compelled to do military work, nor work which is dangerous, unhealthy, or degrading.

When taken prisoner, they will be enabled to advise their next-of-kin and the Central Prisoners-of-War Agency (i.e. the International Committee of the Red Cross) and, afterwards, they can correspond regularly with their relatives, receive food parcels and other "relief",

FR. 5298

BOCHUM Westfälisches
Stahlwerk, dépendant de
Senne, (abt. Fisten I)
7e Région. 96 p.g.
dont 36 français.

Biscuits: arrive bien
Correspondance: met 2 mois
pour arriver
Colis: arrive bien
Logement: ds un édifice
près de la fabrique—pas
de modification depuis
dernière visite. pas de
réclamation.

Travail: charg. et déchar
du charbon. 1o heures
par jour.
Salaire: de 1,2o à 1,4omk
Alimentation: insuffisante
pour le travail exigé
Traitement :pas de plainte
spéciales
Santé: service médical
bon.

Impression: bonne

Visité le 14.5.18 sur
préavis en présence e té
moins par Federico G. DELEI
TO Fernando PEREZ

Report from neutral delegates who are sent to prison camps by the Geneva Agency to obtain information on conditions (food, sleeping accommodation, medical supplies, etc.).

and be attended by clergymen of their own religion. Moreover, they are entitled to elect a spokesman or prisoners' representative who acts for them with the authorities of the Detaining Power and with welfare organisations assisting them. They also have the right to address complaints and requests to representatives of the Protecting Power who are authorised—as are the "delegates" of the International Committee of the Red Cross—to visit the camps, and talk with them either directly or through their representatives. Finally, prisoners-of-war who are certified seriously ill or wounded must be repatriated, but must not afterwards take up active military duties; while, at the end of hostilities, all prisoners must be released and repatriated *without delay*. (As the League of Red Cross Societies is considering adopting Russian as one of its "working" languages—a most desirable step, incidentally— it is suggested that this last portion of the Third Convention, which Russia ratified in 1954, should be printed in heavy type.)

That, in outline, is the new P.O.W. Code.

Now, let us select from this many-sided piece of international "legislation"—for a universal Convention, in the absence of a World Parliament, is a good step towards World Law—a few instances which bring out the special responsibilities of the International Red Cross.

IMPROVING HEARTBREAK HOUSE

Much unnecessary anxiety on the part of relatives was due, during the two World Wars, to delays caused in the transmission to their home country of particulars concerning newly-captured P.O.W.s. This might be caused by a sudden influx of prisoners, breakdown of transport, or priority given to national defence. Serious delays might similarly occur in forwarding cards, written by the prisoners themselves, as was the earlier practice. To overcome the above drawbacks, the 1949 Convention provides for additional means of notification— as was actually put into use by the International Committee during the last war. Prisoners will announce their capture to the Central Prisoners-of-War Agency in Geneva by means of a *capture card*. The uniform type and limited contents of this card, and the fact that it is addressed to the Agency, should facilitate rapid transmission and allow the information to be forwarded at once to the families concerned. That is one improvement.

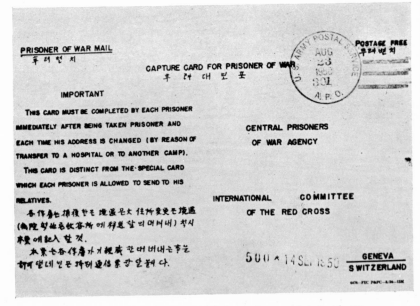

Present-day version of Capture Card. (This card was used during the Korean War bearing Chinese characters.)

Many similar improvements follow in the Convention regarding capture procedure—too numerous to specify here. Prisoners are permitted, under the new rules, to send cards when they are transferred to another camp, i.e., whenever their address is changed. The same applies to men who are ill, whenever there is any significant change in their state of health.

The last war abundantly showed the great importance which prisoners and their relatives attach to a regular postal service. Even the most favourable living conditions do not compensate, in the eyes of the prisoner, for absence of news or slowness in mail delivery. Endeavours were made in drawing up the 1949 Convention, therefore, to find a solution to a number of problems which had occurred in practice, and for which the earlier Conventions had not provided. For example, provisions relating to P.O.W. correspondence have had somehow to get around the nuisance of censorship. Belligerents must perforce censor all written matter which leaves their territory—this is the first limitation imposed on the content of the P.O.W. mail. Yet increase in the number of prisoners, and their anxiety to correspond with next-of-kin, may lead to congestion in the censor's office. So Detaining Powers have been inclined to restrict the number of letters despatched or received. The present Convention therefore allows Detaining Powers to reduce the number of letters and cards despatched individually, but attaches two new conditions: first, the number of communications allowed shall not be *less* than two letters and four cards monthly for each man; secondly, such reductions are permissible only if the Detaining Power "deems it necessary". It would, for instance, be inadmissible for a Great Power, holding a small number of men whose language is no obstacle to censoring, to place any restriction on their correspondence.

One further innovation must be mentioned before leaving the Third Convention. It concerns the organisation of food parcels and other forms of relief. During the last war this work became so extensive that in many countries the Red Cross was asked to co-ordinate and supervise it entirely. Moreover, the blockade and the critical food situation, in most countries, made relief to the prisoners interned in them of decisive importance. Accordingly, after the war, experts who assisted in the revision of the old Prisoners-of-War Convention gave special care to the question of relief, and the new Convention, in large measure, adopted their recommendations.

For example, the old Convention, by making prisoners' rations the same as those for the base troops of the Detaining Power, sometimes led to insufficient feeding, which only outside relief would bring to a normal level. This difficulty now appears to be got over by the wording of a new rule dealing with food: "The basic daily food ration shall be sufficient in quantity, quality, and variety to keep prisoners-of-war in good health and to prevent loss of weight or the development of nutritional deficiencies. Account shall also be taken of the habitual diet of the prisoners."

Another new rule obliges the Detaining Power to supply prisoners with sufficient clothing, underwear, and footwear, making allowance for the climate. And so on. Indeed, the extraordinary situation has been reached, since Dunant's modest efforts of 1864, that the all-round *legal* standards of a prisoner-of-war have been raised, by international agreement, above those of his fellow serviceman who remains uncaptured! (This particular legal point may not, however, be so germane to any future war between the Nuclear Powers, because even what are designated today as "tactical" atomic weapons—approximating to the power of the Hiroshima bomb—are believed to make the normal operation of capture cards, prisoners' mail, food parcels, and other forms of relief extremely precarious over wide areas

Label from a mail-bag transmitting corre-spondence from the crew of the German battleship Dresden, interned in Chile.

of completely devastated and radio-active territory and for considerable periods of time, possibly for years.)

When the Second World War broke out, there was no Red Cross law on behalf of *civilian* war victims, except under the neglected and incomplete Hague "rules of war". People of occupied countries, refugees, and political deportees found themselves subjected to the most arbitrary treatment, culminating in the horrors of the concentration camps, without any effective *legal* rights under International Law. It is true that the International Red Cross had been working on a draft Convention for the Protection of Civilians ever since 1921, but the governments—for the motives we have reiterated—had again and again frustrated the endeavours of the Red Cross pioneers. By 1939, no text had been accepted in time to avoid these terrible happenings taking place as *legally* permissible. Commenting on this lamentable delay, Dr. Jean S. Pictet, Director for General Affairs of the International Committee, states:

> War prevented the adoption of an agreement which would have assured to all civilians, including those in occupied territory, protection equal at least to that enjoyed by prisoners-of-war under the 1929 Convention. There is no need here to dwell on the persecution suffered by so many civilians, the massacres of hostages, mass deportations, death camps. No one would now dare to say that it was wrong to establish finally, in 1949, a Geneva Convention for the protection of civilians.

Now, at last, the Fourth Convention of 1949 gives legal protection to civilians in occupied countries and to persons arbitrarily arrested by the Occupying Power. In short, it adapts to civilians the principles laid down for the protection of military personnel in the other Geneva Conventions. Amongst other things, it prohibits mass deportations, the arbitrary arrest of individuals, and the taking and shooting of hostages.

But let us begin at the beginning and—as with the other three Conventions—consider in bare outline what the 1949 decisions have attempted to do for the "civilian" man or woman or child, in occupied territory, who has today moved into the front line of war victims. Unfortunately, the Convention stops short of giving civilians, in general, protection against the ordinary course of hostilities—hence the insistent need for the new "draft rules" discussed in Chapter IX.

First, a "civilian" is defined as a person who does not belong to the armed forces and takes no part in the actual hostilities. As a consequence of this, civilians may never be attacked. On the contrary, they must be respected, protected, and at all times "humanely treated". Civilian wounded and sick, civilian hospitals and staff, and civilian ambulances must be the object of particular respect and may be placed under protection of the Red Cross emblem.

As regards civilians who are living in the enemy's territory, unless security reasons forbid, they must be allowed to leave. If they do not leave or are detained, they must be treated in the same way as aliens in general. But if security reasons make their internment imperative, they shall have a right to appeal, and to have their cases impartially reviewed. When territory is occupied, the civilian population shall, as far as possible, be enabled to continue as usual. Deportations and transfers of population being, in general, prohibited, every compulsory enlisting of manpower shall be subject to strict regulation. Persons under eighteen years of age are entirely excepted, and enlisted workers may not be forced to do labour which would make them participate in military operations. The Occupying Power shall be especially responsible for the welfare of the children, the maintenance of the medical and health services, and the feeding of the population, and must allow the entry of relief consignments and facilitate their transport. In general, the civil authorities, administration, and public and private institutions should continue to function as normally.

Nevertheless, under the Fourth Convention, the Occupying Power has the right to defend itself against acts hostile to its administration and it may introduce special laws in this connection. And it may try accused persons before its own tribunals, but *no sentence can be pronounced without regular trial*. All such measures, be it noted, are governed by explicit provisions and subject to the supervision of the Protecting Power—which is the "neutral" idea that underpins all these rules.

Civilians in enemy territory and the inhabitants of occupied territories are not only entitled, in all circumstances, to respect for their persons, but for their family rights, religious convictions and practices, and their manners and customs. Women must be especially protected against any attack on their honour, and, in particular, against rape and indecent assault. All civilians have the right of free access to the Protecting Power, the International Committee of the Red Cross and the

National Red Cross of the country where they are, and the representatives of the Protecting Power and of the International Committee should be enabled to visit them freely.

The Convention also envisages the possibility of creating *safety zones* to provide shelter for the wounded, the sick and the children, young mothers and old people. Thanks to these safety zones, entire regions can be spared by war so that those taking no part in the conflict are allowed to survive. (But whether such safety zones can be adapted to the strategy of missile-warfare, conducted from 8,000 or more miles away, is, at present, highly problematical.)

The foregoing summary must, for the time being, mark our concern for the rights of certain civilians in wartime, until we can turn, in our final chapter, to the legally unprotected civilians who would be at the receiving end of tomorrow's "unlimited" warfare.

A passage which concludes a detailed analysis of these four Conventions, published by the International Committee in 1950—on which the foregoing brief survey has been based—provides a clear perspective of the objectives which still lie ahead:

> The Fourth Convention remains faithful to the classic idea of International Law. The individual is subject to law only inside the framework of the State, and the Convention ignores differences which may exist between the State and its nationals. . . . The Universal Declaration of Human Rights is still only a common ideal towards which peoples and nations are striving. The Conventions have gradually taken in the wounded and sick on the field of battle, then the prisoners-of-war, and finally, civilians, to the exclusion of "nationals". It does not seem impossible that they will one day cover the actual citizen, thus realising in law the original and guiding idea of the Red Cross, that suffering should be relieved wherever it may be found, without any political consideration, in the sufficient name of the dignity of the human person.

CHAPTER FOUR

Inter Arma Caritas

"EVEN in the midst of battle, let there be charity!" brought a deeper meaning, during the First World War, to the multitude who were its tragic victims than so vast a concourse of mortal beings had ever known before.

Here is shown a Red Cross Information Card dated 21st September, 1918, which came from a French prisoner-of-war, B—— A——, in a P.O.W. camp at Darmstadt, Germany, answering questions as to the whereabouts of his Captain. Following concise details of date, time and place, the card terminates with the sentence:

"Refused to surrender, he was killed by a revolver shot."

This tiny document, browning with the passing years of man's irrational cruelty to his fellows, is one forgotten item among 90,000 others, collected in 228 volumes, of some 400 pages each, evidence given by prisoners-of-war concerning their missing comrades during the four weary years of the War-to-End-War.

In trying to trace one soldier reported as missing, it was sometimes necessary to question, on the spot, in their scattered prison camps, anywhere from ten to twenty prisoners, before obtaining definite information. In the case of the missing Captain, who was shot out of hand for refusing to surrender at 8 o'clock in the morning of 27th May, 1918, it took five months to elicit the required information and to transmit it to the International Prisoners of War Agency in Geneva, and, from thence, to the stricken parents in Paris.

For some, the answer never came. But for hundreds of thousands of "missing" men and for their sorrowing relatives in every country of the world, the Red Cross, which set up its Agency on the same day that the armies marched, stood for a charity which never forsook them and a light which never left them in darkness.

Aid to prisoners-of-war was the International Committee's chief concern during the 1914-1918 War. The International Prisoners of War Agency was opened in Geneva with an eventual staff of some 1,200 assistants, who wrote out *seven million* Information Cards. Forty-one Red Cross delegates made 524 visits to camps; nearly *two million* parcels and 1,800 wagon-loads of bulk supplies were sent to the camps, and funds amounting to ten million gold francs were forwarded to prisoners and civilian internees. The innumerable services rendered by the many Red Cross and similar relief societies behind their own national fighting forces in all theatres of the war—activities which have since been the subject of an enormous literature—were in addition to, though associated at many points with, the lesser known work of the Geneva organisation, which is the central theme of this chapter.

The most amazing thing is that this immense undertaking and the work on behalf of civilian internees and civilian population as well, were not covered at that time by the provisions of the old Geneva Convention and so had the most slender legal basis in the regulations made by certain Governments under the Laws of War on Land, based on the Hague Convention of 1907. In other words, the humanitarian vision and the prestige of the International Red Cross had already,

Actual Information Card from a prisoner containing a message regarding his Captain, described in the text.

by 1914, become so universally accepted that it could improvise new rules of mercy which were, in the event, able to withstand the savage impact of the first of the global wars, when the "masses" were conscripted and thrown against each other on a scale never before attempted or conceived.

> War, which used to be cruel and magnificent, has now become cruel and squalid. . . . Instead of a small number of well-trained professionals, championing their country's cause with ancient weapons and a beautiful intricacy of archaic manoeuvre, sustained at every moment by the applause of their nation, we now have entire populations, including even women and children, pitted against one another in brutish mutual extermination. . . . War has ceased to be a gentleman's game. To Hell with it!

So wrote Sir Winston Churchill, half a century ago, in one of his first books, *My Early Life*, published about the time that M.K. Gandhi was experimenting with his altogether different technique of passive resistance to human wrong-doing in Darkest Africa.

This almost forgotten opinion, coming from the greatest war leader of our century, is quoted now because it sets forth a master strategist's discovery that the ancient institution of war has fundamentally changed, not merely in degree, but in *kind*. Dunant said much the same thing about the nobility of this legitimised process of killing people, in his own book on Solferino. "From the midst of all this fighting," wrote Dunant, "which went on and on all over the battlefield, arose the oaths and curses of men of all the different nations engaged—men, of whom many had been made into murderers at the age of twenty!"

Yet, even in the confusion of the battle—as Dunant himself was careful to record—charity prevailed, in spite of what men had been made to do to each other in the sacred names of "all the different nations", from which they came. Dunant singles out two such instances —the chaplains and the women. "In the thickest of the fight," he notes, "Napoleon's chaplain, the Abbé Laine, went from one field hospital to the next bringing consolation and sympathy to the dying." And, again, "The canteen women moved about the field under enemy fire like soldiers. They were often wounded themselves as they went among the wounded men, lifting their heads and giving them drink as they cried piteously for water."

The "canteen women"—this was in 1859!

How many a man, now living, looks back at the "canteen women" of 1914-18? Regardless of themselves, of fatigue, of hardship and danger, in a thousand thousand improvised shelters in all the continents, they served, not as warriors, but as *women*. At least 40 million men were torn from their homes and loved ones, during those four endless years, as the tides of battle swept relentlessly across, first, Europe and then gradually engulfed all the Continents, leaving *twelve million* slain or grievously wounded. Yet in no battle sector on land or sea, just back of the immediate fighting, did the ministrations of the Red Cross women desert their menfolk. In canteen huts, in hospital wards, in ambulances and social centres, Dunant's own concern for the rights of the *individual* in wartime—when the individual becomes a cog in a war-machine over which he has no control whatsoever—rested mainly on the shoulders of the women.

It was, in fact, during the First World War that the two trends which have done so much for the building of the National Societies crossed and merged in a united service. The national traditions created by Florence Nightingale in England and by Clara Barton in the United States blended with the centralising functions of the International Committee, and they have never since been separated.

It is not in the least surprising—as we shall consider further in the next chapter—that a League of Red Cross Societies, organically linked with the International Committee of the Red Cross, should have been formed immediately after the conclusion of the war in 1919, for such an organic union had become indispensable, and, indeed, inevitable as a result of the war-time experience.

In the First World War, Red Cross nurses visited the soldiers in the trenches.

A canteen at Bordeaux, France, run by the American Red Cross.

THE BRITISH MOVEMENT BEGINS

In Britain, we might recall briefly in retrospect that Red Cross work, within the terms of the Geneva Convention, had its earliest beginning in 1870, when, as a result of a letter written to *The Times* by Colonel Loyd-Lindsay, the "National Society for the Sick and Wounded in War" was formed and a fund was opened by the Lord Mayor of London. By the end of the Franco-Prussian War in 1871, in which the new society actively participated, at least 200 surgeons, nurses, and other helpers had actual experience in the European field.

By 1877, the English organisation had become known as the "British Red Cross Society" and had established firm links with the budding Societies in other countries. It sent competent workers to assist in the almost uninterrupted series of "little" wars on the Continent of Europe, to which reference has already been made in Chapter II. So impressed was the Geneva Committee with the British record that its Chairman, the indefatigable Gustave Moynier, wrote of the Society's efforts during the Turco-Serbian War: "It would have been difficult for foreigners to do more. We can only admire the generosity, the energy and the administrative ability which the English Red Cross Society displayed on these sad occasions."

In 1899, the South African War broke out, and the Central British Red Cross Committee established a number of hospitals; and doctors, nurses, and medical supplies were sent out. Following the Boer War, the British Red Cross Society was reconstructed in 1905 on its present basis and in 1908 a Royal Charter was granted to the Society, its primary object being "to furnish aid to the sick and wounded in time of war". While, shortly before the First World War, "Voluntary Aid Detachments", consisting of men and women trained in first aid and nursing, were formed in different parts of the country.

When war came to Britain in 1914, the Joint Committee of the British Red Cross Society and Order of St. John was set up and thousands of men and women enrolled for service in hospitals and ambulances, and for the transport of the wounded. Similarly, the Voluntary Aid Detachments served in every sector of the war, acting as the British agency of the International Red Cross. After the war, the British Society was granted a Supplemental Charter which widened the original objects of the Society to include "the improvement of health, the prevention of disease, and the mitigation of suffering throughout the world", thus permitting it to participate fully in the broader aims of the League of Red Cross Societies. Yet, like the American Society, it would not appear to be permitted, under its Charter, to engage in activities specifically concerned with the *prevention* of war and the *promotion* of peace.

British V.A.D. with her motor-ambulance at Étaples, 1917.

The origins of the Red Cross movement in the United States may be said to be earlier than those of the sister society in the British Isles, though, for reasons which we shall review briefly, it did not become organised as a fully-fledged National Society until after the British Red Cross had got well into its stride.

It is worthy of note that, when Dr. Max Huber, then President of the International Committee, spoke at the celebration of the fiftieth anniversary of the foundation of the American Red Cross in Washington on 21st May, 1931, he related certain dates and some interesting facts, which could be better known than they are, perhaps, among Red Cross workers everywhere, carrying us back to the important service with which the present chapter began:

> From 1861 to the end of the War of Secession, a brave woman, Clara Barton, the first President of the American Red Cross, hastened from one encampment, from one battlefield to another, helping the sick and wounded. In 1863 the International Committee was created by five citizens of Geneva, and succeeded in convening a Conference at which the main principles of the Red Cross were laid down. In 1863, too, President Lincoln issued his

Clara Barton, from a portrait by Cornelia Adele Strong Fassett.

historic "Instructions for the Government of Armies of the U.S. in The Field", the forerunner of the work done by the Hague Peace Conferences for the mitigation of the horrors and hardships of war. Finally, in 1866, Clara Barton threw herself into a work which was to become so important during the last Great War, and has remained no less so—namely, the search for missing soldiers.

Worn out with her work for the wounded and missing in the Civil War, Clara Barton went to Switzerland in 1869 to rest; but soon found new avenues for her devotion in the Franco-Prussian War, acting as authorised agent of the International Committee on the continental battlefield. At that date, the United States Government had still not ratified the 1864 Geneva Convention, and it became Clara Barton's great mission to secure America's adhesion to the Convention and the establishment of a Voluntary Aid Society. Clara Barton returned home, but her health did not allow her to begin her campaign until 1877, when she delivered to President Hayes a letter from Gustave Moynier, President of the International Committee. This letter appears to have become buried in the archives of the State Department. But she never relaxed her efforts to convince her own Government of the necessity of ratifying the Geneva Convention, publishing innumerable tracts and articles so as to create public opinion behind the Red Cross idea—until she won, like Dunant before her.

As Dr. Huber has emphasised: "It was certainly no light task for a woman to obtain single-handed this ratification of a treaty concluded seventeen years previously, of no immediate interest to the American Government at that moment, and a matter of all but complete indifference to the public. Yet she never lost hope; even when all her efforts seemed doomed to failure, she persevered in her faith that she would be victorious in the end." At long last, the American Association of the Red Cross was founded, the Convention ratified, and the new Association recognised by the Government on 11th August, 1882, in accordance with the rules laid down by the International Committee—though the American Red Cross Society was not granted federal charter authority by the United States Government until 1900.

From 1905 until the entry of the United States into the First World War in 1917, the leading personality in the American Red Cross was Mrs. Mabel Boardman. It was largely she who secured its new Charter from Congress in 1905, and it was she who was its guiding spirit for

93

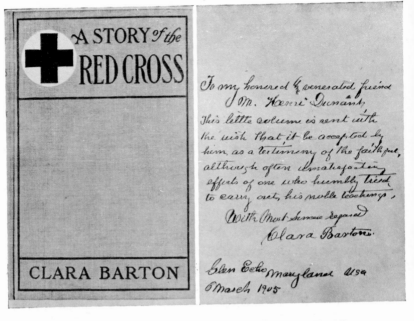

Clara Barton dedicated her book, A Story of the Red Cross, *to Henri Dunant.*

many years. During these formative years the American Society never ceased to enlarge the field of its activities, realising from the first that effectiveness in wartime would be dependent on efficiency in peacetime. Thus, hospital work, instruction of nurses, relief in civic calamities, and the promotion of public health assumed even greater dimensions.

In his fascinating volume, *The American Red Cross* (Harper & Brothers, New York, 1950), Dr. Foster Rhea Dulles has undertaken an almost unique and certainly monumental study of the United States movement as a constructive and evolutionary force in American life, relating its various phases to contemporary political, economic and social developments. Some of the war-time episodes and many human incidents given in this graphic and, at times, heartbreaking account of nearly 70 years of institutional growth, enforce all too plainly the endemic contradiction which has always underlain Red Cross activity from the moment it moves from the national to the international plane —the paradox which tears the human race asunder and yet offers it its only chance of unity:

"War, the utter denial of human brotherhood; and Charity, which knows no foe!"

THE UNFINISHED TASK

Many masterly biographies have been written on and round the lives of both Florence Nightingale and Clara Barton. In certain important ways their careers, like their personal qualities and their ultimate achievements, ran parallel. But in other respects they were as strikingly different as were their surrounding nurtures. Both were fairly rich women; and it might be noticed, in passing, that, but for this primary advantage, neither could have won the place in history which she later attained. In this regard, they were joined by Dunant—who began as a banker, though he died a pauper.

Henri Dunant, like Florence Nightingale, also enjoyed the immense advantage—a *sine qua non* of all humanitarian reforms before the twentieth century—of being able to move freely among the top social strata of Europe and to talk with the accents of aristocracy. But, unlike Switzerland and England, which were much smaller in their size and more settled in their political habits, the United States was, at this time, still pursuing its fast receding frontiers along the new railroad trails. Clara Barton's background therefore called for the simple bravery and tenacity of the kind of woman who could drive by herself an ox-drawn covered wagon over almost virgin territories and across high mountains and swift rivers, rather than for the drawing-room diplomacy of the "Lady of the Lamp" who could, over the afternoon

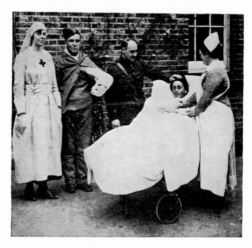

American Red Cross Gray Lady and soldier patients.

95

teacups, amidst the ancestral décor of the Verney family mansion at Claydon, Buckinghamshire, talk persuasively to her Minister-of-War cousin, Sidney Herbert, and his fellow Cabinet Ministers, as well as to the Commanders-in-Chief, as equals or—as was frequently the case —less than equals within the rigid Victorian hierarchy.

Dunant and Nightingale worked downwards, as it were, from the *élite* to the populace. Clara Barton had to cope with a fundamentally different social texture. Starting with the popular vote, she stormed the portals of the White House and of the Capitol from the common street, carried on the shoulders of a mighty mob of convinced citizens, which might have filled Pennsylvania Avenue from end to end, until the official doors were forced open and the United States finally joined the civilised world by agreeing to adopt principles of world humanitarian law which their own representatives had agreed, 17 years earlier in Geneva, were good for the world and, on that account, good enough for the American people. It is as well to bear in mind that governments exist (as was once said) to stop things from being done; and that each generation needs its Clara Barton to see that they *are* done.

The wonderful story of her campaign—told so many times and now known (or ought to be known) by heart by every American adolescent —is as much a reflection of today's "American problem", as many Europeans see it, as it is a success story of the quality of the American pioneer who can—and who will—eventually solve it. Thanks largely to the world view which her training with the Geneva Committee had given her, Clara Barton was among the first of modern Americans to realise that the enshrining of the ideals of formal democracy in a political constitution a century or so earlier was still a long, long way from creating the vigilant social conscience which alone can safeguard individual liberty from the assaults of its enemies and make a nation great in its own eyes, as well as in the estimation of a critical world.

For seventeen years of unrelenting struggle—save when she was too ill to work—as in effect the Ambassador High-Plenipotentiary of the Geneva Committee, who backed her efforts by unceasing appeals to the American State Department to ratify the Convention, Clara Barton preached and wrote, pamphleteered and lobbied, travelled and pulled every available string, until she virtually dragged America into the Red Cross orbit by the tail. In the course of this contest for national righteousness, which has since made the American Red Cross the paragon of twentieth-century philanthropy and voluntary public service, Clara

Barton encountered every delaying tactic of military obstinacy, every subterfuge of political opportunism, and those intangible forces of vested selfishness which parochial-minded Senators can always marshal against practical idealism such as hers—to the continual detriment of the American people.

Yet Clara Barton's place in the modern world, like Dunant's, did not finish with the initial achievements of her heroic life nor with her final success in interweaving the Red Cross pattern of disinterested service into the American dream. As we may have to recognise before the end of this book, what challenges the American belief in the importance of moral values more at this moment than at any time in its history, is *not* the lack of that "profuse liberality of our people", to which Clara Barton appealed in her powerful pioneer pamphlet published in 1878, but the humility (which is ever the mark of true greatness) to accept a rôle in contemporary international society which does not constantly equate *might* with *right*. It is more necessary now than ever for this the most powerful nation, as Clara Barton so well phrased it in her own time, "if not for our own safety, at least [for] our honour, to signify our approval of the principles of humanity acknowledged by every other civilised nation".

MEN ARE MORE THAN NATIONS

Returning now to the international organisation of Red Cross activities under the unprecedented conditions of the First World War, it would require several volumes merely to summarise what was attempted and what was achieved. Yet we can at least glance inside the Musée Rath to observe how the Geneva Committee tackled its many problems during that war, and, finally, how it faced the aftermath of the war with five million ex-combatants of 30 nations in its charge to get back to their homes.

At the beginning of hostilities in August, 1914, the International Committee of the Red Cross, which had been authorised by the diplomatic conference in Washington in 1912 to act as the official intermediary in aiding prisoners-of-war, set up, as noted above, the International Agency under its President, Gustave Ador. One of the towering personalities of Swiss political and intellectual life, who had succeeded Gustave Moynier as President on the latter's death in 1910, Gustave Ador—who later became President of the Swiss Confederation—at once showed his exceptional organising ability in devising an overall plan of prisoners' aid and his courageous neutralism in dealing firmly with the belligerent governments. Gustave Ador—precursor of Count Bernadotte, Dag Hammarskjold, Ralph Bunche, and a score of other outstanding mediators and conciliators of our own times—proved not only that he was the right man in the right place, but also that a man "above the battle" can work miracles for human beings trapped in the conflagration of global war or caught between the passions of rival ideologies.

Yet Gustave Ador could have done nothing without his wonderful team of Swiss citizens. The workaday world knows little and cares less what ordinary men and women have done to guide their fellows to a fuller life, or even to preserve life at all. It is only in lingering over the shining pages, as the author has done, of *this* side of war, recording literally thousands of quiet and simple deeds of kindness and sympathy, done more often than not by volunteers, that one can believe again in Man's alleged "progress".

When one contrasts such a record as this, built and sustained by thousands and thousands of average men and women, who would never regard themselves as heroic or exceptional beings, with the tawdry headlines of the popular Press, reflecting the lowest denominator among human follies and the untamed animal in the behaviour of states, one recalls the assessment of Dr. Fridtjof Nansen, begging the post-war governments of the early 20's to aid him in clearing up the human wreckage of the war by succouring the millions of desperate refugees under his care. Dr. Nansen put his finger on the root problem of all war—namely, the double standard which governments practise in their mutual relations—when he said: "Although, as individuals, we behave like good Christians, and wouldn't dream of hurting anyone, the nations, made up of the same individuals, behave between themselves like beasts in a menagerie."

Here, in the central workshop of the Red Cross, was exhibited over and over again that loyalty to the future, that real patriotism which is not cancelled out by somebody else's patriotism, but which echoes the eternal values with Ralph Waldo Emerson: "How much more are *men* than nations!" In Geneva, there were no "nations"—either "enemy" or "friendly"—only MEN.

When the war reached its height, over a thousand workers at the Geneva centre were handling 30,000 letters *a day*, coming from and going to prisoners-of-war and internees. The Agency was divided into

During the First World War, the British Section of the Central P.O.W. Agency employed 83 workers, used half a million index cards, and handled 100,000 letters from relatives.

four major departments: the first providing information about missing persons to their families; the second transmitting letters, parcels and money; the third dealing with the supervision and improvement of the prison camps on both sides of the various fronts; and the fourth handling questions of repatriation and the care of prisoners interned in neutral countries. The Agency was also divided into sub-divisions of British, French, German, and the other national categories, both for the Allies and for the Central Powers. Later on, when the United States entered the war in 1917, an American Section was added.

The Agency's general method of work was first to obtain lists of prisoners or, at least, information about them in any way possible, such as by enquiries of their compatriots or by questions sent on a reply-card to the belligerent authorities. Soon, an elaborate but spartan system of enquiry—which was the same for each belligerent—was developed by trial and experiment, which was later to become the basis of a more effective method of working during the Second World War. An indication of the amount of clerical work involved can be judged from the fact that the French Section alone produced $2\frac{1}{2}$ million Information Cards and the German $1\frac{1}{2}$ million; while a hundred thousand separate enquiries were sent by the Geneva office to the Allies and sixty thousand to the Central Powers.

One Geneva firm alone, appointed by the Red Cross, handled 2,000,000 parcels for P.O.W.s from September 1914, to November 1918.

Civilians, domiciled behind the various enemy fronts, were by no means overlooked, and the Civil Department, which was set up at the beginning of 1915, added to its duties as the war expanded. For the return of a girl of seven to her family, innumerable letters and telegrams were exchanged between Berlin, Paris, Marseilles, New York, Berne, and Geneva, and the file in front of the present author is headed with the child's name, "Marthe Jeanne Gollmer" and contains 78 separate papers! Meanwhile, the new department which was established in May, 1918, for the transmission of civilian messages between U.S.A. and the Central Powers had, up to 31st December, communicated 21,000 messages from Europe and 53,000 from U.S.A.; and 17,000 answers from the Central Powers and 1,000 answers from U.S.A. This was during the period when much of the Continent of Europe was collapsing fast.

HOPE LIVES IN A CARD-INDEX

As soon as the daily mail came in at the Musée Rath, lists of prisoners were immediately handed over to the proper section and great pains were taken in checking and cross-checking the names. It should be remembered that, towards the end of the war, lists of prisoners were coming in from over 30 nations. Working in day and night shifts, the typing pool alone occupied a hundred full-time typists. It is difficult to describe, when so much detail was involved in so many languages, how scrupulous was the care given to even the tiniest difference of spelling. For example, in dealing with Russian prisoners-of-war, there were many identical or almost similar names. A mistake in a Christian name or in an initial or regimental digit might result in a desperate human being, thousands of miles away, being "lost" to the world.

Enquiries from relatives and friends pouring in from every corner of the globe accounted for much of the enormous correspondence, handled almost entirely by women. But those families that could manage to do so came in person to Geneva to explain their case and obtain news of their loved ones. In four years, more than 120,000 people were received in the Geneva office.

It was found that the best way to handle this mountain of information —always on the move—was to build it into a gigantic card-index, divided into the national sections, with workers knowing the particular languages being allocated to their special section. Some of these devoted workers shepherded their always-growing flock of index cards—each standing for a son, a father, a husband—for two, three, or four years. The British Section, for instance, comprised 83 workers and 500,000 index cards, and received 100,000 letters from relatives and 6,000

As soon as the mail comes in, lists of prisoners are handed to National Sections.

telegrams. The Franco-Belgian Section was even bigger and collected 2½ million Information Cards. Of its 40 workers, 30 were volunteer helpers, and each had charge of a definite number of index boxes, over which she took as much precious care as if they were her own children.

Outside the Geneva headquarters altogether, the Agency's delegates were, throughout the war, on continual missions, often facing danger and hardship themselves, on land and sea, inspecting the P.O.W. camps and negotiating for repatriation of prisoners wherever possible. No less than 450,000 prisoners were repatriated through their efforts, as repatriation had to be carried out through neutral agencies. If ever the principle of "neutralisation", for which Dunant had fought so hard, were justified by its results, here was proof abundant.

As the war developed, with its increasing burdens on the Geneva headquarters, minor Agencies were established in Copenhagen and in Paris and Frankfurt. But most important, perhaps, was the constant effort on the part of the Central Agency to keep the principles of the Geneva Convention before the belligerent governments and to insist on their military commands respecting the immunity of the Red Cross. Reprisals and breaches of the laws of war—such as the sinking of hospital ships—were many and were taken up immediately with the offending governments. Likewise, the International Committee did its

Information Card (in Russian) concerning a Russian P.O.W. traced to Austria.

best to defend, where necessary, the National Societies against the misuse of their services by their own governments. Frequent protests at the use of poison gas and other terror weapons were made, rarely with effect, as well as constant attempts to mitigate the suffering of civilians,

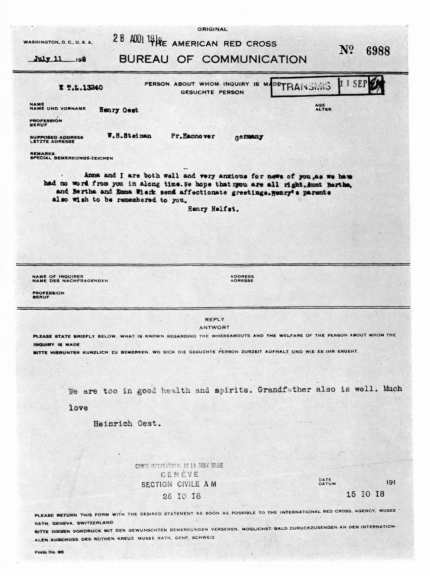

A message from a German civilian (translated by the Agency) for transmission to the U.S.A. in September, 1918.

due to the blockade. But the attitude of governments towards the laws of humanity deteriorates as the "necessities" of total victory take a stronger hold of them and a swirling vortex of unreason and hatred towards the enemy submerges their peoples.

It should surprise no-one today, looking back on the disastrous consequences of the War-to-End-War and, even more, on the Second World War (to end the War-to-End-War), that the International Committee, with this long experience behind it of the behaviour-pattern of modern belligerents, has warned the world's governments in the plainest possible terms—the topic of our final Chapter—that, not only do terror tactics *not* pay, but that the advocates of "total war", on the pretence that excessive suffering by the civil population will shorten the fighting and "save human lives", are talking the language of executioners. Dr. Jean S. Pictet, the present Director of General Affairs of the International Committee, has, in his brochure *The Red Cross and Peace*, summarised the Red Cross experience in unambiguous terms:

> If war is a crime, to wage war inhumanely is a double crime. . . .
> The experience of two World Wars has adequately shown that the brutality of war does not affect its duration, and that terroristic measures prolong the hatred and spirit of revenge to which they give rise or save up for the future.

"THE SIMPLE ELEMENTAL THINGS"

Contrary to popular belief, the most important aspect of modern war is not how it begins, but how it finishes. It is not possible, however, to follow the immense labours of the Central Agency into the "Peace" which—as always—followed the war with even worse consequences for many of the survivors, than had the four years of slaughter. The raging influenza epidemic alone, which followed close on the heels of the war's privations, carried off twice as many dead as the war itself, while the collapse of the Central European economies soon brought Mussolini and Hitler to power—to save the "Peace". After *both* World Wars, Communism, the offspring of human despair, doubled or trebled its geographical area and its political strength. Yet there are still some individuals who believe that a Third World War is needed to *destroy* Communism!

It is nevertheless true that, early in 1919, the new-born League of

Nations, inspired by the idealism and intelligence of one of the greatest world-minded Americans, President Woodrow Wilson, and guided by Lord Robert Cecil's practical genius, began to bring a semblance of order into the European chaos. But the sombre appraisal of General Jan Smuts—also one of the joint-authors of the League of Nations Covenant—summed up what has undoubtedly become the verdict of history on the War-to-End-War:

> *There are only two ways in the world: the way of force and the way of understanding. We have tried the way of force to the uttermost and seen it reduce the earth to a heap of ruins.*

The work of the Red Cross shone like a beacon of hope across the resultant desert, which was Peace only in name. The repatriating of millions of prisoners-of-war, after the major fighting ceased—though minor wars continued in Eastern Europe—makes an epic in itself which, again, would fill many volumes.

Early in 1917, the International Committee had already thought it advisable to draw attention to the difficulties, which would have to be overcome as soon as hostilities ceased, in returning several million prisoners to their homes. The Committee appealed to all the belligerent Powers to prepare for repatriation of war prisoners in good health, even though having undergone several years' captivity. At the Treaty of Brest-Litovsk, for example, in the spring of 1918, the terms of the exchange of war prisoners were agreed between Russia and the Central Powers, and this repatriation was started through the efforts of the German, Austro-Hungarian and Russian Red Cross missions and

Many years passed before some of the prisoners found their way home.

French refugees troop into an American Red Cross canteen for food and shelter, 1918.

carried out fairly regularly for several months. Political events at home, however, soon put an end to normal relations between Russia and the Central States, and organised repatriation of war prisoners and internees to their respective countries was brought to a standstill.

This was the beginning of utter confusion in Central Europe. The Russians, of whom over a million were still in the Central States, attempted to return home unaided. The governments of the countries through which they passed, especially the Polish authorities, attempted to organise convoys with a view to directing these masses of stragglers as quickly as possible towards their Eastern frontiers. Thousands of these unfortunate men died on the way of privation or sickness, while many who were unable to overcome the difficulties of such a journey turned back once more to their former prison camps. At the same time, Hungarians, coming from the East and moving westwards, began to return unaided from Russia and even from Siberia. This haphazard migration of crowds of entirely destitute men, often in a pitiful physical condition, was not only the chief cause of the spread of epidemics which broke out in Central Europe and soon spread across the world, but created dangerous social conditions in areas which were already in revolt against the governments that had sent them to war and then betrayed them.

As it soon proved impossible for the Red Cross to set up any general evacuation scheme as the problem grew bigger, the most urgent task became the maintenance and feeding on the spot of prisoners who were still in the Central States. The next step was the evacuation in organised groups, according to the available means, of the masses of prisoners who were already on the march throughout Lithuania, Poland, Czechoslovakia, Austria, Hungary, Rumania and Turkey. The Committee's delegates concluded agreements with the authorities of these various States, facilitating the evacuation and passage through their territories of groups of prisoners who had already started on their way. Likewise, the delegates were successful in helping the transit of groups coming from Russia, through Poland, Ukraine and Rumania, and moving towards the Central States. The number of prisoners-of-war who were thus able to return home through the arrangements made by the International Committee cannot be accurately estimated, but reached hundreds of thousands.

This is only one corner of Operation Salvation, of which the English-speaking peoples, on both sides of the Atlantic, knew so little, as their repatriation problems were altogether simpler and easier.

The Peace treaties of 1919 stipulated that repatriation of German, Austrian and Hungarian prisoners should take place only after the treaties came into force, or were ratified by three of the principal

A special committee went to work to help Dr. Nansen feed the millions of starving Russians.

A contemporary sketch of Fridtjof Nansen.

Powers; but months elapsed before these conditions were fulfilled. The International Committee therefore approached the Paris Peace Conference and stressed the need for negotiating repatriation of prisoners-of-war of all nationalities separately. But time dragged on while men were dying. Not until the Council of the League of Nations decided on 11th April, 1920, to appoint a Special Commissioner to deal with the repatriation of prisoners-of-war, and placed this humanitarian work in the remarkable hands of Dr. Fridtjof Nansen, did hope come back to the world.

The heaven-inspired work of Fridtjof Nansen, for the flotsam and jetsam of the War-to-End-War, has passed into legend. Standing head and shoulders above his fellows, scientist, world-champion athlete, hero of Farthest North, this Great Neutral was the very embodiment of the Red Cross ideal. He proved that war was no longer a "gentleman's game" by becoming himself the First Gentleman of Peace. Shortly before he died, worn out by his labours of love for the stricken remnants of other men's hatred, he gave this message to the younger generation, when concluding his address to the students of St. Andrew's University, Scotland, urging them to turn their backs on the sordid illusions of war and become themselves heroes of peace:

> We need you, young friends, with fresh eyes, capable of seeing the simple elemental things, ready to run risks, to try new trails, and to dare the unknown.

CHAPTER FIVE

A League is Founded

In the beginning, the Red Cross had no other aim than to second the regular Medical Services of armies in time of war. But Henri Dunant had even then foreseen that wider horizons must open out before the movement, and indeed its scope of action was very soon enlarged. The first stage was the creation of peacetime work in favour of the sick, designed as training for the mission to be fulfilled in the tragic contingencies envisaged by the Geneva Convention. . . . But that was not all. Reaching out beyond its original work with wounded and sick soldiers, the Red Cross had long been active among the victims of natural calamities, and in a number of other humanitarian endeavours. It was, however, chiefly just after the World War that its action was extended and generalised.

In these words, written in the early thirties, Max Huber introduces us to a movement which had emerged from the First World War as an international institution of the first importance. In fact, when the world's statesmen drew up the Covenant of the League of Nations in 1919—eventually ratified by over 50 governments—they included a special provision (Article 25) recognising the legal standing of the International Red Cross and inviting all the Member Governments to co-operate with it and to support it.

The heading over this chapter, however, does not refer to the League of Nations, but to the League of Red Cross Societies, formed in the same year. It is with the latter League that we are concerned and with that League's relations with the International Committee, on the one hand, and with the National Red Cross Societies, on the other hand. These are the three elements which make up what we term "THE INTERNATIONAL RED CROSS".

Their mutual relations, as well as their distinctive functions, are

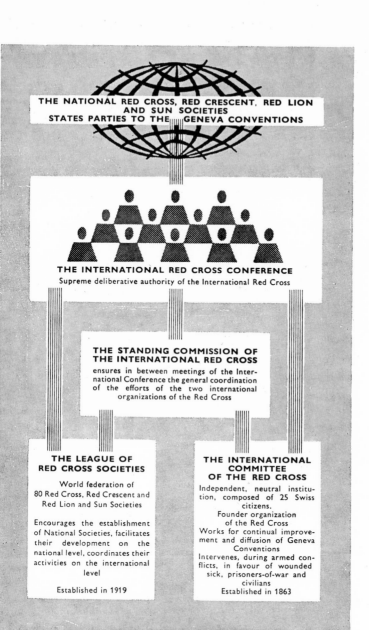

THE NATIONAL RED CROSS, RED CRESCENT, RED LION
AND SUN SOCIETIES
STATES PARTIES TO THE GENEVA CONVENTIONS

THE INTERNATIONAL RED CROSS CONFERENCE
Supreme deliberative authority of the International Red Cross

**THE STANDING COMMISSION OF
THE INTERNATIONAL RED CROSS**
ensures in between meetings of the International Conference the general coordination
of the efforts of the two international
organizations of the Red Cross

**THE LEAGUE OF
RED CROSS SOCIETIES**

World federation of
80 Red Cross, Red Crescent and
Red Lion and Sun Societies

Encourages the establishment
of National Societies, facilitates
their development on the
national level, coordinates their
activities on the international
level

Established in 1919

**THE INTERNATIONAL
COMMITTEE
OF THE RED CROSS**

Independent, neutral institution, composed of 25 Swiss
citizens.
Founder organization
of the Red Cross
Works for continual improvement and diffusion of Geneva
Conventions
Intervenes, during armed conflicts, in favour of wounded
sick, prisoners-of-war and
civilians
Established in 1863

How the International Red Cross is organised.

defined in statutes which were agreed in 1928. The governing authority of the whole movement is the International Red Cross Conference, which normally meets every fourth year. The most recent—the nineteenth—Conference (discussed in Chapter IX) met at New Delhi in 1957. The Conference is attended by representatives of the National Societies, the International Committee, the League, *and also*—be it specially noted—the Governments signatory to the Geneva Conventions. In this way, the Conference has a composition which is undoubtedly unique among international organisations.

Although this short chapter is mainly descriptive of the way in which the Red Cross is organised, on a world basis, it is essential to dwell for a time on this part of the Red Cross story, as too many Red Cross adherents and supporters, in the 80 member countries, as well as the public, have generally little knowledge of the *international* movement. They therefore tend to think of the Red Cross as a national institution, confined to their particular country. Others, again, wonder why there should be two Red Cross headquarters in Geneva; and, sometimes, there are grumblings to be heard at international conferences at "overlapping" or "duplication".

To see the complete picture, we should first glance at the manner in which the International Committee has developed since it was founded in 1863; then, having already seen the Red Cross in action in earlier chapters, we can review the chief principles on which its work proceeds. Finally, we can trace the growth of the League up to that sad day, in September, 1939, when it underwent its greatest trial in the Second World War, but emerged much stronger in 1945 in order to tackle the problems of "peace".

Firstly, then, the International Committee of the Red Cross is an independent body, neutral in regard to politics and religious faith, and composed of 25 Swiss citizens, who are elected by co-option. The word "international" does not, in fact, describe the composition of the Committee, but the nature of its activities, which are international in scope. The headquarters of the International Committee are permanently in Geneva, as we have seen. Up to the present time, the presidents of the International Committee have been General Dufour (in 1863); Gustave Moynier (1864-1910); Gustave Ador (1910-1928); Max Huber (1928-1945); Carl J. Burckhardt (1945-1948); and Paul Ruegger (1948-1955), who was succeeded by Leopold Boissier in September, 1955.

The International Committee is founded upon the principle of voluntary unremunerated service. For this reason alone its membership is bound to be limited, and is further restricted by the unconditional rule of neutral citizenship. Yet this small Committee has built a world-wide organisation so adaptable that it can instantly double, triple, or multiply its work tenfold or more at a few hours' notice. Indeed, the International Committee has managed to find the number of collaborators needed for each emergency, and enrol them in its service so far as means have allowed. But even in "normal" times, it cannot reduce its permanent secretariat below a certain level.

Under its Statutes, the Committee in time of war—whether international or civil—is authorised to act as a neutral intermediary for all questions of a humanitarian nature, on behalf of Governments, National Red Cross Societies, or private individuals separated from their families by war. The Committee is also qualified, on its own authority, to act in favour of war victims, anywhere, as it may consider expedient.

The Prisoners of War Convention gave the Committee its mandate in 1929 to organise a Central Prisoners of War Information Bureau; though—as is obvious from the previous chapter—it was this gigantic task which had already been performed so creditably throughout the First World War. The Conventions of 1949 extended this function still further to cases of civil war. These war-time duties consist, particularly, in tracing the wounded, prisoners, and missing; visiting prisoners-of-

In Iran (Persia) the Red Lion and Sun helps during floods with tents, clothing, food and cooking utensils for disaster victims whose homes have been swept away.

I

war or internee camps; reporting on these visits to the Detaining Power and the home country; forwarding and issuing relief supplies to all classes of war victims, including the population of occupied countries; and acting for Protecting Powers in carrying out welfare work which the latter might no longer be able to perform.

Among the Committee's administrative duties are: to give official recognition to new National Red Cross Societies as they come along; to extend the application of the Geneva Conventions and to take suitable action on any complaints regarding breaches of the Conventions; to promote the improvement of humanitarian law and the better understanding of the Conventions; to encourage the development of medical personnel and medical equipment, in co-operation with Red Cross organisations, the Medical Services of the armed forces, and other authorities; and to carry out the special responsibilities entrusted to it by decisions of the International Conferences.

The Committee's budget comprises two kinds of revenue, ordinary and extraordinary. The ordinary revenue consists of the National Societies' annual contributions and voluntary contributions from governments, parties to the Convention, as well as income from a certain number of title-deeds owned by the Committee. But the extraordinary revenues, from outside sources, have varied as widely as the emergencies which have occasioned their use.

As noted at the end of the last chapter, the consequences of the First World War kept the Committee busily engaged until 1923, in repatriating some 450,000 prisoners-of-war captured on the Eastern Front and detained in Central Europe, Russia, and Siberia. This scheme was carried out in close co-operation with the League of Nations, who supplied a fleet of sixteen vessels. Further action included international relief for the victims of famine and disease in Central Europe and the Balkans.

Minor wars continued in different parts of the world—sometimes checked by the League of Nations, sometimes not. For instance, hostilities between Bolivia and Paraguay in the Gran Chaco continued from 1932 to 1935; there were wars in Abyssinia during 1935 and 1936, and in China ever since 1937. In all these the International Committee acted as a neutral intermediary for the transmission of Red Cross relief supplies, and appointed delegates in each new theatre of war to assist prisoners, civilian internees, and other classes of war victims.

"The invincible spirit of the Red Cross" has been well described in

Belinda Peacey's *The True Book About the Red Cross;* and the account
of the hair's-breadth escapes of a young Swiss doctor, Marcel Junod,
at a time when "the protective symbol of the Red Cross was riddled
with bullets and shattered by bombs, on plain and hillside", and
Mussolini's troops were proving the superiority of European civilisation
in Abyssinia, unfortunately does not stand alone in the annals of the
International Committee. "The rules laid down by the Geneva Convention," she asserts, "had been faithfully observed by the ambulances;
the tents sufficiently far removed from any military objective and clearly
identified by the Red Cross flags fluttering above them and spread out
over the ground around them. Repeated bombings, however, showed
that the Red Cross afforded no protection and first one unit, then
another, removed all signs of it and continued their work of mercy
under cover of trees or camouflaged."

To the fratricidal Spanish Civil War, which lasted from 1936-1939,
the Geneva Convention did not apply, but the Red Cross Committee
nevertheless carried out relief activities on a large scale. The Civil War
had hardly finished before the Second World War broke out. Thus, the
experience gained during these two decades of insecure armistice—
seeing that "peace" can never rest secure on competitive armed force,
even if the weapons are standing still—gave the International Committee the assurance, if such were needed, that the principles on which
it had taken its stand were the durable ones.

So much for a bare outline of the functions of the International
Committee and its almost limitless field of operation between the two
World Wars. Now it may be useful to bring together, under a few
simple heads, the basic principles by which the Committee has, from
the beginning, guided its work.

FOUR PILLARS OF PEACE

The Red Cross is both an *idea* and an *organisation* or, rather, it is an idea
working through an organisation. As such, it expresses an intimate
relationship between the end to be attained and the means towards that
end. The history of the Red Cross has clearly shown that both the means
and the end must be consistent if a human institution is to do its proper
job in the real world. The Red Cross doesn't say one thing and do
another. Its ideals and its practices have harmonised to a remarkable
degree. That is why it has succeeded and belongs to man's future.

By studying the constant interplay of ends and means in the traditional work of the Red Cross, we suddenly become aware of the fact that War —or War-preparation to "keep" the Peace—is the complete antithesis of the Red Cross. For the object of War is, or is represented to be, PEACE. But the *means* which War uses to attain its objective become more and more inconsistent with Peace, as weapons become more and more inhuman and destructive. The Red Cross, in fact, far from encouraging war-preparations, as some people tend to believe, shows them up for what they are—destroyers of Peace.

The evil consequences of the War-to-End-War we have discussed briefly in the previous chapter, and the similar consequences of the War-to-End-Totalitarianism we shall have to consider in the next chapter. After that, we have left over for a later chapter the strange behaviour of those incredible people—who have forgotten nothing and learnt nothing—who look for a War-to-End-Communism.

But the Red Cross, by its irresistible vitality in the face of all the follies and disasters of the past century, is an ever-present reminder that War, by its very nature, can *never* bring us Peace, but only more War. For Peace must be built, as the Red Cross has been built, by peaceful means. There is no road to Peace through War—Peace is the only road to Peace.

At the end of his book, *Red Cross Principles* (1956), Dr. Jean S. Pictet, Director for General Affairs of the International Committee, has provided a convenient summary of Red Cross principles which, as the foundation stones of the world organisation, have never been so simply described. For present purposes, we can arrange them in a single paragraph, as follows:

> The Red Cross fights against suffering and death, and demands that man shall be treated humanely under all circumstances. It is ready to come to the help of each individual equally and without any form of discrimination. The help available will be apportioned according to the relative importance of individual needs and in their order of urgency. The Red Cross acts without favour or prejudice towards or against anyone. It observes strict neutrality in the military, political and philosophical spheres, and is independent of all authorities and free from every influence. Finally, the work of the Red Cross extends to all men and all countries.

On the above foundation, well and truly laid by Dunant himself and his Geneva Committee, the Red Cross has been firmly erected over the intervening years. Here, in Dr. Pictet's words, we can summarise, again in a single paragraph, the organisational principles which have shaped its world-wide structure:

> The Red Cross must not reap any advantage from its activities; it is only concerned with the humanitarian interest of the persons who require help. It offers its services free of charge. It is an expression of private charity and a spirit of service, an institution for the provision of voluntary relief. It co-operates with the public authorities, but it must have a sufficient degree of autonomy in its relations with them. The ranks of a National Red Cross Society must be open to all the citizens of the country concerned, and the Society must be organised on a democratic basis. All National Societies have the same international rights. In each State there can be only one Red Cross Society, directed by one central body. The activities of the Society must embrace the whole country. Having the same aims, Red Cross Societies have established mutual relationships and recognise that it is their duty to help one another. The Red Cross must always be ready for the tasks with which it may be faced.

"It is ready to come to the help of each individual." Austrian Red Cross Volunteers giving first-aid in the mountains.

*"The Red Cross is an expression of private charity and a spirit of service";
a British Red Cross worker collects from Sir Winston Churchill outside
10, Downing Street.*

Consequently, there are four distinct elements which, over and over
again in this book, have revealed themselves as the pillars of the movement and the source of its strength: *Humanity, Impartiality, Neutrality,*
and *Universality*. When we turn these concepts over in our minds, the
thought again presents itself: But these are also the principles of Peace!
If nations—if their governments—were to base their foreign policies
on these same principles, they would begin to practise peace. It is
*in*humanity, it is the "ganging up" of groups of nations against other
groups, it is the national reliance on the use of force, and it is the
refusal to act in terms of the whole human race, that give us our
recurrent wars.

The question naturally follows: If nations—if their governments—
began to base their foreign policies on humanity and impartiality, on
neutrality and universality, like the Red Cross, would they not also
gain the mutual security they are losing today? The strategy of peace
in our time will, therefore, become our chief concern before we close
this book. But, meantime, by comparing in the course of these chapters

the techniques employed so consistently by the International Red Cross in its dealings with men and nations, with the techniques normally employed by national governments in their dealings with each other, the truth of Dr. Jean-G. Lossier's appraisal of the historic mission of the Red Cross will become more apparent:

> As a symbol of mankind's efforts to wrench itself free from the constant and ubiquitous fatality of war, it stands out as one of the greatest triumphs of the Nineteenth Century.

SUPERSTRUCTURE OF SANITY

Coming now to the organisation of the League of Red Cross Societies, we discover another interesting parallel. Just as the League of Nations began its life in 1919 under the persuasive personality of Woodrow Wilson, President of the United States, so did the League of Red Cross Societies begin its existence on the initiative of another American public servant, Henry P. Davison, Chairman of the American Red Cross Council.

It was Davison's idea to carry into peacetime the momentum gained during the war, and to increase the efficacy of the National Red Cross Societies by welding them into a federation, thus bringing about

The League of Red Cross Societies was founded by an International Medical Conference at Cannes, France, in April, 1919.

Presentation of Nansen Medal to the League of Red Cross Societies in recognition of its Hungarian relief work, Geneva, September, 1957; Dr. Auguste R. Lindt, U.N. High Commissioner for refugees, centre; Mr. Odd Nansen (son of Dr. Fridtjof Nansen), on his right; Mr. B. de Rougé, at right, received the medal as Secretary-General of the League.

greater co-ordination of effort. In February 1919, a Committee of Red Cross Societies was formed, comprising the American, British, French, Italian and Japanese Societies, whose aim was to "work out and propose to the Red Cross Societies a programme of action on behalf of the general welfare of humanity".

In April of that year a general medical conference met at Cannes, France, for the purpose of examining the Davison plan. This conference, under the presidency of Professor Emile Roux, Director of the Pasteur Institute, was composed of the leading medical authorities of the world, who approved the programme of action submitted by the Red Cross Committee. Thus, on 5th May, 1919, the League of Red Cross Societies was founded, grouping 26 Societies. Since then, this federation has grown until it now comprises 80 or more National Societies and over one hundred and twenty-five million individual members.

The League is, then, essentially a "parliament" of the National

Societies, where their representatives regularly assemble. As a federal body, the League performs the following major duties:

(a) to encourage the establishment and development in every country of a national, independent, and duly authorised Red Cross Society, working in accordance with the principles outlined above;

(b) to act as a permanent liaison between National Red Cross Societies, to represent them on the international level and, when necessary, to be the spokesman to express the opinions of the members as a whole;

(c) to co-operate with the Red Cross Societies in all spheres, in particular for the improvement of health, the prevention of disease, and the mitigation of suffering;

(d) to work closely with the International Committee of the Red Cross in matters affecting the work of either body.

It is important to observe that the League of Red Cross Societies receives no Government grants, and is free from any political, racial or religious ties. Its programme is financed by the contributions of Member Societies. The governing bodies consist of a Board of Governors and an Executive Committee, which are assisted by Advisory Committees.

Canadian Red Cross bringing emergency aid to loggers and miners.

The Board of Governors is composed of representatives from all the National Societies, members of the League, and meets every two years. It entrusts the execution of its programme to a Secretary-General, who is appointed by the Board itself, and other permanent officers; while an Executive Committee exercises the powers of the Board of Governors, when the latter is not sitting. Advisory Committees and a standing Finance Commission study technical questions concerning Medico-Social, Nursing, Junior Red Cross, and Finance, respectively, and they guide the action of the Secretariat's specialised Bureaux.

In view of their importance, both to the Societies and to the impact of their services on the public at large, a few paragraphs at least are needed to indicate the wide duties undertaken by the League's "bureaux".

For example, the Relief Bureau is constituted to assist National Societies develop their own relief organisations and to co-ordinate their international activities. Since the end of the Second World War, it has acted as a clearing house for international relief action undertaken by the Red Cross on behalf of victims of natural disasters and of refugees. Donor Societies send their gifts either directly or through the Relief Bureau. It obtains import and export permits and assists National Societies on all transport questions. At the present time, the League is

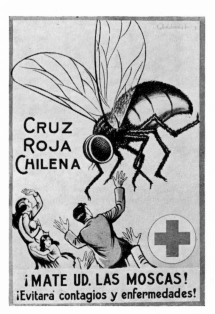

The World Health Organisation ran a "Destroy Disease-Carrying Insects" campaign in 1956 and 23 National Societies co-operated.

An isolated Red Cross outpost in Northern Canada.

maintaining, with the assistance of the Societies, emergency depots in Australia, Austria, France and Turkey, from which relief can be rushed to disaster-stricken countries.

The main work of the Medico-Social Bureau consists in studying the medico-social activities of National Societies and offering assistance to Societies wishing to organise or extend these activities. The Medico-Social Bureau gives priority to certain programmes, such as first aid, accident prevention, maternal and child welfare, the fight against social disease, social service and aid to the handicapped—an ever-expanding area—and it naturally maintains contacts with other international organisations, in particular with the World Health Organisation.

The chief responsibility of the Nursing Bureau is to assist National Societies in developing their nursing services and to act as a co-ordinating agent between the Societies. It gives technical assistance on such matters as the organisation of nursing schools, training programmes for nurses' aids, the development of home nursing programmes and the enrolment of nursing personnel for all Red Cross activities. Personal visits are made to National Societies and an intensive correspondence is exchanged. It also acts as adviser to the National Societies in selecting qualified candidates for Red Cross scholarships and fellowships and organises international meetings for Red Cross nursing personnel.

The Information and Publications Bureau operates in two stages: the first stage is the collecting of textual, visual and statistical information from the movement throughout the world; and the second stage is to spread this information through publications and Press releases, and

Poster designed by the American Junior Red Cross, who form part of 50 million Junior members.

through visual materials, making full use of those produced by National Societies. The Bureau also edits *The Red Cross World*, an illustrated quarterly, in English, French, Spanish; and produces special materials for the annual commemoration of World Red Cross Day, for League meetings, and for the International Conference.

The Junior Red Cross also has a Bureau to act as a co-ordinating centre for Junior Red Cross throughout the world. Today, there are

Junior Red Cross Sections in over seventy countries, and this branch of the movement already counts about *fifty million members*. But the work of this particular Bureau, aimed at "inspiring young people with the spirit of the Red Cross and providing them with the opportunities of Red Cross Service", is so important (at least, in the mind of the present writer) that a fuller treatment of the activities of the Junior Red Cross can best be dealt with later on in Chapter VII.

Finally, it should be stressed once again that the League maintains continuous liaison with kindred international governmental and non-governmental organisations. Among these, particular mention has already been made of the United Nations and its Specialised Agencies, notably WHO, UNESCO, FAO, UNICEF, ILO, as well as the U.N. High Commissioner for Refugees, and other operative units of the U.N. family who are constantly engaged in helping the human race to *live*. The Red Cross does not stand alone, therefore, sufficient unto itself, but first among the universal organisations which have come in answer to modern man's universal needs, the Red Cross emblem—historically and geographically—floats high over its Geneva headquarters, with the later comers proudly spread out beneath it.

CHAPTER SIX

The Last of the World Wars

❧

IN the early hours of a morning which gave promise of a very hot day, a squadron of six medical aircraft took off. "We were leaving an aerodrome near Athens," wrote a special reporter of the German Army Medical Service afterwards, "heading in the direction of Mersa Matruh, with the object of collecting on the African coast—as we were then doing several times each week—those of our men who had been seriously wounded on the El Alamein front, and whom we were to take back to Athens for admission to army hospitals."

The writer of those lines was on board the first aircraft, piloted by the squadron leader, a medical officer. "I hope that we shall not be attacked during our flight," remarked the latter. For the past week no enemy aircraft had been reported in the neighbourhood. Nevertheless, the squadron flew at about ten yards above the sea, so as to escape the enemy's notice as far as possible. After flying for about an hour the planes made a short stop in Crete, to take in fuel, but very soon took off again and, skimming the rocky cliffs of the island, continued flying just above the sea.

After a flight of about five hours, the rescue squadron came in sight of the African coast where there could still be seen the remains of armoured cars and other vehicles knocked out during the fighting. On the edge of a temporary airstrip, ambulances containing the seriously wounded Germans were waiting in the scorching African climate.

"I will refrain from describing the painful task of carrying the wounded from the ambulances and placing them on board the aircraft," continued the narrator. "When the ambulance doors were opened, the unbearable heat, the stench of suppurating wounds and the swarms of flies made us recoil. None of us thought that there could be much hope of saving the lives of the men placed in our care in such a pitiful state—but whoever saw those same wounded men, a week later, in

Sysmanoglion Hospital, Athens, in the care of Red Cross doctors and nurses, could believe in miracles!"

Less than an hour later, the medical craft took off again, so as to be back in Athens before nightfall. "I know," said the medical officer who piloted the aircraft himself, "what seriously wounded men are in my care and I am adapting the flight to circumstances. Let us hope we shall not meet the enemy; we know from experience that we must expect anything to happen."

He was right; for an hour later, just before they arrived at Crete, and were expecting to see the escort which had been promised, a British fighter-plane bore down upon them from the rear. He swept round the German formation at full speed and after tracing a wide circle, again followed them, but more slowly. "Get ready for an emergency," said the medical officer, "I told you, when we left, what to do in case of trouble."

The British aircraft again drew near. It was at a distance of a dozen yards and the pilot was examining the German aircraft with a field-glass. He was certainly trying to see what was in the cabins. So the medical staff placed a wounded man at the front of each plane; his bandaged head, on a pillow, near the window. Thus, the British pilot was bound to see that they were, in fact, carrying the wounded.

The British aircraft circled round twice. The medical officer said, "I think it is going to be all right." The British pilot swept round once more and approached them from the rear; then, passing alongside, the pilot raised his hand to his helmet, saluted, flew off at full speed, and the Germans saw him no more.

"I have a pleasant memory of that 'enemy' for whom the Red Cross emblem was sacred," concluded Willy Heudtlass, now head of the Press Department of the National Red Cross of the German Federal Republic.

But not all the personal experiences and episodes of the Second World War—which forms the basis of this chapter—ended on so chivalrous a note. Nevertheless, we begin by recalling this incident, because it takes us back to Henri Dunant, who never lost an opportunity, in describing the horrors of Solferino, to point out that the man who had been drilled and driven by his government to destroy his fellows in battle could still remain a man in himself, and seize every occasion which came his way to prove his manliness. The whole Red Cross achievement, during past times of war, was built on the ordinary humanity of the ordinary man, even though, again and again, "superior orders" have turned some men into butchers and torturers, contrary to their true human nature.

But not so today. Now that directors of national strategy, ensconsed deep down beneath the earth in impregnable concrete caverns, are rehearsing how to push buttons which will release atomic-warheads on to the inhabited towns and cities of their invisible targets 8,000 or more miles away, the essential manliness of the common soldier, which alone gave war its passing glory, has been stripped from him by the military machine itself, leaving him naked before his God and his conscience. *"The greatest courage and devotion would be unavailing under such circumstances,"* insist the International Committee in their report on the latest developments in the art of making war (which forms the subject of our final chapter), "and the recent Geneva Conventions would themselves be ineffective if the belligerents were unrestricted in their choice of means and methods of warfare."

In recounting, therefore, some of the unproclaimed acts of chivalry associated with the Red Cross during the last of the World Wars, the truth must be kept in mind—a truth constantly obscured by the flood of "war" books and films, which befog and delude the public attitude as to the real character of modern war—that no man can be a hero any more within the five-hundred-square-miles or more radius of a nuclear bomb.

Even so, the incalculable loss and evil inflicted on the human race by the Second World War is only adequately revealed when approached from the angle, which we are now doing, of those dauntless men and women who sought to save and succour some of its unnumbered victims. In fact, one of the major psychological problems in the adjustment of peaceful relations between the different areas of the world today is the fact—too little understood and too little discussed—that, while all of Europe and much of Asia was torn with indescribable mental anguish and unprecedented physical destruction, day and night for over six years, a New World across the Atlantic was physically immune from this ever-present terror of death and annihilation, except at second-hand. Thus, today, the *approach* to world peace is necessarily a different one to a population which, in the main, had no personal experience of imminent death on the rooftops, instant destruction at the door, and constant deprivation of the elements of life, year after year. How they can sense the utter revulsion against war

of those millions upon millions of simple human creatures who underwent this appalling experience, stretching right from the Atlantic coasts
of Europe, across the Urals, to the Sea of Japan and beyond? It is not
solely because of different politics or ideologies that peace and war
mean different things in Moscow and Washington, or in Pekin and
San Francisco. Emotion counts infinitely more than logic.

"When, on a Sunday in October 1943, I left New York in the
Atlantic Clipper to return to my Swiss homeland," said a well-known
Red Cross leader, "I had the feeling that I was bidding farewell to the
uncrushed Continent, to be once more absorbed into the crushed, the
tragic Continent. . . . The nearer we came to the Continent of suffering,
the darker and more impenetrable grew the night. Lowering clouds
rose up, and hovered soundlessly over the sea, like huge, mysterious
wings. Was the Spirit of God brooding again over the dark waters of
chaos?"

So wrote Dr. Adolf Keller, Director of the European Central Office
for Inter-Church Aid, in introducing Max Huber's little testament of
faith, published during the war: *The Good Samaritan* (Victor Gollancz,
London, 1945). This awful picture of the crushed Continent can be
forgotten too easily today—especially by those who never saw it or
who have no imagination to envisage what war could do to daily

Max Huber.

human existence, even when its extent could still be limited. "I passed through Spain," recalled Dr. Keller, "and saw the pale, hungry faces of fading children searching for food among the refuse at the back doors of the houses. I travelled through France, which, from a land of smiles and the joy of living, had become an empty desert and a place of bitterness. And then I reached that haven, that white spot on the map of Europe which is Switzerland, where war is not. There, in the midst of darkest Europe, it seemed to send out, from its Alpine summits, a light of Hope, as if to show the way to a refuge of love and charity in the vast welter of horror and despair."

THE REFUGE OF LOVE

What, then, is this light shining in the prevailing darkness of despair?

On to the tables at the former Palais Electoral, given over to the Central Prisoners of War Agency, mountains of letters are shovelled daily. Three thousand five hundred persons are working here and in other buildings occupied by the International Committee, with its twenty-six sections established in different towns of Switzerland. Day in and day out, and often at night they toil throughout the years of the war. Letters are pouring in all the time from prisoners-of-war and civilian internees, and from their families in thirty, forty, fifty different countries, anxious to know where their loved ones are and how they are.

But for the bridge which the Red Cross has built across the constantly-changing battle lines, mothers, wives, husbands, and children would be lost to them. Within the Palais, hundreds of Red Cross workers, barely able to keep pace with the ever-piling letters, try to re-write them into the twenty-five-word message established by the International Red Cross—the length of a night-letter telegram. What a master-work of peace, expressed in the grammar of love, is here? Names of places and needs of the lost and the missing, the imprisoned and the suffering, all compressed into these twenty-five words!

Between the belligerent countries, the world over, stand the forbidding walls of fear and hate; but here is a small door opened for the welled-up waters of humanity to flow through, watering the arid places of the war-scorched earth. These fragile, twenty-five word messages, telling of pain and tragedy, of hope and confidence, of a mother's anxious care for her far-distant boy and a man's tender thought for his vanished home, mean a concentration of words, charged with deepest emotional experience, which could only be written by men and women of the International Red Cross, who are sharing within themselves the unspoken tragedy of unknown soldiers, parents, and loved ones, and who can suffer along with them as members of the same unbroken family.

Outside the Agency building, in the City of Geneva and in neighbouring towns, there grew up in an amazingly short time the biggest importing, warehousing and export enterprise the world has ever seen. This colossal relief and supply organisation was directed by men and women, all neutrals, who had to guide the Red Cross over political mountains and through a wilderness of international jealousy and official obstructiveness; and bring food and clothing and other means of comfort from their Swiss refuge to the millions of deprived men, women and children who needed them so badly.

It was not always the obvious relief which mattered most. Not only were millions of books distributed to keep minds alive during those dead years, but at least a hundred thousand spare pairs of spectacles were sent to the P.O.W. and internee camps, so that men could, in fact, read the books they received—an aspect of war-time solicitude

(LEFT) *Stock-pile of Red Cross parcels in the Depot, Geneva, for despatch to P.O.W.s.* (RIGHT) *Belgian prisoners receive American parcels in Oflag II in 1941.*

which reveals the practical humaneness of the manner in which the Red Cross thought out and achieved its tasks. Nevertheless, as Dr. Keller himself wrote at the time:

> The best of what is done at the Red Cross remains invisible. It is the meticulous exactitude with which the daily work is done, the orderliness which must be in the mind before it is in the files, the effort of the human heart, the passion of aiding unknown persons. Such is the faith that underlies all those activities.

As noted earlier, the experience which had been built up by the fierce pressure of human necessity during the First World War had subsequently been "legalised" by the Prisoners-of-War Convention of 1929. Hence, when war was renewed, the internal organisation of the Agency and the well-tried filing procedures had reached as high a degree of perfection as is conceivable; soon the gigantic central Card Index had reached a total of fifteen million cards—each one of which demanded the utmost accuracy in recording the smallest details. For each one meant a man.

As this wonderful system of keeping track of the whereabouts and the movements of millions of men, in spite of the chaos around them, has already been described in some detail in Chapter IV, and as the Agency's general functioning remained the same for the Second World War, further description is unnecessary now, though the complexity of the new tasks must never be forgotten.

One thing should be stressed especially, however, namely that the Second World War was one of immense and unceasing fluctuation of men and material. For the most part, battle-lines were constantly changing, except for short periods of time. Hence, the technical tasks which confronted the International Red Cross, involved in moving so much physical material around the earth, surpassed anything that had ever been attempted before. Again, the paradox of its continuing challenge appeared in a new form: the same mechanical means which the governments of the world were employing to destroy each other, the Red Cross was using to save them all from themselves. Railways and ships were bringing home the wounded and carrying foodstuffs to the starving countries; airplanes were taking Red Cross delegates to inspect P.O.W. camps; wireless, cables, and telephones were sending out messages of consolation across the earth; and all the standard procedures of international diplomacy, conducted by men of high integrity

A section of the great Card Index at the Central Agency in the Palais Electoral, Geneva.

and exceptional experience, were being used to the full—in spite of cruel blockades, savage war crimes, and all the subterfuges of "military necessity"—to uphold the right of the individual to his life and soul in the midst of this prevailing conspiracy of death.

By the end of 1946, the Agency's Card Index for prisoners-of-war and civilian internees contained no less than 39,000,000 cards. Here are a few other figures:

Mail items received and despatched	120,669,000
Telegrams received and despatched	567,251
Official lists of prisoners-of-war	3,600,000
Civilian 25-word messages forwarded	24,000,000
Photostat copies made	3,719,814
Visits to camps by Delegates	11,175

The relief supplies despatched to prisoners-of-war and civilian internees through the International Committee represented 445,702 tons, valued at 3,400 millions Swiss francs (close on a billion dollars). 1,500,000 printed volumes (educational or fictional) were also forwarded by the Committee to the camps—a vital activity to which we revert below. While the total cost of this universal public enterprise amounted to 54,875,000 Swiss francs, and contributions—half of which were subscribed by the Swiss themselves—reached over 50 million Swiss francs.

Although statistics of this order have only a quantitative significance, and the present book is more concerned with the human values involved, these overall figures go far to show that the sheer size of an organisation, when directed to human welfare and not to human destruction, need not make it "totalitarian" or even autocratic. Nor need it become corrupt or inefficient, because it is so big and responsibility is so widely shared. Localised misappropriation or official obstruction has been astonishingly rare even in the midst of the worst war conditions—except where questions of high policy have been involved. In fact, the war-time planning and administration of the International Red Cross, based partly on the finest professional skill at the centre, and partly—perhaps mostly—on the diversified use of voluntary service at the circumference, presents a powerful argument in support of those world-based public services which, especially under the auspices of the Economic and Social Council of the United Nations, are now being put forward as the normal and sensible way for the world to conduct its peace-time economic and commercial affairs, in place of the Cold War techniques which linger from the cut-throat rivalries of the past and still appear to be favoured in some unenlightened quarters. There is, surely, something morally or mentally wrong with people who won't do willingly for peace what they will gladly do for war?

The above figures relate only to the International Committee's own initiative. The total Red Cross war effort would not be complete, of course, unless the stupendous efforts of the League and its National Societies were added to this list. But only passing reference to these other two indispensable arms of the Red Cross endeavour can be included at this point, so as not to stray too far from the main narrative.

On the outbreak of the Second World War, the League of Red Cross Societies moved its headquarters from Paris to Geneva, and collaborated with the International Committee in operating a Joint Relief Commission, which, during the next six years, *distributed* aid valued at more than 200 million dollars to distressed civilian populations. Meanwhile, the National Societies greatly expanded their own relief services, and many independent groups—of which the Friends' Ambulance Unit was among the most conspicuously successful—worked alongside them.

Inevitably, the American Red Cross—for reasons which need not be stressed, but which in no way lessen the incalculable value of its achievement—surpassed its already unique humanitarian record. Its field directors assisted in some 12,000,000 cases brought up by soldiers and sailors in camps and hospitals; the headquarters Communications Service in Washington handled 42,000,000 messages between Army and Navy personnel and their families or friends; while over 2,000,000 loans, totalling 60 million dollars, were made to servicemen. Volunteer workers made 2,500,000,000 surgical dressings and assembled 28,000,000 P.O.W. packages; members of the Motor Corps drove 43,000,000 miles; and canteen workers served 86,000,000 meals. Not least, 6,600,000 volunteers contributed over 13,000,000 pints of blood at the Red Cross blood centres. All this in the country which had resisted the ratification of the first Geneva Convention for seventeen years—and now leads the world in Red Cross activity!

These and similar breath-taking figures are given in Dr. F. R.

The American Section of the Central Agency, Geneva, 1944.

Dulles' impressive volume, already cited as the unrivalled classic in this field. It will doubtless stir the imagination of the more austere European reader to learn that (to quote the compiler's own terminology): "The recreational and morale supplies distributed to members of the armed forces added up to several billion individual items . . . ranging from pianos to fishhooks. In carrying out its programme, the Red Cross purchased 1,498,000,000 cigarettes, 31,000,000 packages of chewing-gum, 17,000,000 decks of playing cards, 121,000,000 razor blades, and 58,000,000 pounds of doughnut flour."

How the American Red Cross, quite apart from these general activities, conducted a far-reaching operation in providing relief for American and Allied prisoners-of-war held by the Axis powers, supplying nearly 200,000 tons of goods, valued at 168 million dollars, is referred to by Dr. Dulles in terms which bring us back again to the heart of the subject: "How many lives were saved, or serious cases of illness averted, by these relief operations can hardly be known. But whether from the point of view of the physical welfare of the war prisoners, or of their morale and that of their families, this steady flow of food and other supplies across the Atlantic was of utmost value." And he makes clear that the United States, as with the other National Societies, depended on the International Committee in Geneva to channel all food and relief packages to the P.O.W. camps. "The real rôle of the American Red Cross," he emphasizes, "was that of a procurement and shipping agency. It undertook to assemble and package the supplies, arrange their transportation overseas, and otherwise co-operate with the International Red Cross in whatever ways it could. . . . In practice, it was the International Red Cross that assumed the major responsibility for such operations, and in its neutral capacity undertook to investigate conditions in the prisoner-of-war camps and supervise the proper distribution of all supplies forwarded through its Central Agency for Prisoners of War."

BREACHING THE WALLS

Before concluding the present chapter by selecting for special examination one of the most fruitful examples of this invincible war-time collaboration, attention must be drawn, however briefly, to some of the chief obstacles—legal and material—which stood in the path of the full development of the Red Cross experiment.

Total warfare confronted the International Committee with problems which the Conventions did not foresee. There were—as explained in an earlier chapter—no legal provisions in International Law which allowed for the Committee's intervention in the unspeakably dreadful concentration camps. The Detaining Authorities regarded these camps as a purely domestic affair, and access to them was strictly denied to the Committee's delegates. Finally, after protracted negotiations, the Committee was given permission, in the autumn of 1943, to send food parcels to internees whose addresses were known. This was an important breach in the whole hideous system. During the last period of the war, however, several of the Committee's delegates succeeded in entering certain concentration camps and, at great personal risk, in saving the lives of many thousands of inmates.

Moreover, two of the chief belligerents, Soviet Russia and Japan, had failed to ratify the Prisoners-of-War Convention. The Committee was consequently unable, despite repeated efforts, to bring about agreement

American ship carrying Red Cross supplies in the Second World War.

between Russia on the one hand, and Germany and her allies on the other, for the transmission of relief supplies to their respective war prisoners. Even the exchange of family news between citizens, which the Committee offered to organise, was refused. Nevertheless, throughout the war the German Nazi Government co-operated with the International Red Cross, *and P.O.W. supplies were given priority*, subject only to military transport.

In the Far East, the Committee's relief schemes met with systematic opposition from Japan, and Red Cross delegates had access only to a small number of camps in Japan, Shanghai, and Hong Kong. The Japanese Government obdurately refused safe conduct for neutral relief ships and notoriously failed to maintain the standards in its P.O.W. camps anywhere approaching those prescribed by the Geneva Convention.

On the other hand, the International Committee was more successful in solving some of its gigantic transport problems, in spite of the enormous physical obstacles. No less than forty-three vessels were necessary for the transport of relief supplies for prisoners-of-war and the civilian victims of war. The ships, which all sailed under neutral colours and under the protection of the Red Cross flag, enjoyed special privileges granted by the Blockade Authorities, each vessel carrying a supercargo representing the Committee. By the end of hostilities, these mercy ships made 383 trips and conveyed 470,000 tons. By the spring of 1942 the expansion of the relief schemes and the growing shortage of neutral vessels, due to the intensification of submarine warfare, compelled the Committee to set up its own shipping agency. The "Foundation for the Organisation of Red Cross Transports" was thereupon created with a fleet of three vessels, and nine vessels were chartered in addition.

In the last phase of the war, another delicate transport problem had to be solved—at once. Destruction of railways and the total disorder which reigned made it impossible to carry food supplies to millions of detainees in Germany facing starvation in the camps and on the roads. But, by the immediate establishment of a new transport system, consisting of 474 vehicles and 137 trailers, relief supplies were rushed across the borders of the defeated countries to save those who could be reached in time. In 1945, the white lorries of the Red Cross made 3,140 journeys, travelled over two million miles, and repatriated 23,481 persons, amongst whom were a large number of utterly helpless deportees.

BARBED WIRE UNIVERSITIES

Minds must be fed as well as bodies. And one of the greatest triumphs of the human spirit, in all the organised welter of animal fury and

The International Tracing Service was divided under the names of the concentration camps, though these records were never completed.

criminal stupidity, which we call war, was revealed in the intellectual activity promoted in P.O.W. camps. The British Red Cross Society, as a case in point, published in 1943 a prospectus of study for use in one of the "Barbed Wire Universities"—Stalag Luft VI. Largely representative of the educational ferment in over 50 camps in enemy countries, it reported that, out of 4,686 prisoners, 4,259 attended classes and 40 per cent were taking examinations.

The supply base of these courageous schemes was provided by the Intellectual Relief Service at Geneva which, in one typical year alone, collected and despatched over 270,000 books to P.O.W. camp libraries. It was through the Geneva Committee, too, that more than a hundred examining bodies, university and professional, held their examinations in the prison camps.

"Hundreds of thousands, not to say millions, of men, women and children," said the members of the International Committee in their fourth Annual Report, "now know from first-hand bitter experience the material hardships of life in prison camps; together with its boredom, loneliness, and monotony. Some of them have known it for many years now. Whether occupied or not—officers, non-commissioned officers, privates, or interned civilians—all camp inmates are overwhelmed, from time to time, by the hopelessness and uncertainty engendered by their exile in the camps . . . thus our Service is able to help all these unfortunate victims to react against the depressing effect of a life wasted away in sterile inactivity behind barbed wire."

Now we can glance at some prisoners' letters.

"I belong to a small group of isolated prisoners-of-war," writes a French P.O.W., "and would be very grateful indeed if you could be so good as to get me a work on botany; as well as something on the treatment, planting and pruning of fruit trees, which would give us particular pleasure. Furthermore, a grammar and a book on hotel-management would also be welcome. Could you send us a book on the rules of bridge as well?" From a Mohammedan prisoner-of-war comes the request: "I take the liberty of requesting you to send me a copy of the holy Koran, in Arabic, in order to help me better to bear my captivity." A British camp-leader writes: "Lieut. X., who is preparing for his matric., needs the following articles: a compass, a square rule, a protractor, a graduated ruler (flat), a paper gripper, flat on one side, which will be very useful to him in order to help him hold his papers, as he has lost his right arm."

In Geneva the Service was housed in the Hotel Metropole, then the headquarters of the International Committee, and placed under the control of one of its members, assisted by the representatives of various educational and religious bodies which constituted the Advisory Committee on Reading Matter for Prisoners of War and Civilian Internees, which met at regular intervals. There one could find anything from a paper-bound pamphlet to rare editions which would not shame a collector's shelves. Magnificently-bound volumes printed in folio, ornamented with wood-cuts, stood side by side with complete collections on medicine, religion, and law, or full editions depicting the history of art, profusely illustrated. In another room were games for the blind, as well as shelves full of grammars and alphabets in braille; further on, indoor games, sports gear, and musical instruments were stored. The Commercial Section of the Intellectual Relief Service stocked individual and collective consignments of paper, copy-books, rulers, pencils and water colours; and established a system of export and import permits, as well as bills of lading and so on, for the transmission of gramophones, records, musical instruments, sports gear and games.

"I was so glad to receive, on the 6th January, 1943," is the testimony of a Hindu prisoner-of-war, "your two parcels containing complete

When the war ended, fleets of white trucks of the Red Cross swept into Germany with food and medical supplies to save the civil population.

141

drawing materials which came to hand intact. The objects which you included therein, such as the slide-rule, the box for drawing instruments, the paper and other objects, are of very fine quality indeed. You have replied more generously than I could ever have hoped for. I feel, and am, so thankful that I cannot find words to express my gratitude. With my very best wishes, Yours sincerely, Bhogat Singh."

The arts flourished out in the camps. Designers, painters, sculptors, interior decorators were only too happy to be able to follow their inspiration; and the Intellectual Relief Service sent them abundant material, comprising drawing boards, papers, brushes, charcoal, and drawing pins. In one civilian internment camp there was an arts and crafts school with 89 students inscribed on its rolls, of whom 48 were children from 9 to 18 years of age. Newspapers in the camps were as varied as were their contents. Some were printed in ink on newspaper by press-men by profession, working in a neighbouring printer's. The more luxurious periodicals looked almost like reviews, their cover was on brilliant paper, depicting a detailed country-scene in black and white, or even printed in three or four different colours. Social, educational and sports news, as well as jokes, puzzles and chess problems, follow each other—just as at home. The doctor's corner is next to the page of science. On the same sheet Catholic and Protestant padres give their comrades messages of advice and good cheer.

Thus, man conquers his environment—again—just as he has done all down the ages; as he assuredly will, one day, conquer war itself.

"Man was born free," cried Jean-Jacques Rousseau, Citizen of Geneva, in the opening words of his world-changing *Social Contract*, "yet everywhere he is in chains!"

Henri Dunant, also Citizen of Geneva, who toiled to save and liberate the common soldiers of his day, was among the first of modern revolutionaries to perceive that the shackles of the prison-camp over men's bodies would only finally be broken when men broke the power of war over their minds.

CHAPTER SEVEN

Peace Hath Her Victories

❧❧

THE Malaria Cavalry advances. The fight is on and the enemy retreats. Not at Solferino this time, but in the High Sierras. This also is War—but to save lives, not to sacrifice them. It demands the thoroughness of military organisation in planning and in logistics, and calls for devoted men and women, trained in the tactics of peace, to carry it through to a successful conclusion.

Mexico, which has decided to eradicate MALARIA and deliver its 30,000,000 inhabitants from the disease which has crippled empires and destroyed civilisations, has put it on war-footing. High-ranking officers direct the campaign from operational headquarters, from which they deploy their spray-teams as if they were combat troops. "Supreme Headquarters" is WHO's Regional Office, the Pan-American Sanitary Bureau, which sees Mexico as a sector of the wider battle-front of all Latin-America. The U.N. Specialised Agencies are linked together on a wide front. The U.N. Children's Fund has provided equipment. There are motorised columns alongside the Malaria Cavalry, with their mounted spraymen and pack-horses, climbing the bridle-paths into the High Sierras. And the Red Cross, of course, is there—part of the world team.

The next enemy is LEPROSY; in the Far East, especially. In all recorded history this dread contagion has stood apart from all others and set men apart from men. The warning bell, the wailing cries of "Leper!" have echoed down the centuries—symbols of despair and of the outcasts expelled from human society.

Leprosy is still widespread in the world. In Burma, alone, 200,000 cases have recently been reported; and more and more secret sufferers are appealing for medical aid. Just like the sufferers from tuberculosis, its victims can now seek treatment by new-found drugs, and in the wonderful organisation of modern medicine—but organisation across

The Malaria Cavalry advances. This also is war, but to save lives, not to sacrifice them.

frontiers, based on a One World strategy. Now segregation need only apply to the contagious period; it no longer means the dreaded leprosy asylum.

In the leprosy colonies and centres of today, the despair of an isolated doom has given place to the radiant faces of hope. And, since poverty and malnutrition are the allies of this disease, the whole world-team is at work on it—with the Red Cross out in front.

It is the same with POLIO. "East is East and West is West," but they meet wherever human need calls forth the first law of human nature: self-defence against man's common enemies. But, this time, self-defence means that the *individual*, not the nation, has become the unit of universal concern. Man, ceasing to war against man, is no longer a cog in the war-machine, a slave of the state, demanding him body and soul; but he has returned to his heritage as a citizen of the world and become a man again in his own right and dignity.

Such was little Shigenori's case. No longer a "target for tonight," but the child of everyone's care. The virus found him in the tiny hamlet of Tsukuni on Kyushu, far from Tokyo, and farther still from Hiroshima and Nagasaki.

Polio paralysed him. Shigenori could not lift a hand nor move a leg. He was eight years old when he was taken to Tokyo, to the Seishi Ryogo En. There, in the Hospital school and home for crippled children, he began the long wrestle with infirmity. In that hospital there are many like him, children who, only a few years ago, would have been forsaken as helpless, useless, cripples for life.

The Japanese Government's rehabilitation campaign, which WHO and UNICEF began to help in 1952, by providing fellowships for Japanese health personnel to go abroad and learn how such handicaps are overcome, is yet another sector of this real war in which all governments are allied, not *against* each other, by fears and threats, but *with* each other, by science and understanding. They are carrying to its logical conclusion the humanitarian incentive which had its origin, a hundred years ago, in the Geneva Convention.

But how did it happen that the Red Cross, which is still looked upon by some people as a sort of welfare branch of the national war ministries (or "defence departments", as they are nowadays called), became so closely identified with this world-wide campaign against disease, poverty, and malnutrition?

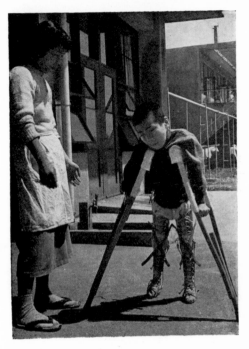

"Shigenori could not lift a hand or move a leg." (A full-page picture of Shigenori appears on page 245 at the end of the Postscript.)

Has the Red Cross changed its masters, and has it at last become what it was *intended* to be—a mighty Peace Army?

THE DEFEAT OF DISASTER

At its first post-war meeting in Oxford in 1946, the Board of Governors of the League of Red Cross Societies reconstituted its Relief Bureau to co-ordinate the peace-time activities of the National Societies. At first, their work fell into two categories: relief for civilian war-victims, and emergency needs created by public disasters. But, as time went on, and the U.N. Specialised Agencies developed—Health, Food, Refugees, Children's Fund, and so forth—the League and its National Societies found themselves more and more involved. They became the shock-troops in the World War against WANT. The century-old dream of Henri Dunant had become true.

Looking back, it is clear that the Red Cross has not only become universal in scope; it has also become an essential part of an emerging One World social order, which—not a moment too soon—is gradually replacing the anarchic régime of "sovereign states". So let us now trace this most significant development since the end of the last war, and then ask: *Where is it carrying the Red Cross today?*

In 1948, for instance, the League accepted a direct mandate from the United Nations to care for no less than 330,000 Palestine refugees in Lebanon, Syria, and Jordan. At the same time, the International Committee of the Red Cross accepted a similar mandate for those in Palestine. Refugees—a symptom of the failure of the sovereign state to solve its internal problems—have become a special object of solicitude to the organisation which reaches through the artificial barriers of the impersonal state and lays its hand on the shoulder of the homeless and the persecuted.

Assistance of the same kind has been given, on a systematic scale, to thousands of refugees in Western Germany, Austria, Italy, and Greece. In 1956, the Hungarian tragedy (*see* Chapter VIII) brought the Red Cross to the highest point of its achievement. But the U.N. Office of the High Commissioner for Refugees, and other official organisations, such as the U.N. Works and Rehabilitation Agency and the Inter-Governmental Committee for European Migration, as they came into being or grew in strength, gradually took over much of this side of the work of the Red Cross. Yet, as always, it was the Red Cross which was the pioneer and then continued as an auxiliary to the others.

On the other side of the picture, as countries devastated by the war regained their equilibrium, the Red Cross societies of those same

In Palestine, in 1948, the wounded are carried to safety under the protection of a Red Cross delegate.

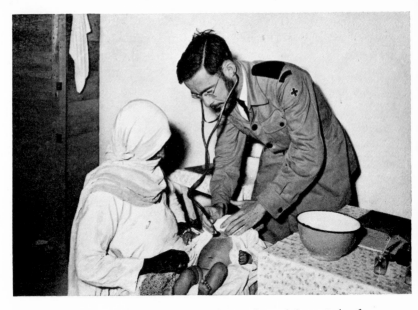

Co-operating with the U.N., the Red Cross brings help to Arab refugees fleeing from Palestine.

countries responded with enthusiasm to any appeal from the League when disaster struck other countries. In 1949, for example, 31 National Societies donated three-quarters of a million dollars in cash and in kind for earthquake victims in Ecuador and nearly 60 thousand dollars for victims of a typhoon in the Philippines. In 1950, the Canadian Red Cross spent more than a million dollars for flood victims in that country. Shortly after that, sixteen National Societies contributed to alleviate the suffering of earthquake victims in Peru. So the story of mutual aid and common service has grown with the years.

However, it was disastrous 1951 that saw the Red Cross leap forward as the outstanding world-wide organisation to provide disaster relief. This tragic year for so many started with floods in the United States, a hurricane over Jamaica, a cyclone in Martinique and, in October-November, terrible floods in Italy.

During this calamity, the League's Relief Bureau demonstrated the value of its international co-ordination centre in Geneva. Forty National Societies contributed assistance, valued at some three million dollars, which was administered by the Italian Red Cross. Planes were used to rush international relief to the scene of disaster; special trains and long lines of ambulances and motor trucks sped across Europe. And, after the flood waters receded, entire villages were reconstructed with pre-fabricated houses from Scandinavia.

The North Sea floods in 1953, which caused the death of 2,000 persons in Great Britain, Belgium and the Netherlands, and left 80,000 homeless, were the next big test. Within a matter of hours, planes carrying Red Cross relief were winging their way to the scene, ships carrying Red Cross supplies were plying the Atlantic; special trains started from Italy and truck convoys from West Germany, France and Switzerland.

Along with forty sister societies operating through the League, the three National Societies directly concerned contributed an estimated total of nearly five million dollars. Commercial air-lines granted free space for relief supplies; military and naval planes of half a dozen countries were placed at the call of National Societies or the League; state railways carried thousands of tons of relief free of charge and steamship lines carried supplies at reduced rates.

Later in the same year, there were floods in Yugoslavia, Japan, and India, and earthquakes in Turkey and Greece. With the same ex-pedition, nearly two million dollars' worth of supplies were sent to these countries. All of these movements were co-ordinated by the

In the Po Valley floods, Italian Red Cross volunteers answer the calls.

President Eisenhower with a Junior Red Cross member.

League's Relief Bureau, which has thus become the universal head-quarters for emergency relief anywhere around the globe.

One result of this vast living network of humanitarian action has been that the whole Red Cross movement has been brought into intimate and continuous association with the other international and regional organisations concerned with our One World economic and social life. Starting with the Organisation of American States, the Caribbean Commission and the Council of Europe, and leading on to the U.N. World Health Organisation (WHO), the U.N. Food and Agriculture Organisation (FAO), the United Nations Children's Fund (UNICEF) and the International Civil Aviation Organisation (ICAO), the Red Cross today stands for common action in all cases of international calamities.

Incidentally, the example of the Red Cross as an instrument in the cause of peace was well illustrated in 1954 when President Eisenhower offered relief supplies, valued at nearly six million dollars, to flood sufferers in East Germany, Czechoslovakia, and Hungary, and an equal amount to those in West Germany, Austria and Yugoslavia. When the governments of those countries accepted this offer, the League of Red Cross Societies was chosen to supervise its distribution and did so in East and West Germany, Czechoslovakia, Hungary and Yugoslavia, the Red Cross Societies of these countries actually carrying out the distribution. This was the first large-scale relief operation conducted simultaneously on both sides of the so-called "iron curtain" since the Second World War. It was so eminently successful that people are gradually awaking to the thought—thanks to the Red Cross experience—that this is the *normal* way for countries to conduct their relations.

Ten thousand Red Cross volunteers made this operation possible, and, in a letter of congratulation addressed to the League, President Eisenhower remarked that "the most notable fact about this programme has been the strict adherence by everyone to the humanitarian principles of the Red Cross. Relief was given to the most needy, regardless of race, colour, creed or political convictions. For the first time in many years it was possible to surmount political boundaries in the administration of relief."

It is no wonder that Dag Hammarskjold, Secretary-General of the United Nations, in his 1956 personal message for Red Cross Day, declared: "It has happened many times in the last ten years that the

Dag Hammarskjold.

international community has appealed to the Red Cross to give aid and comfort to some of its stricken members. Whether the occasion has been disaster in the form of earthquakes in Asia or Latin America, floods inundating the lowlands of Europe, political upheavals rendering millions homeless and helpless in the Middle East or Korea, the answer has always been the same: a prompt 'Yes' followed by immediate practical and selfless service, without which many of the sufferers would have been unable to survive."

UNIVERSALITY IN ACTION

In the most recent of the four-yearly Reports of the League, appropriately entitled *Universality in Action*, the author states: "In every field of Red Cross activity throughout the world, the League and its federated Red Cross, Red Crescent, and Red Lion and Sun Societies have made dynamic progress in the service of mankind. Yet this is no time for complacency—far from it. The needs of distressed humanity were never greater than they are today; and their volume, which is incalculable, is steadily increasing. Up to now, all efforts to deal with universal human suffering have produced no more than palliative results: for it is largely caused by complex forces which have hitherto defied control—*and many of them are closely linked with those of war.*"

Thus, even in taking up the ever-present challenge of peace-time needs, the words which have been italicised remind us that the whole movement is overshadowed with the constant threat of war or the results of war.

For this reason alone, the present book would have been justified in insisting from the beginning that the *prevention* of war is Red Cross responsibility No. 1.

This distinct trend in the thinking of, especially, the international leadership—though it has not yet been reflected so strongly in all the National Societies—is presenting problems of great magnitude to the international movement, with its hundred-and-a-quarter-million individual members in all lands. For the "prevention" of war does not mean the same thing to the International Red Cross as it means to the national Governments.

Hitherto, some National Societies appear to have been content to follow the lead of their respective Governments and, unreservedly, back them in preparations for war, which have always led—and *must* always lead—to war. But, "Universality in action" can only mean

This little Greek girl has reason to remember Geneva (1954).

that the National Societies must, unitedly, persuade or compel their respective Governments to follow *them*—and to prepare for peace. The implications of this new direction in Red Cross philosophy are certainly earth-shaking—though, up to the present, they have not been thought through on the national level.

Nevertheless, this realisation is clearly becoming a deepening concern of an increasing number of Red Cross leaders working in the centre of the movement today. These men and women have caught the flaming spirit of their intrepid founder, and are guiding the movement where he undoubtedly would have led it, had he been alive in body.

This underlying motive definitely revealed itself in the career and the dedicated life-work of John Wills, the author of the Report which forms the substance of the present pages. John Wills died in September 1957, before his final task was quite complete. This is what the Secretary-General of the League wrote of him:

> The value of the Red Cross as a force in the service of peace came as a revelation to him when he began to write. Although he was in intense suffering, he persevered in the expression of what he fervently believed. Up to his very last breath, he kept before his

eyes the vision of the great destiny which was to be that of the movement he had learned to know.

It is such a revelation of the "great destiny" of the Red Cross "as a force in the service of peace" which must inspire, not only its international leaders, but the rank and file of its fast-growing membership. If it does, it will assuredly carry a united Red Cross forward to the next phase of universality in action—the abolition of war.

Meanwhile, the techniques of peace are being strengthened in every corner of the world. In Chapter VIII we shall return to the unremitting ministrations of the International Committee's delegates—in Hungary, Algeria, Korea—but, in the present chapter, let us travel awhile with the missionaries of the League of Red Cross Societies. In every continent their presence complements and sustains that of the Geneva delegates.

These frequent missions serve several main purposes: to strengthen the bonds between the League and its member Societies, to help launch new Societies—or to reconstitute existing ones, and to help expand the programmes and activities of all the established Societies. Study visits and exchange of staff likewise play an important part in this round-the-world work. But the League's missionaries are discovering every year that, in today's fast-moving context, they have much more to do than preach the simple Red Cross word. "For, in a world," runs the Report, "where two-thirds of mankind are under-nourished—and so deprived of reasonable health, expectation of life, and productive capacity—new ways must be found without delay to stem the tide of human suffering. The fact that the hardships besetting the less fortunate two-thirds of humanity have steadily increased during the last ten years, proves once and for all that official machinery, both national and international, moves far too slowly to provide, by its own efforts alone, an adequate remedy for this tragic situation."

It follows, therefore, that people in distress cannot rely solely on administrative health and social services, however well organised these may be. Rather, they must strive to ease the burden on such services by learning to look after themselves as far as possible. Thus, practical experience gained in all parts of the world must be provided to help them to improve the medical and social services in their countries. The Red Cross, so admirably equipped to play a pioneer part in all these campaigns, as we have noted through its countless volunteer

154

workers, is in close touch with the ordinary people of every land, and most important, it has their confidence. With its wide knowledge of the most advanced methods of dealing with human suffering, it can render the "official" health and other welfare services invaluable aid in developing new techniques, especially in the under-developed countries.

To fulfil these multiple aims, the Red Cross has to plan and operate on the broadest international lines (as we studied at the beginning of this chapter), thus giving to the passive concept of "neutrality"— which Dunant strove so strenuously to include in his first Convention —a dynamic meaning which marks a new era in Red Cross achievements, and which must, eventually, re-create the Red Cross in a new image.

TO THE ENDS OF THE EARTH

The Afghan Red Crescent became a member of the International Red Cross in November 1954. The Society's aims were summed up by Prince Ahmed Sha Khan, its Honorary President, in the words: "Humanity stands in desperate need of mutual co-operation and mutual assistance." How true these words are, was clear from the manner in which the Red Cross campaign proceeded in this rugged mountainous kingdom, secluded by natural barriers from the outside world.

Early in 1952, Dr. Anne-Marie Gade, the Danish expert on the staff of WHO, was sent by that organisation on a three-years' mission to Afghanistan, to develop mother and child services; but she also acted for the League in assisting the Afghan Red Crescent Society to qualify for League membership. The problem of organising national health services in this country is obvious from the fact that it lacks railways and has only one navigable waterway; camels and mules provide its chief means of normal transport.

Nevertheless, when Dr. Gade arrived in Kabul in 1952, she found the Red Crescent Society striving to meet the needs of the people and to gain their active support. It possessed first-aid tents, ambulances, and trucks; while a 100-bed hospital and polyclinic was under construction in Kabul. The Society was engaged in the provision of medical and health services, the recruiting and training of staff, the development of branches in all the provinces and the organisation of relief work. Furthermore, a Red Crescent programme was heard weekly from Radio Kabul. Dr. Gade's valuable work in helping the

Thailand Red Cross Juniors prepare to meet tomorrow's emergencies.

Society to qualify for League membership, while carrying out her main mission on behalf of the WHO, is one more example of how the League co-operates with international bodies on the U.N. level.

From Asia, we now pass to the African scene, where, in February 1956, General François Daubenton, M.D., the Medico-Social Consultant to the League and former Director of the WHO Regional Office for Africa, left Geneva on a mission to Libya and the Sudan in order to advise on the formation of National Societies in these newly independent countries. One of the objects of General Daubenton's mission was to determine how far in each country a new Society could supplement the official health services. On his recommendation, the Government of Libya has since ratified the Geneva Convention and appointed a special commission to frame statutes for a national Red Crescent Society, and the Government of the Sudan has likewise agreed to ratify the Geneva Convention and intends to establish a Red Crescent Society.

But perhaps the round-the-world expert tour *par excellence* was undertaken in 1954 by the present Under Secretary-General, Mr. W. J. Phillips, then Director of the Bureau of Organisation and

Development, who left Geneva on a five months' mission to South and South-East Asia and Australia, in the course of which he travelled 40,000 miles and visited the Societies of nine countries: Thailand, Indonesia, Australia, New Zealand, the Philippines, Burma, India, Ceylon and Pakistan.

Every year that passes brings this important area into greater world prominence. Six hundred million people—nearly a quarter of the world's population—inhabit it. In many of these countries independence has given to their young Governments the heavy responsibility of meeting long-standing problems relating to health, housing, and diet, particularly in those countries which were devastated by the Second World War and subsequent social disturbances.

Since the war, however, the U.N. Economic Commission for Asia and the Far East (ECAFE), the Colombo Plan, and other international schemes, as well as the American Point Four programme, have been launched to aid economic development in South and South-East Asia. But the ultimate success of these efforts depends on the active support of the ordinary peoples of South and South-East Asia. These peoples must be helped to improve their own health and living conditions, so as to build up energy both to produce more food and other necessities, and to resist the hardships that must still await them. Here the

American Red Cross dropping sorely needed food and medical supplies to a flood-isolated mountain family in Greece.

157

Red Cross is playing a vital rôle in helping the broader plans to succeed; and it is, once again, in the light of this close relationship that the value of the League delegate's mission can best be appreciated.

The people of Indonesia, for example, which has a population of 77 million, suffered severely during the Second World War, and their distress was later intensified by a war for national independence, followed by a further period of disturbance. The problems facing the Indonesian Red Cross were, therefore, immense; but their leaders recognised that success could only be achieved by far-sighted planning and perseverance. They accordingly turned to the League for advice.

Mr. Phillips met all the members of the Central Council and head-quarters staff of the Indonesian Red Cross and discussed their problems with them. Then he visited thirty of the Society's seventy-five branches and so gained a clear picture of its general activities. He addressed meetings in every town, sometimes as many as three a day, visited institutions and paid courtesy calls on prominent officials. He saw blood transfusion centres operating in Semarang, Surabaya and Bandung, a home for crippled children in Solo, a home for the aged and a hospital for tubercular ex-service men in Bandung.

Travelling along the main roads from Djakarta to Tegal and from Tegal to Semarang, he noticed that Red Cross first-aid posts lined the highway at regular intervals of five kilometres; and in Djakarta and Macassar he saw the work of the newly constituted volunteer corps. But, more important, he also pointed out that the Society's great hope for the future lay in the seven million children attending Indonesian schools and urged that steps should be taken to teach them Red Cross ideas and methods. Suiting the action to the word, he at once took up this question with the Ministry of Education; and a few months later the Ministry recommended that Junior Red Cross sections should be formed in all Indonesian schools.

This was only the beginning of his tour, and many arduous weeks followed. In regard to general policy, the League delegate suggested that, in view of the difficult conditions existing in Indonesia, the Society should concentrate its main efforts on dealing with basic needs —such as public health instruction and preventive measures; and he accordingly advised priority development of its first-aid, nursing, and blood transfusion services.

During his stay in Canberra, Mr. Phillips accompanied the Secretary-General of the Australian Red Cross on a visit to the Department of

External Affairs to discuss methods by which the Australian Red Cross could help National Societies in South and South-East Asia under the provisions of the Colombo Plan—especially in connection with staff training. It was arranged that the Australian Red Cross should send, at the expense of the Australian Government, a blood transfusion expert to Burma, Indonesia, and Thailand, in order to advise on the establishment in those countries of national blood transfusion services staffed by technicians trained by the Australian Red Cross. During his visit to Australia, the League delegate also addressed many meetings in the divisions through which he passed, and broadcast talks to the Australian people on the aims and work of the League.

He likewise toured the principal towns of New Zealand and called on the Mayors to explain the Society's special position with regard to the Community Chest scheme, which the Society had been invited to join, but found it impossible to do, because of the terms of the Geneva Convention and the Red Cross principle of independence. Mr. Phillips, found himself, therefore, carrying out a mission of some delicacy and one requiring tact and impartiality of a high order.

Under-Secretary-General Mr. Wilfrid J. Phillips pauses in Ceylon during a 40,000 mile tour of National Societies in Asia.

Leaving New Zealand, the League's delegate flew to Manila, where he conferred with leaders of the Philippine Red Cross at its headquarters. He then toured the country, travelling many hundreds of miles to tell provincial branches of the work and structure of the international movement. After visiting the branches of the British Red Cross in North Borneo and Malaya, he flew to Rangoon, where he had conferences with the officers of the Burma Red Cross Society. With the approval of the Minister of Education, he addressed a meeting of teachers and pupils of Government Secondary Schools on the work of the Junior Red Cross, and in this way, a Junior Red Cross Section was created in Burma.

And so on through India, Ceylon, Pakistan, this inexhaustible and imperturbable humanitarian diplomat and negotiator travelled day after day, to report finally in Geneva the following January that he had studied on the spot the special Red Cross problems of many lands—problems affecting the health and happiness of nearly one-quarter of mankind; he had been able to advise many Societies on the solution of their particular difficulties; and he had abundantly confirmed the extraordinary adaptability of Red Cross methods to widely differing economic, social, and climatic conditions.

If there were ever a one-man embodiment of "Universality in Action", then Wilfrid J. Phillips is that man.

YOUTH FINDS ITS IDEAL

"What is brotherhood?" asked John Wills at the beginning of the last—and finest—Report he ever wrote for the League. And he answered in terms which both carry us back to Henri Dunant and forward to Mahatma Gandhi and Albert Schweitzer, and which leave no doubt as to the future rôle of the Red Cross in the earth-wide Crusade to destroy the war-system once and for all:

It is primarily an attitude of mind; a personal outlook—free, kindly and spontaneous—which is not in the gift of governments. On the contrary, the spirit of brotherhood has itself created common law and good government—on which the internal peace and unity of nations depend. There is but a single step from national to international brotherhood. And that universal outlook, *once shared by enough people*, can be the mightiest force on earth—a force which could, without violence or blood-

shed of any kind, banish arbitrary power overnight and set up true authority in its place, true authority which tolerates neither inequality nor violence.

It is this world-ideal of a just, tolerant and non-violent international order, based on mutual consent and not on force or the threat of force, which the International Red Cross holds up before every one of its hundred and a quarter million members today—but, above all, its 50 million Junior members.

To its Junior Branch the Red Cross has assigned a task which (in John Wills' own words) "consists of establishing bonds of real affection between young people of every country. By offering them practical means whereby they may get to know one another, the Junior Red Cross seeks to create an atmosphere of mutual esteem and greater understanding, and breaks down the only real barrier that separates the different races: ignorance on both sides, and the nursing of old grievances which have ceased to exist."

This constructive approach to the handling of world problems is, perhaps, the most original contribution the Junior Red Cross has made to the modern conception of education. While belonging to a long-established and powerful organisation, which has gained world

Yugoslav Juniors making toys for refugee children.

recognition and respect, the Junior Red Cross offers a tool to the schools for continuous human contacts between the different countries which is almost unique. The different means by which the Junior Red Cross carries out its international friendship programme have today advanced far beyond the familiar traditional form, consisting usually of school correspondence. The exchanges of school art, begun after the war by means of drawings and paintings, depict the countryside and surroundings, and daily happenings at school and at home. They have been a mounting success and, in 1955, the Junior Red Cross Bureau was able to carry out a plan for simultaneous exchanges between 28 National Sections.

During recent years, many of the National Sections have asked the Bureau to help them organise large exhibitions of art and school work, and these have always met with a good response from sister sections. The exchange of recorded songs and messages is still in its experimental stage, despite the fact that at least ten National Sections are now doing this fairly regularly. What appears to be, however, the most significant demonstration, during the last few years, of the desire of the Junior Red Cross to provide its members with real opportunities of affirming their ideals, and of forging solid links between the different countries, are the Study Centres. The main features of this innovation in the international life of the Junior Red Cross have now clearly emerged from the experience gained in different parts of the world, and all the National Sections are expected in the near future to organise such Centres on lines approved by the Advisory Committee.

Again, the Junior Red Cross has forged its own links with the growing circle of international associations making for a world community. The Junior Red Cross Bureau decided, however, to concentrate its efforts on UNESCO, whose aims and programmes had many points in common with those of the Junior Red Cross, besides becoming a focal point for nearly all the international non-governmental organisations concerned with childhood and adolescence. The League has been regularly represented at the Conferences and technical meetings of UNESCO, in particular the sessions of the Conference of International Youth Organisations.

The League's connections have also become increasingly intimate with the International Bureau of Education, the World Health Organisation, the U.N. Children's Fund, the International Labour Organisation, and the Food and Agriculture Organisation. In addition, a

wide network of personal contacts has been woven, enabling the Junior Red Cross to be better informed on specific problems and to pass on necessary information to the National Sections.

There is no doubt that participation by young people in well-planned international projects has inestimable educational possibilities. Those who have had personal experience of such world-wide co-operation will be better armed to meet international difficulties as resolute defenders of understanding and peace.

For example, one of the biggest relief actions in which the Juniors have joined, in recent years, was due to the previously-mentioned tidal wave which swept over the North Sea Coasts of Great Britain, Belgium, and the Netherlands in 1953, bringing merciless floods in its wake. The Juniors' contributions to their National Societies' relief actions came to well over a million Swiss francs. "Henri Dunant House", at Woudschoten in the Netherlands, stands as a permanent memorial to this disaster. It was built during the summer following the floods, mainly with funds collected by the Austrian Juniors—nearly 350,000 Swiss francs—who sent a group of their members to help with its building for several weeks. Whole families came in turn to escape from the wretched conditions in the devastated areas. The House is furnished with gifts in cash and in kind from the Juniors of

In 1953, Netherlands Junior members battle at the dykes with their elders against the raging North Sea.

American Junior members, since 1950, have come to Geneva to study Red Cross principles and practice. In the historic Alabama Room hangs the painting by Armand Dumaresq of the signing of the first Geneva Convention of 1864.

various countries. The British Red Cross also launched an appeal to this end, and the House is now filled with books, paintings, gramophone records and handiwork from the Juniors of nearly forty different countries. It has since become a real international Junior Red Cross meeting place, and, in 1956, the Netherlands Red Cross organised an International Study Centre there. Every year groups of crippled boys and girls now spend welcome holidays there, which are entirely financed by the Netherlands Juniors.

Again, the League's relief action in aid of Hungarian refugees, described in detail later on in Chapter VIII, included an appeal launched by the Junior Red Cross in December 1956, which met with such a generous response from 17 of the National Sections that it was possible to make Christmas presents to nearly 7,500 refugee children in Austria, consisting of complete sets of warm clothing; and later appeals duplicated these results.

When, in October 1957, the expansion of the work of this worldwide Junior Red Cross movement was discussed at New Delhi, Mr. Charles A. Schussete, Director of the Junior Red Cross Bureau, League of Red Cross Societies, referred to the sad fact of how disillusioned young people of today feel because of the lack of security in the world bequeathed them by the older generation. He urged the necessity of impressing Red Cross principles on these young people, who are going to lead the world of tomorrow. It was necessary to create a respect for the human personality, the spirit of which is embodied in the Geneva Conventions, and he suggested that a copy of the Geneva Conventions should be in every school library. He also said that Juniors should be acquainted with the problems of the modern world, such as protection of civilian population during a war.

In the same discussion, the U.S.S.R. delegate, Mrs. Emilia Salenick, emphasised that the ideas of the Red Cross were dear to Soviet youth. There were $7\frac{1}{2}$ million Juniors in the U.S.S.R., and the Red Cross had extra-scholastic classes in health education. Great attention was being paid to the prevention of accidents among school children, and traffic rules were taught thoroughly to the children. Children were also taught to organise their leisure hours so as to become fitter citizens.

It is, nevertheless, significant that—at least, in the reports available— neither the traditional "West" nor the Communist spokesmen in New Delhi dared to face frankly the revolutionary effects which the Red Cross ideas, cited at the beginning of this section, would be

New Zealand Junior Red Cross helps the needy and finds happiness on the doorstep.

bound to have on the minds and outlook of young people today if these new concepts of Red Cross responsibility in the atomic age were openly expounded by the adult Societies.

Mr. K. Shanken Nigam, Director of the Indian Junior Red Cross, in fact confessed that he could not understand how problems created by war, such as the protection of the civilian population, should be of such vital importance to Juniors, who should primarily be made familiar with the problems of *peace*. He advocated a re-orientation of Junior Red Cross Services to suit the conditions of modern times. In this connection, he declared that a great "silent revolution" was spreading throughout his own country, affecting every aspect of life, and that Juniors were part and parcel of this movement, helping as they did in the work of revitalisation of the villages, taking part in community projects, and participating in sanitation drives, digging wells, and other village welfare work.

As one listens to the voice of the East, urging *both* the West and the Communist countries to re-orient their outlooks and methods "to suit the conditions of modern times", one turns back to the heart appeal of John Wills and asks whether the adult Societies in all countries are prepared to give to their own youth *his* answer to the question: "What is brotherhood?"

CHAPTER EIGHT

Limited War: Today

❦

ON 27th October, 1956, the International Committee received its first appeal from the Hungarian Red Cross for blood plasma, blood transfusion equipment and dressings, as the fighting which was going on in Budapest had already caused many casualties. The first delegate of the Committee left for Vienna that same day.

The Red Cross had got through. It was the *only* international relief organisation, as events were soon to prove, to be allowed to cross the frontiers of that ravished country during the whole period of the rebellion and its aftermath—with the sole exception of Dag Hammarskjold's top three officials some weeks later who, like the Geneva Committee, stood "above the battle" and put humanity unreservedly before politics.

The next day a telephone conversation took place with the Hungarian Red Cross, whose headquarters had suffered heavy damage. The situation was more serious and relief supplies urgently required. The same day the International Committee obtained 600 units of human albumen and chartered a Swissair plane which took off that evening to carry the supplies to Hungary. The aircraft landed at Feri-Hegy Airport, with two delegates of the Committee, Mr. Bovey and Mr. Beckh, on board. They handed over the relief supplies to the Hungarian Red Cross, and left immediately for Vienna to pick up the gift supplies which were beginning to arrive in Austria. So the airlift had begun.

During the next few days the blood plasma requirements appeared to have been met, but the frontiers had been shut and the general strike prevented food supplies from reaching the capital. Powdered milk and infant foods were badly lacking. At the same time the refugees started to arrive in Austria. Relief columns of various National Red Cross Societies now started to cross the frontier, and a relief train of the

The arrival at Feri-Hegy Airport, Budapest, of the first plane from Geneva with relief supplies for Hungary.

German Red Cross managed to reach Budapest under a safe-conduct supplied by the Committee. Another of the Committee's delegates, Mr. de Preux, accompanied a food convoy of the Austrian Red Cross as far as Budapest and managed to return to Vienna the same evening. The Hungarian Red Cross, however, then announced the loss of all its vehicles and made an urgent request for ambulances, surgical instruments, medicaments, food, and building materials for the rebuilding of hospitals. But on 4th November, all communications were cut off. Two delegates, Mr. Bovey and Mr. de Preux, remained at Budapest where violent fighting was in progress. Attempts were made, from 5th to 8th November, to obtain authority to pass through Czechoslovakian and Yugoslav territory, while the motor convoys of several national Red Cross Societies were held up in Vienna.

On 9th November, a convoy composed of 15 lorries, carrying 27 tons of foodstuffs, medicaments and medical equipment, left Vienna for the frontier. The Committee in Geneva notified the Hungarian and Soviet authorities of the departure of this convoy and requested them to help it to pass the frontier. Neutrality worked again: the convoy passed the frontier at 11 p.m., under the responsibility of Dr. Willener, another Swiss delegate, who proceeded immediately to Budapest, where the relief supplies were handed over to the Hungarian Red Cross. Thus began the second phase of the reach-through—that of the road transports. The Committee immediately made up a second convoy of 38 lorries, loaded with 120 tons of foodstuffs and medicaments for Budapest, and from that time, up to 15th March, 1957, the white lorries with the Red Crosses were seen regularly on the road from Vienna to Budapest, to be followed later on by supplies by rail and by barge along the Danube.

The following appeal, which was broadcast over the Swiss Short Wave Service and on its own wavelength, was an explicit reminder of the meaning and purpose of the Red Cross in times of civil war:

> At a time when the International Committee of the Red Cross, in conjunction with the principal National Red Cross Societies, is endeavouring to give Hungary, so sorely tried, the charitable aid the country requires, it wishes to recall several fundamental principles contained in the Geneva Conventions by which all peoples are bound:
>
> (1) All those who take no part in the fighting must be respected. The taking of hostages, in particular, is forbidden.
> (2) It is prohibited to kill or to wound an enemy who gives himself up. Prisoners must be treated humanely. In no case can any

Columns of Red Cross trucks leaving Vienna for the Hungarian frontier.

sentence be passed on them without previous judgment pronounced by a regularly constituted court.

(3) The wounded and sick shall be collected and cared for without discrimination.

The International Committee appeals to all concerned for the principles of these Conventions, which Hungary ratified in 1954, to be strictly respected.

This was followed, a few days later, by another broadcast from Geneva, the terms of which are self-evident:

The International Committee of the Red Cross makes a solemn appeal to commanders and combatants in Hungary. The International Committee of the Red Cross is informed that combats are still raging in Budapest, and that numerous wounded have not yet been collected and cared for. It makes an urgent appeal to commanders and combatants to call a truce by mutual agreement in order that the wounded may be collected and evacuated, in accordance with the provisions of Article 15 of the Fourth Geneva Convention.

At the same time, the Red Cross delegates tried, unsuccessfully, to obtain an armistice to allow the collection of the wounded lying in the streets. In East Hungary, another delegate, Mr. H. Beckh, was successful in preventing the shooting of some two or three hundred prisoners, who had fallen into the *insurgents'* hands. Other delegates in Budapest endeavoured later to obtain authority to visit persons detained or interned on account of their participation in the rising, but their efforts were unavailing. Russians were then in charge and, although the relief work went forward on an increasing scale, the clamp came down on any personal intervention.

Meantime, mass arrivals of relief supplies from all parts of the world and the magnitude of the overall action on behalf of the victims of the fighting in Hungary, as well as for the assistance of the refugees in Austria, necessitated a division of responsibility between the various Red Cross bodies. An agreement was therefore made between the international Red Cross organisations. The League of Red Cross Societies was entrusted with the reception and co-ordination in Vienna of the gift supplies sent by the National Societies, while the International Committee was to forward the supplies to Hungary and distribute them in co-operation with the Hungarian Red Cross. Out-

The Swiss Red Cross helps Hungarian refugees on their long journeys to new lands.

side Hungary, assistance to the refugees was to be the concern of the Austrian Red Cross. But very soon the flow of refugees from Hungary grew to such proportions that the International Committee undertook also the handling in Vienna of gifts for relief in Hungarian territory, and the League distributed relief supplies assigned to Hungarian refugees on Austrian soil.

In its arrangements with the Hungarian Red Cross, it is important to note that the International Committee retained the control of the distribution *in Hungary* of the gifts supplied to it, and ensured that the distribution was carried out in accordance with the fundamental Red Cross principles, "with strict impartiality and without any discrimination whatsoever other than that based on the urgency of the needs of the persons to be assisted". This agreement was ratified by the Hungarian Minister in Vienna, in the name of the then Hungarian Government, and all facilities were granted to the Committee for carrying out the tasks entrusted to it.

UNITED NATIONS WINS THROUGH

Turning away from Europe, for a time, to the United Nations proceedings in New York, it will be recalled that a Special Emergency Session

Stock-pile of American Red Cross parcels waiting in Vienna for transport and distribution.

of the General Assembly, convened at the beginning of November 1956, to get the British, French and Israelis out of Egypt, suddenly found itself confronted by the Russian aggression, too. These momentous day and night sessions marked for most of those who (like the author) were present, the supreme test of the United Nations as an effective barrier to a Third World War. The United Nations not only survived that test, but emerged a greatly strengthened body, much to the surprise—if not dismay—of its detractors.

Amidst the mutual recriminations of that double crisis and the repeated condemnations levelled at the world organisation because it did not, or could not, push the Russian invaders back, it is easily forgotten that the United Nations *did* succeed in carrying out its rightful and proper function as a humanitarian body—which was not to drop atom-bombs on recalcitrant member-states, but to aid the Hungarian people in spite of the costly, but not unforeseen, *military* failure of their rebellion. The U.N. resolutions calling for large-scale relief programmes to assist the Hungarian people, resulted in large funds being transferred over the following months from the U.N. to the International Committee of the Red Cross, which agreed to use the funds to provide immediate aid.

The agreement, which recognised the total *independence* of the International Red Cross, stipulated that distribution would be made in accordance with Red Cross principles and in the spirit of the Geneva Conventions, and stated that the Committee would be the *sole agency* to carry out the relief progamme on behalf of the United Nations. It would be difficult to find a more striking example of how effectively the Red Cross has become integrated—yet retaining its complete independence of action—with the world's chief organ of political decision.

It is only possible, in this very general review of what the Red Cross has meant to the Hungarian people, to add a bare outline of the basic civilian needs and the results actually attained. According to investigations made in December 1956, 8,000 dwellings had been completely destroyed, and 35,000 had suffered partial damage. Several hospitals, where the fighting had been particularly severe, were badly damaged. Casualties were estimated at 2,700 dead and 20,000 wounded. Coal supplies were extremely precarious; weeks of strikes and damage to the mines had considerably reduced output. Heating in the hospitals was barely adequate. Although the threat of famine in Budapest was dispelled when the transport strike came to an end, victims of the events, destitute through the loss of their dwelling or their bread-winner, were

Parcels are distributed as soon as possible after arrival in Hungary.

173

"Operation Milk", supplied daily to nearly 100,000 Hungarian children.

unable to obtain even essential foodstuffs. There were also great difficulties as regards textiles and footwear, since large stocks had been
destroyed by fire and factories had been shut down for weeks at a time.
The only essential medicament in urgent need at first was insulin, but
further investigation showed that antibiotics, dressings and X-Ray films
were also urgently required for hospitals. In Budapest alone, at least
250,000 persons were in need of assistance.

Of the 167 separate relief programmes set up and administered by
the Hungarian Red Cross, with a staff mainly composed of voluntary
workers, with the addition of 500 salaried workers, the following few
items are indicative of their size and effectiveness of achievement:

> 1,861,076 food parcels were distributed (each containing sugar,
> fats, tinned meat, powdered milk and, so far as possible, chocolate,
> coffee, tea and cigarettes), of which 745,000 were packed by the
> Committee in Budapest by means of the gift supplies received from
> the various countries. The total amount of powdered milk reached
> 1,707,000 kilograms.
>
> A hot meal *daily* was planned for 66,000 Budapest children under
> 14 years of age, but, owing to circumstances, the programme had
> to be limited to children up to 6 years.

From the great quantity of gifts, 1,460,607 kilograms of clothing and footwear, and 205,000 blankets were distributed to those in need.

A delivery of 8,696 tons of coal enabled the hospitals to overcome the acute shortage of coal. The welcome gift of American CARE made available 92,335 parcels of 25 kilograms of coal for families.

The influx of nearly 200,000 refugees to Austria and the necessity of organising transit camps and assisting the Austrian authorities brought together not only the International Committee and the League of Red Cross Societies, as far as the local arrangements were concerned, but also the Office of the U.N. High Commissioner for Refugees and the Intergovernmental Committee for European Migration (ICEM) to fulfil their obligations on the world level. Dr. Auguste Lindt, U.N. High Commissioner for Refugees, remarked especially on this extremely important matter of co-ordination, looking back on the biggest rescue operation yet carried through within a matter of barely three months. He said:

The magnitude of the new problem created by this exodus from one small country in such a short space of time has been revealed not only by the extent of individual human suffering, but also by

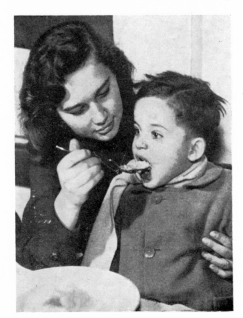

A little orphan of Budapest receives the first warm meal that he has eaten for several days.

the urgent measures taken to deal with the situation. The League of Red Cross Societies is shouldering a substantial proportion of this heavy burden, while the Intergovernmental Committee for European Migration and a host of voluntary agencies have also played their part in the operation of aid and assistance with efficiency and complete devotion.

Much rescue work remains and the Geneva Committee's scheme for re-uniting broken families still goes ahead—though the wider problem of the Hungarian refugees lies outside the scope of this book. But it should be added that, in compiling the Hungarian Central Card Index, all the National Red Cross Societies in the countries of refuge have given their utmost co-operation in the setting up and operating the Card Index in Geneva, by filling in the personal history cards, printed in four languages, or by supplying lists of names. However, in accordance with the practice followed by the International Committee in such cases, no information concerning a refugee is supplied without his consent. This work is being continued, since requests and enquiries continue to flow in to the Geneva Office. Once again, a card index, where hope lives, has proved mightier than an "iron curtain", where hope dies.

THE SUEZ DEBACLE

While the citizens of Budapest were being mowed down by Russian tanks, the citizens of Port Saïd were being blitzed by British planes. Grotesque though it may now seem, the arguments that were being, at that moment, so strenuously bandied around in the Assembly Hall in New York by both Russians and British, simultaneously, were fundamentally the same. They have been used a thousand times before, and always come down, in the end, to a simple proposition: the "right" of a Great Power to walk over a little one when the little one does not do as it is told. However that may be—and the U.N. debates have put the record straight for all time—the physical effect of the explosives on the human beings in the Suez region was the same as that on the inhabitants of Hungary. But, in addition to the British bombing of the usual points of "military importance", the Egyptians also had to bear the assault of the French and Israelis by land and sea.

But as the Suez adventure—like the Hungarian—was not called a "War" and as its attempted justification by the parties themselves was contumaciously rejected by the United Nations Assembly in a vote of

64 to 5 which, up to that time, was unique in its overwhelming condemnation of a premeditated act of military aggression, our concern here must be directed to the humanitarian action taken internationally to help the sufferers. Once again, about the justification of Red Cross action there could be no dispute.

An estimated 135,000 refugees had fled from Port Saïd alone—two-thirds as large as the exodus from Hungary, yet this phase of the episode was remarkable for its lack of publicity value to the world's Press. Thanks to the unexpected success of the United Nations Assembly —supported by the bulk of public opinion throughout the civilised world, and, also, inside the United Kingdom itself—the situation in Egypt was saved in time. In circumstances known so well, the invaders withdrew, under almost unanimous U.N. pressure, from the brink of World War III.

Not least among the beneficent results arising from the third-party judgment exercised by the United Nations plenary body on behalf of the threatened world community, was the speedy improvisation of the United Nations Emergency Force. UNEF stepped swiftly—like the Red Cross itself—between the belligerents. Furthermore, in addition to operating on the same basic principles which have made the Red Cross such a steadying influence in world crises, UNEF was endowed with political powers, which the Red Cross has never possessed. By remaining in the Gaza danger zone, the virtually unarmed UNEF has clearly demonstrated to the world that the Red Cross traditional principles of independence and impartiality, operating as an entirely neutral intervention between the belligerents, are the sure foundation on which the United Nations itself can build a permanent barricade against war.

With that perspective in mind, we can now pass on to review the manner in which the International Committee fulfilled its obligations in this other "limited" war.

On the outbreak of the Suez conflict, the International Committee appealed immediately to the Governments of the four countries involved in the hostilities to ensure the application of the four Geneva Conventions. Three of the Governments—Egypt, France and Israel— were already bound by these Conventions; but the United Kingdom, as we noted in Chapter III, had signed the new Conventions of 1949, but had not ratified them. Nevertheless, the British Prime Minister stated that, pending their ratification, the British Government accepted the Conventions and intended to apply their provisions.

Once more, the Committee assumed its traditional duties. As a neutral institution, enjoying the trust of all the countries involved in the conflict, it could endeavour, with every chance of success, to ensure that the military and civilian victims of the events were given protection and assistance, and intervene—on strictly humanitarian grounds—between the parties concerned. It immediately drew the four Governments' attention to the duties assigned to it by the Geneva Conventions and to the existence in Geneva of the Central Prisoners-of-War Agency, which would collect the names of the prisoners and detained or interned civilians, and transmit this information to the belligerent Governments, as well as arrange for the exchange of correspondence between prisoners and their families.

The Committee's General-Delegate in the Near East went immediately from Beirut to Israel, to receive the authorities' agreement to the nomination of a doctor-delegate from Geneva, whose headquarters were then fixed in Tel Aviv, where the Egyptian wounded were held. At the same time the central Committee invited the Egyptian Red Crescent to make known its needs of material relief and informed other National Societies of this action. The Egyptian Red Crescent accepted the Committee's offer of assistance and made an urgent request for large quantities of medicaments and medical supplies. The International Committee at once appealed to the National Societies and their response was immediate and favourable. The National Societies, it will be remembered, had already been asked to do all in their power in connection with the similar events in Hungary, but they at once began sending further important gifts to the Near East.

At the Headquarters of the Egyptian Red Crescent in Cairo, hundreds of people—all volunteers—came to offer their services to the Society. In all, 2,472 persons were registered and divided into teams for emergency care, welfare work and training of new volunteers. It was the first time that the Egyptian Red Crescent had recruited so large a number of volunteers. They were to fulfil many tasks in aid of the families made homeless in Port Saïd and of repatriated P.O.Ws. and civilians. The Egyptian Junior Red Crescent also took an active part in the Society's relief programme, helping in camps and hospitals.

In Geneva, the Central Prisoners-of-War Agency analysed and registered lists of prisoners as they came in, as well as information concerning releases, repatriations and deaths, received in accordance with the

Repatriation of Egyptian prisoners-of-war captured by Israeli forces at Bir-el-Babd in January 1957.

Geneva Convention. It forwarded family news and civilian messages sent through Geneva and investigated cases of death and disappearances. One unexpected difficulty arose, however, because most of the communications about Egyptian prisoners-of-war led to considerable correspondence with the delegations. In many cases the names given did not agree with those on the lists supplied by Britain, France and Israel, this trouble arising from the difficulty of rendering Arabic names phonetically, which caused extra research work.

To Port Saïd, completely cut off from the rest of Egypt, the Committee sent one of its delegates, Mr. M. Thudichum, who from 12th November took over the Committee's tasks on behalf of the victims of events, in particular the prisoners-of-war at Port Saïd and Port Fuad, forwarding family messages and opening enquiries concerning the missing. Urgent representations were made to the British and French Commands, calling attention to the Geneva provisions concerning repatriation of prisoners-of-war. The Egyptian prisoners at Port Saïd and the British civilian internees at Cairo were accordingly released and the exchange took place on 21st December.

Gifts in cash were meantime coming in from the National Societies, enabling emergency supplies to be purchased. The interruption of com-

179

munications by the British and French bombardments, however, made the despatch of supplies to Egypt subject to many difficulties. A DC-4 aircraft was therefore chartered by the International Committee for the Geneva-Cairo run. It had to be marked with the Red Cross emblem and follow a specific route in the Egyptian air space. The aircraft left Geneva on 11th November, loaded with $4\frac{1}{2}$ tons of relief supplies and with another delegate on board, and landed in Egypt 24 hours later. The following week, a second plane, also from Geneva, but placed at the Committee's disposal by the Danish Red Cross, carried to Cairo three tons of medicaments and dressings. Precautions were taken in distributing these consignments to make sure that they were used in conformity with the donors' wishes and the Red Cross spirit. The first two consignments by air alone weighed 7 tons, and were worth 300,000 Swiss francs.

In agreement with the Egyptian Red Crescent, the Committee, in order to meet the needs of the unfortunate civilians beleaguered in Port Saïd, sent trains loaded with medicaments and clothing to that city; they obtained permission for the trains to cross the lines held by the occupation forces and, on 16th November, the first convoy arrived at its destination. During this period, the delegate in Port Saïd strove to co-ordinate and develop the work of the various philanthropic societies working there, who elected him Chairman of their Committee. He directed the distribution of relief to the families in greatest need, in agreement with the medical authorities. At the end of November, the Red Cross General-Delegate for the region also went to Port Saïd with sufficient quantities of vaccine to immunise 100,000 persons against epidemic diseases. The two delegates discussed with the High Command and the Egyptian Government the steps to be taken to send convoys to the city and they also succeeded in having the ban lifted on the entry of Egyptian Red Crescent personnel into Port Saïd. Thus, thanks to these two Swiss, the trains organised by the Egyptian Red Crescent arrived at Port Saïd at regular intervals until 22nd December, when the last contingent of the Anglo-French expeditionary force left the badly-damaged port for their own countries, their mission of military force unfulfilled.

Meanwhile, the Red Cross International Committee continued, at the request of the Egyptian authorities and of embassies and consulates, to assist the nationals of various countries who had been equally the sufferers, without news of their families because of the events. Up to the end of 1956, for instance, the Red Cross transmitted no less than 65,000 personal messages between Egypt and the occupied territories of Port Saïd, Port Fuad, Gaza and Sinai. At the same time, the over-worked Red Cross delegates also dealt with the cases of stateless persons, particularly Jews. Several thousands of these harmless and peaceful people had been forced to leave Egypt, where they and their families had, in most cases, lived for generations on perfectly good terms with the Arabs, and could so have continued to live in peace—but for the aggression of their northern co-religionists. The Geneva Committee took steps, as ever, to help these unfortunate Jewish refugees and arranged for their transport by sea from Alexandria to Greece and Italy. In both of those countries the stateless persons in the Committee's charge were assisted by the National Red Cross and by charitable Jewish organisations, until they left for a country of asylum, in most cases Israel.

Finally, on the other side of the battle-front, the doctor-delegate, Dr. L. A. Gailland, sent specially from Geneva to Israel at the beginning of the conflict, took steps to co-ordinate relief measures there. He gave all possible material assistance to the Egyptian prisoners-of-war in Israeli hands, made regular visits to the camps where the members of the

Jewish refugees leaving Egypt on board a Red Cross transport as a result of the Suez conflict.

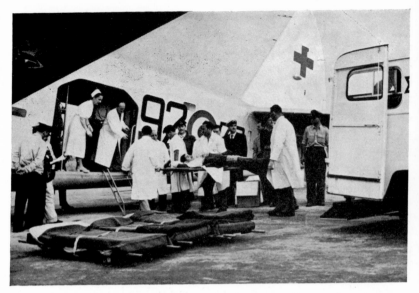

On their way to hospital, badly wounded Egyptian prisoners-of-war are repatriated by the Red Cross.

armed forces, captured during the Gaza fighting, were detained, and to the hospitals where wounded and sick prisoners were being treated, and sent a list of these prisoners to Geneva. The repatriation of a first group of seriously wounded Egyptians involved delicate negotiations. Two medical aircraft, placed at the Committee's disposal by the Italian authorities, flew from Cairo to Lydda in Israel, and brought back to Cairo 26 seriously wounded, accompanied by the doctor-delegate, an Italian doctor, and two Swiss nurses. Further repatriations were made later when the two medical aircraft flew from Cairo to Tel Aviv with a cargo of relief supplies, which the delegate in Israel arranged to have distributed among the Egyptian prisoners-of-war. On their return journey, the aircraft brought back to Egypt a second group of seriously wounded, 22 in all. The flights of the Red Cross medical aircraft between Israel and Egypt constituted *the first direct air link between the two countries since the beginning of the war in Palestine in 1948.*

After the invaders had withdrawn behind their frontiers, in accordance with the unconditional demand of the United Nations, the Red Cross delegate supervised the handing over by Israel of the 5,000 or more Egyptian prisoners to the United Nations Forces, which were then stationed on the Israeli border.

The delegate also undertook missions of enquiry into the living conditions of the inhabitants and some of the 700,000 pathetic Arab refugees—for ten years cut off from their homes—in the occupied regions of Gaza and Sinai. In Gaza itself, arrangements were made for him to pay regular visits to suspected Egyptian nationals under house arrest in the city. At El-Arish and Rafah he assisted children in need by distributing powdered milk and eggs, while in the Sinai peninsula he made sure that the people should not suffer unnecessarily from the invasion.

The Suez conflict, in fact, short though it was, provides a perfect example of the way the International Committee carries out its duties under the Geneva Conventions, and especially under the Fourth Convention dealing with the protection of civilians, which was applied for the first time—to the credit, let it be said, not only of the four belligerents, but of the practical visionaries of the International Red Cross who had "thought it through".

FROM NORTH AFRICA TO SOUTH ASIA

Thus far, in this chapter, we have considered only the two "limited" wars, each of a few weeks' duration, which were suddenly thrust upon

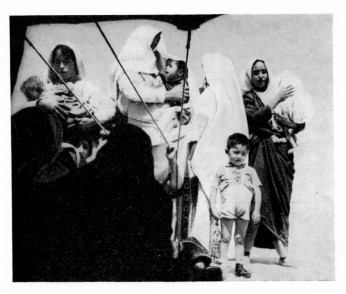

Arab refugees have been living in improvised shelters in Palestine since 1949—a generation of children is growing up in these conditions.

183

the world at the end of 1956 by three out of the five permanent members of the Security Council, *i.e.*, the members on whom the responsibility for safeguarding of peace most heavily lies under the terms of the U.N. Charter. We have noted, however, that it was the United Nations in one capacity and the Red Cross in another capacity which came in immediately to prevent the wars from spreading and to bind up the wounds of the sufferers. Once again, humanitarian law had triumphed, while jungle law had settled nothing, leaving behind its legacy of bitterness and a grave set-back to the cause of disarmament and peace.

From this point we can, within the compass of a few pages, first turn westwards from Suez and pinpoint some of the exceptional services rendered during the last few years by the International Committee in North Africa; and, lastly, glance East of Suez, as far as the tortured Kingdom of Korea, the two "halves" of which were brought together for the first time—since their dismemberment by the victors at the end of the last war—in an international Conference under the auspices of the Red Cross, held at New Delhi in 1957.

Early in 1955, the fighting in North Africa, where the native populations were in revolt against their French colonial masters, led the International Committee to offer its services to the French Government, to perform its humanitarian duties in Algeria, Morocco, and Tunisia. In February of that year, the Premier stated that the French Government was prepared to authorise Red Cross representatives to proceed to Morocco and Algeria to visit places of detention, and, if they wished, to converse without witnesses with persons under detention. Two missions were at once sent to North Africa. The International Committee's delegates visited 41 places of detention in Morocco and were able to converse freely with the prisoners and camp representatives. Conversations were held in French, and internees who spoke French served as interpreters for their comrades who did not speak the language. On account of the remote situation of places of detention, the delegates covered 5,000 miles, even to some far distant regions in South Morocco.

The first mission to Algeria was composed of three delegates from Geneva, who covered the three departments of Algiers, Constantine and Oran, and 43 places of detention were visited. In several cases, the International Committee's representatives were authorised to converse freely with the detained persons, and, after the interviews, their suggestions were placed before the detention-camp commanders. In the summer of 1955, the situation in North Africa having become more serious, the Committee again requested authority to send missions. It also reminded the North African authorities of the fundamental principles of the Geneva Conventions, as many cases were coming to light that the rebels were not being dealt with in accordance with France's solemn undertakings.

As the rebellion in Algeria spread, despite the reiterated promises of the many Resident-Generals that a week or two would suffice to end it, more reliable journalists began to write articles in radical Paris journals, and to write books, on what they had seen with their eyes or personally suffered in their bodies at the hands of their compatriots in Algeria. The tortures and atrocities practised against captured rebels became not only the subject of acrimonious Parliamentary debates by the end of 1957, but became, in fact, "The Question" for the people of France to answer—as one tortured writer entitled his famous exposure, just as Zola, half a century earlier, had courageously denounced the same military chauvinism in *J'Accuse!*

On the other hand, Government propaganda exhibited detailed texts and pictures describing the terrible mutilations, and worse, perpetrated by the rebels against French civilisation and honour. As a result, the

In Morocco, a delegate of the International Committee distributes parcels given by the Egyptian Red Crescent to Algerian refugees.

185

French people, who had had little to say about the Algeria question anyway, were driven to choose between an outright military rebellion on the soil of Metropolitan France itself and the demise of their Republic (which had been held up as an example of democracy to the Moslems abroad) after barely a decade of uncertain existence—all in a completely vain attempt to reconcile the nostalgic myth of *L'Union française* with the reality which was, and still remains, Algeria.

The International Red Cross, however, had to face the realities all the time—that is, in so far as its delegates were able to make contact with the people who needed them most. To these intrepid Swiss, especially the gallant Mr. P. Gaillard and Dr. L. A. Gailland, who made repeated visits, the whole of Northern Algeria must have seemed like a continuous concentration camp. During one of their many missions of mercy in 1957, the International Committee's delegates visited, in the course of barely six weeks, 48 places of detention—prisons, assembly centres, screening and transit centres, and hospitals. These included prison establishments in Constantine, Batna, Algiers, Tizi-Ozou, Berrouaghia, Blida, Mostaganem, Oran and Tlemcen, as well as the assembly centres for suspects and prisons in Djorf, Lodi, Berrouaghia, Paul Gazelles, St. Leu, Arcole, Bossuet, Sidi Chami and the Maréchal Camp. The mission was also able to visit a number of screening and transit centres, under military authority, where suspects arrested during military operations are detained. These were the centres in the Constantine area (Kerrata, Hamma-Plaisance, Alger Sahel, Batna, Bône, Duvivier), the Algiers area (Tizi-Ouzou, Bordj-Menaiel, Tigzirt, Beni-Messous, Boudjima, Dra el Misan, Tizi Reniff, Ouadhias, Château Holden, Aumale, Damiette, Orleansville, Warnier, Ferme des Cinq Palmiers), and the Oran area (Telagh, Chanzy, Ain-Tedeles, Blad Touaria, Rivoli, Tlemcen, Nedromah). Hospitals in Batna and Mustapha were also visited by the mission and during each visit the Committee's delegates were, as customary, authorised to converse without witnesses with detained persons of their choice.

Naturally, the delegates cannot publish their findings to the world, but they have endeavoured to obtain, on the spot, the necessary improvements in detention conditions, and they have had, in particular, interviews in Algiers with the Resident-Minister and the Commander-in-Chief of the Combined Forces in Algeria. Furthermore, detailed reports containing their suggestions were handed to the Head of the French Government. As with the Hungarian revolt, the International

Red Cross has been the *only* international body allowed to penetrate the barbed-wire curtain around Algeria and keep the road open for real civilisation to return one day to the land which was the very country which Henri Dunant chose as the most promising site for his earliest experiments in co-operative agricultural and industrial development, before he took the road which led to Solferino—and back again to Algeria.

Reverting to August 1955, the International Committee also approached the British authorities to inform them of its wish to be allowed to carry out its traditional humanitarian duties on behalf of victims of British action further south in Kenya. But the United Kingdom Government at first said "No!" The British Red Cross informed the Committee, nevertheless, that, in some cases, it did give assistance to child victims of the Mau-Mau rebellion.

Later, however, the British authorities relented and authorised the sending of a Red Cross mission to Kenya, composed of Dr. L. A. Gailland and Mr. H. P. Junod. This mission went to Kenya in March and April, 1957, and was able to visit 52 camps and prisons and 18 "rehabilitation villages" where the British authorities had detained without trial several thousand people—many of them entirely innocent

In Algeria, 1957, Mr. Pierre Gaillard, a Red Cross delegate, samples the food for Algerians under house-arrest at Djorf.

—accused of participation in, or sympathy for, the Mau-Mau movement. A policy of gradual release had, however, by the time the Red Cross delegates were let into the Colony, reduced the number of detained natives to a mere 35,000. This was an enormous native population to keep locked up, but the political and social side of this unhappy story cannot be unfolded here. As is the custom, the delegates investigated all aspects of life in these camps. Several camps contained huts made of aluminium, well insulated against both heat and cold, easy to erect and simple to maintain, which seemed well suited to the climate. Elsewhere, however, hutments were of stone or brick, roofed with thatch, or with plaited-reed walls and roofs of woven palm leaves.

By the date the Committee's delegates were allowed to inspect the conditions under which these 35,000 people were living, special regulations had been promulgated by the British authorities, dealing with life and work in the camps and with their discipline. The detainees were employed particularly on the digging of irrigation canals, the building of roads and the terracing of land for crops near certain villages, as well as in the manufacture of various articles, such as sisal string sleeping mats. In some camps, men who wished could work on large construction schemes, such as the digging of a 43-mile-long canal to carry water

In Kenya, Mr. H. P. Junod and Dr. L. A. Gailland, Red Cross delegates, talk with population in the work-camps, March-August 1957.

from the Thiba river to irrigate the Yatta plain, or the construction of a new aerodrome at Nairobi. Special camps have had to be built for women and juveniles, and apprentice workshops have been opened, where the detained persons can learn a trade. In the new villages, specially built to "rehabilitate" the released persons and their families, nurses and welfare workers of the British Red Cross are carrying out what the International Committee regard as a remarkable work on health and social problems.

During their visit to Kenya, the two delegates had long conversations with Sir Evelyn Baring, the Governor, and passed on to him their general views on what they had seen during their visits to not less than 52 camps. A detailed report on their many findings and suggestions was sent to the British Government, though it is yet too early to comment on the positive results.

THE INDOMITABLE MR. DE TRAZ

Meantime—again in 1955—the fresh outbreak of political strife in the island of Cyprus, where the irresistible force of the Cypriot independence movement met head-on with the immovable object of British intention to hold the island at all costs as a NATO military base, brought the Greek Red Cross to appeal for the intervention of the International Committee on behalf of detained Cypriots. So, in December 1955, Mr. de Traz, one of the Committee's most experienced delegates, who was then on a mission to the Middle East, was called back to get in touch with the British authorities on the spot.

Mr. de Traz proceeded to Nicosia and, with the authorities' consent, visited Cypriots deprived of their liberty (again without trial) in camps in Kokkino-Trimithia and Dekhelia and also in the Central Prison, Nicosia.

For the next two years, Mr. de Traz seems to have had an exceptionally busy time at the Eastern end of the Mediterranean coping almost single-handed with the results of the combined U.K.-U.S. Middle-East doctrine. In the spring of 1957, we find him back again in Cyprus visiting the detention camps and the central prison of Nicosia, where about 1,300 persons were being detained. In these detention centres the Red Cross delegate was able to have long interviews, without witnesses, with the internees' committees; but he was not able to obtain access to the police stations where suspects are interrogated before their internment. We must, therefore, leave him for the time being doing all he can for the detained men and youths on this tormented island—which had unfortunately for the inhabitants become one of the most valuable pawns on the Middle-East strategic chessboard—and keeping a check on the use of relief supplies sent by the International Committee and distributed in the two main camps. Before leaving Cyprus on the last occasion, Mr. de Traz had an interview with the Acting Governor-General, and gave him his own impressions and made appropriate suggestions to relieve the lot of the detainees. As is the custom with Red Cross visits of this nature, the results of these missions were contained in a detailed confidential report sent to the British authorities.

In the summer of 1958, however, we follow Mr. de Traz at post-haste to Lebanon, with yet another "limited" war on his hands; this time travelling at the head of a Red Cross convoy up the mountain roads to the rebel opposition headquarters in the Druze region. He now found himself working alongside an entirely new arm of world humanitarian law, namely, the United Nations Observers, who were keeping watch on the somewhat vague, but not unnaturally troublesome borders of Lebanon, carved out of the old Turkish Empire by the French 40 years before.

Red Cross truck under the charge of Mr. de Traz on its way from Beirut to Mouktara with medical supplies for the rebels.

The unheralded intrusion of foreign troops at the very moment when Dag Hammarskjold's men were fulfilling their delicate mandate by rapidly combing out the last suspect areas and reporting favourably on their success to the Security Council, hindered the work of the U.N. Observers. It is, again, tempting to contrast this further undisguised use of armed force in the Middle East by a Great Power, acting on its own authority, with the slower but, in the end, only effective method of employing U.N. peaceful procedure by mutual consent. Rarely were the two opposite alternatives of conducting what is still called "foreign policy"—i.e., the way of violence and the way of understanding—more sharply exposed to public gaze for world opinion to take its choice for the future peace of the world.

"In spite of the set-back caused by the landing of United States troops on 15 July," stated the official U.N. report, "which resulted in a sharp reaction in the opposition-held areas, the ground lost was steadily regained through the tact, patience, and perseverance of the military observers." This was pretty strong language for a neutral commission to use, but it appeared as one of the main conclusions of the report of the United Nations Observation Group in Lebanon, submitted to the Security Council in August, 1958, by its three neutral leaders, Galo Plaza of Ecuador (Chairman), Rejeshwar Dayal of India, and Major-General Bull of Norway. How much like the familiar language of the Red Cross mission itself do the concluding passages of their report sound?—

"The presence of the United Nations Observers," they stated, "moving around in their white jeeps from village to village, is welcomed both by Government supporters and by opposition elements. The independence and impartiality of the Observers is universally recognised and appreciated, and they are regarded as the symbol of the United Nations presence; they help to inspire feelings of calm and confidence in the areas patrolled by them. Sometimes local disputes and difficulties have been referred to them by different parties, which they have occasionally been instrumental in solving."

Mr. de Traz, the other neutral, also by-passed the self-appointed "liberators" and continued his work on both sides of the domestic conflict. As the disturbances had worsened earlier in the year, this resourceful and highly popular Swiss, assisted by the Lebanese Red Cross Society, made representations on the spot both to the authorities

In the Lebanon, students from the nursing school parade through the streets of Beirut.

in Beirut and to the various rebel groups, reminding them of the essential humanitarian principles set forth in Article 3 of the 1949 Geneva Convention. As noted in Chapter III, this provision does not give "rebels" any legal status, but it does bring them under the laws of war, just as if they were regular soldiers. Mr. de Traz was soon successful in setting up regular liaison with the rebel chiefs in various areas, and ascertained that a considerable need for medical and other supplies existed among them. Thereupon, the International Committee throughout the summer of 1958, by drawing on emergency relief funds available to it, sent to Mr. de Traz by air from Geneva various consignments of medical relief supplies, in particular blood plasma, surgical equipment and medicaments.

In some cases the Red Cross delegate managed to facilitate the evacuation of the seriously wounded rebels, and, at the worst stage of the rebellion, he himself transported urgent medical supplies and a fully-equipped operating-theatre across the rough Druze country to Mouktara, headquarters of Kemal Jumblatt. Mr. de Traz twice visited the Chouf mountain region held by the insurgents, and took with him medical and surgical equipment sufficient for setting up a field dressing station, where the wounded in this zone were given treatment. A

Lebanese doctor and a nurse, both voluntary workers, accompanied him and remained in attendance there to run the emergency until more stable conditions returned to Lebanon with the newly elected government—as all intelligent people anticipated they would. We shall doubtless hear more before long of the indomitable Mr. de Traz, Swiss citizen, world servant, and hero of peace.

WHEN THE GODS ARE POWERLESS

Peace has its heroines, too, as this record has repeatedly proved. Thus, the twentieth century moved on to another stage when Mrs. Liechti, after Mr. Liechti was called back to Geneva, proceeded with the Red Cross mission through some of the remote regions of Pakistan, in 1957, trying to complete the official list of Pakistani ex-prisoners-of-war. No lists of Pakistani prisoners-of-war were ever transmitted by the Japanese authorities during the last World War, and war compensation was now due to many of them. Furthermore, very many of the Moslem soldiers recruited in the days of British rule had come from areas that subsequently became part of the Republic of India. At the time of the country's partition, the military records had to be split up on the basis of nationality, and a very large proportion had remained in India, or been lost.

Mrs. Liechti took great care to familiarise herself with the work. In Geneva, she had made a preliminary study of the incomplete lists; but, in her own words, "the theoretical description given me of the work, and the situation as I found it in Pakistan, could obviously not coincide at all points. A thorough knowledge of local conditions is needed to make a success of it." As Mrs. Liechti had a total list of some 20,000 names to check, and several thousands of square miles as her "workshop", her task could hardly be regarded as routine. At General Headquarters at Rawalpindi alone, the records left much to the imagination, and her investigation had to be extended to the record offices of fifteen regional military commands.

After a preliminary side-trip across desert country in the direction of the Afghan frontier, the party proceeded by stages to the country's northern frontier and to Kashmir, via Bahawalpur and Lahore. Mr. Liechti's enforced departure placed Mrs. Liechti in—to say the least—a somewhat unusual position. During a journey which turned into a veritable "trek", a lone woman among soldiers, she had for three months to share their life, both during long trips by jeep and in the

Youthful prisoners-of-war from North Vietnam discuss their problems with Mr. A. Durand of the International Committee.

relative comfort of sheltered military posts. Furthermore, she had, in a Moslem country, to do work usually performed by men. At first she had difficulty in making those with whom she had to deal understand what she wanted of them, but she always met with a most courteous reception and eagerness to fulfil her wishes. As her journey progressed, she found local collaborators better informed as to her requirements, and more care was being taken to prepare the ground for her investigations.

Even a few of the difficulties she encountered would be quite impossible to detail here. Each case had to be examined on its merits. The assertion, for example, that a man had been taken prisoner on the Japanese front and not elsewhere—many Pakistanis had fought in Africa and other theatres of war—rested merely on assumption, so corroborative evidence had to be found. Then, a large number of mistakes had their origin in the fluid nature of the military situation in Burma. But, apart from her endless search for corroborative facts, Mrs. Liechti was constantly "on parade"; the day commencing at dawn and finishing at 11 p.m., or even later, with the hurry and scurry of dawn departures and the fatigue caused by interminable journeys by car or truck over rough roads, turned at times into rivers by torrential rain. In addition, she had to carry with her, not only an outfit adapted to extreme changes in temperature, but also her own mattress and bedding. "I was," she said on her return, "the first woman to be lodged in a military post in Pakistan. I had my own guards and orderlies. Nowhere in Europe would I have encountered such correct behaviour."

"Such correct behaviour!" How mixed is human experience, how different the nation from the man—as Fridtjof Nansen had maintained—how unpredictable the conduct of the gregarious herd, how irrational and cruel man-in-the-mass fearing for his collective safety! Such is a natural reaction as we pass, at the end of this chapter, from the single-minded perseverance of Mrs. Liechti, south of the Himalayas, to the sufferings so brutally inflicted on the people of the "Northern King-dom" of old China, in their rocky peninsula. For, throughout long ages, Korea has always been, in the eyes of Eastern peoples, a limb of the Chinese family tree.

Western Europe, where the modern concept of "national sovereignty" was born at the end of the feudal ages, has yet to grasp the fact that, to the Oriental mind—as well as to the Arab and African mind—the

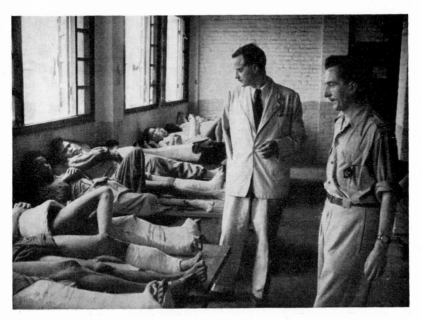

Mr. A. Durand visits the P.O.W. camp hospital in Indo-China, 1952.

West's rigid emotion-charged theory of national sovereignty is unthinkable, if not ridiculous. Although Western colonialism, in its expansive stage, imposed these artificial barriers for a time on non-Western civilisations, leaving so many bitter memories today, the different peoples of Asia and Africa, and what is now called the Middle East, feel, in their great awakening, that they belong to each other, even though many varieties of geography and culture and local loyalty divide them at many points. The Western mind will never be able to come to terms with the true character of the "Eastern", "Arab", "African" (or any other journalistic catch-as-catch-can adjectives) revolt against the West, unless it frees itself from the pagan belief in the "sovereign state" as an end in itself—a justifier of the most diabolical acts, provided "the Government" commands them. National Sovereignty—which the Communists exploit for their own purposes, though they do not allow it for others—becomes ever more an anachronism, as each space-satellite leaves the Earth, as each missile enters the waiting atomic stockpile.

KOREA IN PERSPECTIVE

Korea, which was split in two by the occupation forces of the two major liberators of the last war, knew just what "national sovereignty" was worth to small nations! The unhappy people of this ancient "Northern Kingdom" had never had a joyous existence, as far as human memory went. Successive conquerors had possessed their land, and the resented Japanese overlordship was replaced, barely a dozen years ago, for the 21 millions of modern Koreans, not by a rational "peace" settlement, but by a completely irrational division of their war-swept country. Thus, the limb was torn off and left bleeding to death.

It was only a matter of time—as any historian could have foretold—before worse befell. The incidents along this mock frontier in 1950—preceded by five years of wrangling and threats and many other such incidents—were debated *ad nauseam* at the United Nations, but they were symptoms and not causes. The subsequent attempt at the U.N. to bottle the whole Korean issue behind a label called "aggression" was, as events were to prove, utterly futile and destructive of any agreed solution, and only served to prolong the conflict.

As matters turned out, the monstrosity of the 38th parallel—which has since cost the major contestants so many precious lives—did not even make sense as a valid military line, when the rival High Commands attempted to base an armistice upon it at the termination of the most inconclusive conflict of modern times. Three years of fearful slaughter and devastation of their land brought the Korean people no permanent settlement, but two uncompromising régimes, confronting each other today more suspiciously then ever across that fatal fictitious line. Such is the craven folly of attempting to rebuild a peace on the dogma of "military necessity".

It is necessary to set this dark picture of a dismembered people in its proper perspective, in order to appreciate the magnitude of the problem which presented itself to, especially, the International Red Cross, to whom fell the major task of cleaning up the mess. In fact, the Red Cross was called upon to do very much more than succour the many victims of this unlimited "limited" war—it was instrumental, as we shall show, in finishing the war itself, a result which neither of the belligerents were capable of securing for themselves. In this respect, the Red Cross achievement in Korea far out-distances the tremendous contributions it was making, almost at the same time, to the various other peace-settlements arrived at in Indonesia, Indo-China, Vietnam and other rebellion-torn areas of "limited" war in the East—which space prevents us pursuing here. It must be added, of course, that in coping with the heavier burdens of the Korean Armistice, the International Committee

During the Korean War, life-saving blood plasma was sent from donors thousands of miles away in the United States.

197

found an essential partner in the Indian Red Cross, who were working under the "neutral" government of India, on behalf of the U.N. General Assembly. By handling the extraordinarily difficult on-the-spot problems of repatriating the prisoners-of-war, the Indians placed the whole United Nations and, especially, the United States permanently in their debt.

In truth, during the time that has elapsed since the Korean Armistice, calmer judgments have been brought to bear on the conduct of the diplomatic side of the conflict, which fully sustain the repeated contentions in the present book that the resort to military force to meet dangerous international situations—especially when they arise in other people's countries—defeats its own purpose and destroys the very basis of peaceful action through the United Nations machinery of mutual adjustment.

For example, in Professor Robert E. Riggs' careful research study, based on the United States State Department and United Nations records covering the whole period, entitled *Politics in the United Nations* (Illinois University Press, 1958), the evidence is impartially assembled which would convince any reasonable mind that the Korean conflict could have been ended much sooner—as virtually, all other members of the U.N. were agreed at the time—but for United States long-term policies of hostility against China itself. The Russians, past-masters at intimidation, knew this perfectly well and would not yield an inch in their instigation of their new ally to meet force with force—as the conference table was denied to them. It was Communist policy which was advanced, not the West's, as a result of this insistence on a military solution.

Within this cast-iron framework of opposed positions taken on the debating floor at Lake Success by the chief protagonists of the Cold War, it is obvious that the agencies of moderation and compromise—with the Indians and the International Red Cross in the lead—stood very little chance of making headway. Professor Riggs, for instance, draws particular attention to India's neglected warning that a movement of U.N. troops across the 38th parallel would unquestionably provoke Chinese intervention. It can too easily be overlooked that India is not only a powerful Eastern civilisation, but one having extensive common frontiers with China and, virtually, with Russia. Whereas, since Korea was 8,000 miles distant from the United States, the latter country was not concerned with defending her own territory against Chinese "aggression", but with an entirely different question: namely, a theory which was being experimented with in high places of "containing" Communism by military action "anywhere or everywhere in the world"—a gigantic illusion which has, already, lost the Western world about two-thirds of its potential friends, and accentuated an atomic armaments race which can give no nation any security so long as it continues.

How true to contemporary life was the graphic word-picture of the gravely developing twentieth-century situation—against which Dunant's ideas have had to struggle continuously—painted twenty years ago by the caustic Martin Gumpert, when he wrote that "the masses, who are careless towards responsibility, unaccustomed to thinking and tired of feeling, let adventurers, fanatics and politicians snatch their responsibility for them! Uncontrollable and drunk with their propaganda, these sinister forces are driving humanity to disaster. Well-meaning and decent human behaviour is caught in the barbed wire of its own powerless and effete organisation. Anarchy and national insanity are permitted to parade unpunished as practical politics."

Thus, the deadlock in Korea dragged on from stage to stage, grounded in political misconceptions, diplomatic blunders and military mistakes—which have since produced a whole library of controversial

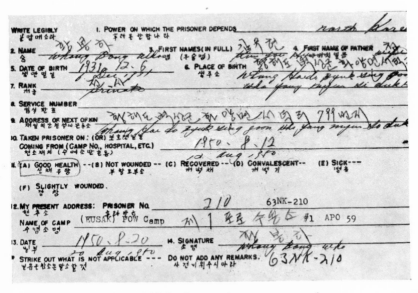

Capture Card filled in by a North Korean prisoner-of-war.

literature, but which leave the normal mind staggered that such blind ineptitude should cost the world so dearly, without any lesson apparently being learnt. British opinion, which was more bitterly divided over the Korean issue than over any similar event—until the Suez campaign provoked the same public revulsion—was largely convinced that, but for the sudden air flight of the Prime Minister (Mr. Attlee) to Washington in December 1950, atom-bombs would almost certainly have been dropped—had the military advisers got their own way—on North China, with consequences which require little imagination to predict today.

But Professor Riggs' factual survey has also set out the ruthless obduracy displayed by the Communist command. We can only refer, for the limited purposes of this narrative, to their many attempts to impede India and the Red Cross achieving their humanitarian objects; but, in the end, the Communists had to yield to reason what they would not yield to force.

At the beginning of hostilities, for instance, the League of Red Cross Societies invited the North Korean Red Cross Society to co-operate— as a matter of course—in applying humanitarian law to the civilian sufferers, on both sides of the fighting line, offering also to assist the Society in its onerous tasks. Though repeated overtures were made, the

An interpreter checks a list of North Korean prisoners-of-war.

North Korean Society did not even bother to reply. A year later, the Indian Red Cross appealed to the Society, but evoked no response. The same implacable attitude—which was a defiance of the Geneva Conventions—also stymied the efforts of the International Committee of the Red Cross, which transmitted to the authorities in North Korea no less than fifty reports by the end of 1952 on the delegates' visits to P.O.W. camps—without the recipients displaying the least sign of interest.

What was most reprehensible, however, were the attacks which the Chinese People's Government at Pekin made upon the International Committee itself—echoed by all the other Communist Governments—on the disputed question of the alleged use of bacteriological weapons by U.N. forces. On the initiative of the United States, the International Committee was invited, and it thereupon consented, to conduct a detailed investigation into these most serious allegations. It proposed to do this, if permitted by both belligerents, by designating an impartial commission, composed of eminent scientists, selected from countries having no part in the Korean conflict, but assisted by specialists chosen by the belligerents themselves. Not only did the Chinese Communists reject any such investigation or accept any alternative kind of enquiry, but the International Red Cross was condemned, especially by radio-broadcasts from Pekin, for having consented to undertake these essentially neutral tasks.

On the other hand, the Red Cross delegates, pursuing their extremely arduous duties of assisting the Indian mediators and the United States military command (who ran the P.O.W. camps), had to carry through the repatriation of hardly less than 100,000 men towards the end of the conflict. In this connection the delegates had to investigate a particularly grave situation, which occurred during the night of 18th February, 1952. In one of the largest camps, where "screening" was being carried out, so as to separate the prisoners who wished to return to North Korea and those who did not, some of the custodian troops fired on the prisoners. sixty-nine of the prisoners were killed outright and at least 142 were wounded, several of these dying later in hospital.

A full account of this ugly episode is given ("to avoid the risk of being misquoted, as on former occasions," say the Committee) in the International Committee's Special Report, published in their *Quarterly Review*, in April 1952. Nobody who reads this shocking account of the treatment meted out to these helpless men, who were in a terrible predicament, anyway—and under the protection of the Geneva

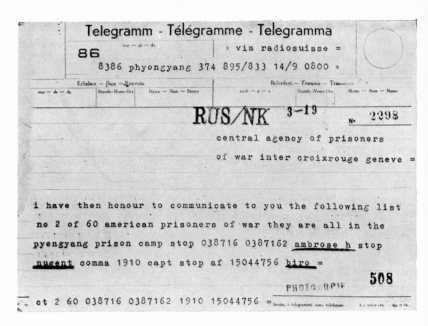

Telegram sent to the Central Agency in Geneva by the authorities in North Korea concerning American prisoners-of-war.

Conventions—can have any doubt that the Red Cross delegates were in the best possible position, by being on the spot and by interviewing many witnesses, to pronounce a considered judgment, as they did, against the military controllers (who were at once removed) of this particular camp.

The foregoing few paragraphs lift only one corner of this unmitigated tragedy of a "limited" war, which left behind it a black shadow of hatred and insecurity, as well as of physical and spiritual loss, for the Korean people, who still look to the peaceful and humanitarian procedures of the United Nations and of the Red Cross for light in their darkness. Since the abject failure of so-called "police action" under the sole military Command of one nation in the Korean conflict, there has been more and more emphasis in U.N. circles on non-violent methods, of which UNEF in the "Gaza Strip" in 1957 and the U.N. Observer Corps in Lebanon in 1958, as we have already noticed, are outstanding examples which many authorities want to see expanded into a permanent non-military U.N. Peace Force. If this does, in fact, happen, then the men who gave their lives in Korea, and the civilians, too, who suffered so much, will be among the last to pay the price of misguided force in a world of anarchy.

THE HEALING TOUCH

It is against this kind of background that the remarkable achievements of the world's neutrals, centred in India's mediation in the political field and the Red Cross's handling of the humanitarian requirements of the armistice, can be seen at their true worth.

In December, 1952, the Executive Committee of the League of Red Cross Societies in Geneva, deeply concerned by the continued deadlock in the armistice negotiations, had issued an appeal which was to inspire the first effective step towards an agreement for peace. In a resolution stressing the untold devastation and suffering caused by the prolongation of the conflict, the Committee urged the parties to take immediate action to implement the Geneva Conventions by repatriating sick and wounded prisoners-of-war. This appeal met with a strong response from public opinion throughout the world; for it offered both belligerents an honourable means of continuing negotiations which might finally lead—as in fact they did—to the conclusion of an armistice.

On 22nd February, 1953, the Commander-in-Chief of the Allied Forces in Korea sent a duplicate letter to the Supreme Commander of the Korean People's Army and to the Commander of the Chinese People's Volunteers, in which he referred to the appeal made two months earlier by the League, and proposed that negotiations be re-opened with a view to repatriating sick and wounded prisoners-of-war. The North Korean and Chinese Commanders accepted and, a few days later, staff officers of both sides met in Panmunjon to arrange details of the repatriation. As a result, within the next few weeks, 7,354 sick and wounded prisoners were exchanged—of whom 6,670 were North Korean and Chinese, and 684 members of the United Nations forces.

Meanwhile, the Korean armistice negotiations dragged on in a wearisome controversy concerning prisoners-of-war in general, as distinct from the sick and wounded—thus prolonging the suffering caused by the war. The Executive Committee of the League accordingly made two new approaches to the belligerents. First, it urged them to arrange a speedy settlement of the general question of prisoners-of-war "on a reasonable basis in accordance with the principles of the Geneva Conventions", so that an armistice might rapidly be brought about in Korea and peace established in the Far East "in compliance with the

Dr. Otto Lehner and Mr. Albert de Cocatrix, Red Cross delegates, confer with Major-General Li Song Cho, chief of the Communist delegation, at Panmunjon, January, 1952.

wishes of the Red Cross members and all peace-loving people throughout the world". Secondly, in view of the needless distress inflicted on the civilian population by the long-drawn-out negotiations, the Executive Committee appealed to the belligerents "immediately to cease all hostilities for an agreed period, in order that the present armistice negotiations may take place in the most propitious circumstances". Incidentally, about this time, the Chinese and Japanese Red Cross Societies were displaying their own belief in mutual understanding by carrying out the repatriation of 30,000 Japanese citizens from China.

Two months later, on 27th July, 1953, the Korean armistice was signed in Panmunjon. The agreement provided for Red Cross assistance in the repatriation of prisoners-of-war from both sides; and authorised the formation of three joint Red Cross teams, consisting of doctors, nurses and social workers recruited from the National Societies of all countries directly engaged in the conflict. Each side supplied seventy Red Cross staff. The first team, composed of twenty members, worked in the reception centres; the second, with sixty members, visited prison camps in North Korea; and the third, also numbering sixty, visited prison camps controlled by the United Nations.

Within six weeks of the signing of the armistice, 70,158 North Korean and 5,639 Chinese able-bodied prisoners were handed over to the armed forces of their countries, and 12,760 prisoners, of fourteen nationalities, had been returned to the U.N. Command. There remained, however, many prisoners-of-war who did not wish to be repatriated—including some 15,000 Chinese, 8,000 North Korean, 300 South Korean, 22 American and one British subject. Under the auspices of a U.N. body, appropriately named the *Neutral Nations* Repatriation Commission, all were transferred to a special camp near Panmunjon.

By the terms of the armistice, the Indian Red Cross was specially entrusted with the task of providing for this large number of stateless persons; and it appointed a team of 113 members to carry it out. During the next 4½ months this splendid group organised a general programme for building up the morale of 23,452 prisoners-of-war, belonging to five nations. It included educational, handicraft, and entertainment schemes; and more than 50,000 class enrolments were registered—showing that on an average each prisoner took instruction in at least two subjects. This was in the midst of the West *versus* East battle for the soul—and what was left of the broken body—of Korea! To the Red Cross, it was the men who mattered, not the nations.

The Indian Red Cross workers also collected and distributed the prisoners' mail, and, when necessary, took up complaints on their behalf with the camp authorities. In January 1954, when their mission came to an end, the Hon. Rajkumari Amrit Kaur, Chairman of the Indian Red Cross, described their achievements, without exaggeration, as "the most important international assignment ever entrusted to any individual Red Cross Society".

In the next chapter, we shall meet this remarkable woman and humanitarian leader again, presiding at the latest four-yearly World Conference of the Red Cross in New Delhi in 1957—a Red Cross, which had passed through the fierce fires of "limited" war, in every continent, and had emerged to face the yet greater challenge of "unlimited" war with its emblem untarnished.

CHAPTER NINE

Unlimited War: Tomorrow?

A N "incident", which abruptly terminated the latest World
Conference of the Red Cross, held in New Delhi in the
autumn of 1957, is so tragically typical of the "War in the
minds of men", which threatens to terminate humanity itself, that
we must devote space in our final chapter to getting this much-publi
cised event into some perspective.

Before the next World Conference meets in 1963, the organisation'
handling of this particular issue might well determine the future
effectiveness of the Red Cross as a real force for peace. In fact, long
before the Red Cross holds its next regular international Conference
—to celebrate, in 1963, the 100th anniversary of the first Geneva
Conference—events are compelling the whole movement to deal
courageously and unequivocally, not merely with this indecent
intrusion of Cold War diplomacy into its internal affairs, but with the
far more pressing question of the renunciation of atomic and similar
weapons of mass destruction. That is why the 1957 Conference marked
a decisive turning-point in Red Cross history—and in the history of
civilisation.

The 19th International Conference of the Red Cross, which met for
the first time in India at the invitation of the Indian Red Cross Society
was such a vital and, in many ways, uplifting experience, that its
positive achievement cannot be compressed into a few paragraphs
but, as the general Press was, not unnaturally, more passionately con
cerned with the fictitious status of Formosa than with the purpose
and programme of the Conference itself, it is first necessary to outline
what the Conference actually was about.★

★ The *New York Times* of 29th October, 1957—to take one example—carried a Special Report
14 inches long, of which over half (8 inches) was devoted to a graphic (though accurate) descrip
tion of the Formosa affair. Both the main headline ("CHINA ISSUE MARS RED CROSS
TALKS") and sub-headline ("PEIPING DELEGATE THREATENS WALK-OUT . . ."
focused attention entirely on this conflict. Even the six remaining inches, reporting the resolu

The 19th Conference was the second ever to be held in Asia—the 15th International Conference having been held at Tokyo in 1934. *Eighty-three countries* were represented at New Delhi by Red Cross and/or governmental delegates or observers. (The previous highest record was the 18th International Conference at Toronto, in 1952, attended by representatives of 63 nations.) Of the over four-score countries thus represented, 14 were attending an International Conference of the Red Cross for the first time. Many of them were States newly created since the 18th International Conference: four from Africa, eight from Asia, and two from Europe. A total of 279 delegates or observers came from the national Red Cross, Red Crescent and Red Lion and Sun Societies, while 160 were delegates or observers of Governments or international organisations. The number of recognised National Societies present was 71; and the number of Governments was also 71—a balance of forces which, as we shall see, had more than a paper meaning.

All continents were well represented; the world's largest nations— the People's Republic of China, India, the U.S.S.R., and the U.S.A.— with populations ranging from 600 millions to 170 millions, as well as the world's smallest—Liechtenstein, Monaco and San Marino— none with over 20,000 population. Some of the countries were not, as yet, members of the United Nations. These included Cambodia, the People's Republic of China, the German Democratic Republic, Ghana, Liberia, Outer Mongolia, Nepal, San Marino, Tunisia, the Democratic Republic of Vietnam, and the Republic of Vietnam.

Not least significant, the "split" countries were brought together under one roof *for the first time since the Cold War began:* Germany, (East and West), Vietnam (North and South), Korea (North and South) and China (Mainland and Formosa). Thus, true to its century-long tradition of absolute neutrality, independence of "politics", and universality of membership, the International Red Cross succeeded, where so many others had failed (or never tried), in its earth-wide mission of reconciliation.

The President of the Republic of India, Dr. Rajendra Prasad, inaugurated the assembly on 28th October, 1957, when over 1,000

tions, included at least three editorialisings on the West's *"weak political position"*. Less responsible newspapers, with mass circulations—if they reported it at all—completely ignored the aims, personalities, and agenda of the Conference. A comparison of these "reports" with the attitude shown by the newspapers of Dunant's day is some indication of the moral slump which modern journalism has suffered in its enthusiasm for the Cold War.

The 19th International Conference of the Red Cross meeting in the House of Wisdom, New Delhi, October/November, 1957. (Compare photo on page 43)

delegates, observers and guests—many in national dress—filled to overflowing the vast auditorium of the "Vigyan Bhavan", the House of Wisdom, decorated with flags from all the nations. For a moment, we can turn back history from this impressive picture of the intellectual and moral élite of the 83 nations assembled in the House of Wisdom, on the other side of the globe, to the simple photograph, which appears on an earlier page, of the handful of men, without any official mandate, who met at the first Conference on 26th October, 1863—94 years before, almost to the day. And we ask ourselves: If the fear of the Lord be the beginning of wisdom, of whom then need this powerful and dedicated assembly be afraid?

The answer to that question is to be found in the course taken by the discussion and in the composition of the assembly itself.

Prime Minister Jawaharlal Nehru, in welcoming the largest international gathering of the Red Cross ever held, set the ethical standard of the discussion at its highest when he declared that, in these times of conflict, suspicion, and hatred, it was the spirit of man that needed the "healing touch" more than his physical suffering. The *new approach* needed to mitigate the suffering of the spirit, Mr. Nehru added, must be based on tolerance and avoidance of violence and hatred. A third Indian philosopher-statesman, Dr. Radhakrishnan, followed a few days later with a similar unmistakable challenge to the whole Red Cross movement to rethink its primary aims and purposes in terms of the revolutionary Gandhian concept of non-violence and a peace strategy of non-involvement. In each case, the "new approach" evoked spontaneous agreement from the great majority of those present, listening as individuals and responding as human beings. This is just what they had been *thinking*, zealous and devoted Red Cross workers, back in their own countries—yet had not always had the courage, perhaps, to say so. But will the "new approach" get back to the National Societies, the national leaders, the national Governments?

WHERE ANGELS FEAR TO TREAD

Coming, now, to the "incident" which was forced upon the Conference during its last 48 hours, the facts are very simple and are not disputed. We have taken the precaution to cite them almost verbatim from the official conference report.

The eventual seating at the Conference of the Government known as the "Republic of China" was the focus point of the trouble. It must be remembered that the host country was India, which does not

Prime Minister Jawaharlal Nehru addressing the delegates from 83 countries.

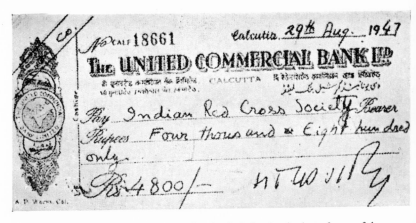

Cheque signed by Mahatma Gandhi, shortly before his death, in favour of the Indian Red Cross.

practise the iron-curtain doctrine in relations with its Asian neighbours. The invitation addressed to the Government which has its seat on the island of Taiwan, or Formosa, was sent under the name of the "Government of Taiwan". The Government in question protested, at a much later stage, on the ground that the Government was not invited under its "official" name. It was, however, the Government of the United States of America which officially brought the question before the Conference in a draft resolution by which the Conference was requested to "decide, on the basis of the traditional principles of the Red Cross" that all the parties invited to participate should receive their "official" title. From declarations made in or outside the proceedings it appeared that the Taiwan Government would not come to the Conference if it were not invited under its official title and that the Government of the Chinese People's Republic (Pekin) would walk out if the American resolution were accepted. Rumours also went about that the American Government delegation would do the same, unless it got its way. Thus, the Cold War, to the chagrin and resentment of most of the "independent" members, showed its ugly head and, once more, the heated arguments followed their usual sterile pattern—so familiar to regular participants in United Nations and other inter-governmental gatherings.

The Swedes and other neutrals, by tact, gentle persuasion, and impeccable logic, valiantly tried to bring the two "sides" together for the sake of unity and dignity—and Red Cross "traditional principles"; but, as *governments* were involved, and committed, the Cold Warriors won. Proposals with the object of avoiding the conflict from being consolidated into a vote were rejected and the resolution which provoked the incident was carried because of the votes of the governments. This decision resulted in about thirty delegations walking out, including the Red Cross delegation of the host country, headed by the President of the Conference, who stated from the rostrum, before she left, that the introduction of the resolution was an act of "grave discourtesy to the Indian Red Cross". With the Hall of Wisdom now half empty—it was the closing session of the Conference—two Formosan delegates, who had been waiting all the week for this crowning event, were then let in and seated behind a piece of cardboard inscribed: "*Republic of China*".

But who was the victim of this unmannerly manoeuvre? *China*? It can hardly be imagined that the 600 millions of present-day China suffered any loss of face—after a century of Western influence in the East, and exclusion from the United Nations itself, under the strange subterfuge that it does not exist. *Russia*? As always, Russia only gains from these unconscionable diplomatic blunders. Who, then, was the victim? *The Red Cross*, undoubtedly—struck down "in the house of its friends".

So let us listen to some of the views expressed at the close of the incident by the three Red Cross leaders who are unquestionably best able to form a mature judgment. First, the noble lady who had presided with such distinction, charm, and diplomacy throughout the arduous sessions of the Conference (until she walked out with the other protestants on the last day), Rajkumari Amrit Kaur, Chairman of the Indian Society, declared that the issues under discussion were *political* issues and completely outside the sphere of the Red Cross organisation. Never during the host country's invitation to the Formosan authorities were they referred to as the "Republic of China". "The first letter to them," she said, "was issued to the Government at Taipeh, Formosa, on 22nd May, 1956, and there was no protest. Again, they were informed of the postponement of the Conference on 21st December, 1956, and this letter was addressed to the Secretary of the Government of Formosa. Again, no protest. It was made perfectly clear to them at Toronto that the People's Republic of China, representing the vast continent of China, were its representatives; but, because Formosa was not in fact under their control, the humanitarian ideals of the Red Cross could not eliminate the Government authority of that part of China from within its orbit." After referring in detail to later correspondence with the Government of Formosa, Rajkumari Amrit Kaur, concluding her statement, said that the Indian Society had actually gone against its inner feelings in sending an invitation to the Formosa authorities, but had done so in the interests of the whole movement; and that, as Chairman of the host Society, she was not going to rescind that invitation or accept anything new.

Secondly, the beloved and highly respected Chairman of the League of Red Cross Societies, Justice Emil Sandström, sternly deprecated that the Red Cross was "forced to take sides in a political fight". In spite of the reference in the offending resolution to "traditional principles of the Red Cross", he wanted to know *which* principles were being evoked by the affronted governments? And he added that "one is far from convinced that the decision was made on Red Cross principles only and not also on essentially political considerations". If the Cold War contestants maintained their present attitudes, "this means that there will be no more International Conferences of the Red Cross having the universal character they have hitherto had," he

Justice Emil Sandström, Chairman of the League of Red Cross Societies, in consultation with Rajkumari Amrit Kaur, Chairman of the Indian Red Cross, who presided at the Conference.

asserted, and "such a situation, of course, will be detrimental to the work of the Conferences, especially to their principal task, namely the preparatory examination of modifications in the Geneva Conventions or of new Conventions in the humanitarian field". Judge Sandström came clearly to the conclusion, therefore, that: "The question must be examined as to what can be done to maintain the useful collaboration of the Red Cross with the governments, without jeopardising the universality of the Red Cross."

Thirdly, we have none other than that peer among diplomats, Ambassador André François-Poncet, President of the French Red Cross Society and highest ranking official of the International Red Cross, as Chairman of its Standing Commission, who had earlier been charged by Madame Li Toh-Huan, Chairman of the Red Cross Society of the People's Republic of China, with having committed an "illegal act" in telegraphing to "the Minister of Foreign Affairs of the Government of the Republic of China" in Taiwan to send a delegation to the Conference, which, she alleged, was a "provocation against this Conference and is intolerable to the Chinese Delegation". Ambassador André François-Poncet most correctly reminded the Conference that the Standing Commission did not concern itself with the legitimacy of governments. It was sufficient for a government to exercise its authority over a particular territory and for it to be a signatory to the Geneva Conventions to have the right to take part, without reservations, in an International Conference. In the application of these principles, the Standing Commission had invited both the Governments of the People's Republic of China and of Taiwan, since both were parties to the Geneva Conventions. Looking back on the Conference, the Ambassador stated categorically, on leaving New Delhi (our italics):

> A by-product of the Formosa incident at the closing session of the 19th Conference is to give strength to the feeling of some Red Cross leaders that *future International Conferences should perhaps be restricted to National Red Cross Societies only*. If there is a vital question to be discussed at the time concerning the Geneva Conventions, then the governments could perhaps be convened at the same time, *but in a separate conference*. This would tend to avoid political situations arising in International Conferences of the Red Cross.

This suggestion, supported by such authority, would seem to be the essence of wisdom—borne out again and again in the course of this book. It is obvious that the direct participation of governments openly committed to "win" the Cold War (whatever that phrase may mean), and unable to divest themselves of the nuclear arms and the other weapons of mass destruction which are so patently incompatible with Red Cross principles and directly contrary to the Geneva Conventions, can only wreck any future Red Cross Conference, or, at least, block progress towards drafting a new Convention or new rules prohibiting the use of the blind weapons on which some governments rely.

Blind weapons, however, are not so dangerous as blind men who cannot see that, by using them or threatening to use them, they cannot preserve "freedom" or "democracy" or even prevent the expansion of Communism, but can only bring about exactly opposite results. As this writer has argued in some detail elsewhere,★ this attitude has as much relevance to the actual world situation as the use of a sledge-hammer to repair the fragile mechanism of a watch. The remedy has no relation to the disease. It is not the split atom which imperils our earth, but the split mind.

No future Red Cross Conference can hope to succeed unless it preserves its integrity and maintains its universality. This means that the Red Cross movement, as it is perfectly capable of doing, should base its decisions, without fear or favour, on humanitarian principles, and on humanitarian principles alone; and then present its decisions— as it has done all through its wonderful century—to the national governments for *them* to take the political decisions necessary to implement and sustain world humanitarian law. If the Red Cross fails in this, it fails in its primary duty and throws away its last hope of saving mankind.

Before turning to matters of substance, however, a minor issue concerning the next World Conference deserves comment. It was, perhaps, unfortunate—no doubt due to the atmosphere created by the Formosa incident—that a proposal coming from Russia to hold the next *regular* Red Cross Conference in that country was (politely, it is true) turned down. The Russian view seemed to be that, because the New Delhi Conference had been almost a year late, the *regular*

★ See the author's *Revolution on East River*, Abelard-Schuman, London and New York (1957).

Conference could still be held at its normal four-year interval, namely in 1960, and, for the first time, it could take place behind the Iron Curtain. As the Russians tactfully remarked, in extending the invitation, this would not interfere with the "Anniversary" Conference being held in Geneva in 1963, at the invitation of the Swiss Red Cross, jointly with both the International Committee and the League of Red Cross Societies.

Was not this rejection evidence of the chilly hand of the Cold War, laid upon the shoulders of the delegates? No one in his senses who knows the Red Cross movement at all, would imagine that, by holding the next world meeting in Moscow, the delegates and observers of 70 or 80 National Red Cross Societies would become converted to Communism. Nor need the "propaganda" appeal, which the Russians would, without doubt, make of such an event, frighten anyone in the West who has a clear conscience on the nuclear question.

On the contrary, yet another opportunity would appear to have been lost for carrying the Red Cross universal and humanitarian outlook into the heart of what is called the "Communist empire", where genuine contacts with the peoples of the world are so obviously lacking and so badly needed. Such a gesture, combining the wisdom and altruism of both the West and the Neutral East, would have been

Chinese Red Cross tackles the emergency hundreds of feet below ground in the mines.

worth infinitely more than much present-day official propaganda which is directed, presumably, at the Russian "people" who see so little of the better side of Western ideals and progress. Can anyone imagine Henri Dunant turning down such an offer?

Fortunately, the 19th International Conference is not to be judged by the manoeuvres of the Cold War protagonists. For instance, notable women health leaders could discuss, in the Medico-Social Commission, their new world projects face to face, in a manner which made the prestige battle over Formosa look infantile. While Miss Margaret Magill, of New Zealand, told how the aged and infirm in her country (which has the highest life expectancy in the world) were looked after through a modern social security programme and other efficient hospital services, and while Mrs. G. C. Scantlebury, from Australia, explained how her National Society provided a Talking Books Library Service for blind military veterans throughout Australia and how the Junior Red Cross did pioneer work among blind children by inviting them to Red Cross camps; from right across the other side of the globe, Mrs. Maria Tour, Deputy Minister of Public Health in the Republic of Byelo-Russia, described the institution of milk kitchens for children provided at Consultant Centres and also the Breast Milk Centres, where working mothers feed their babies at feeding houses, and, likewise, Mrs. Damdin Tumendelger, from Outer Mongolia, gave an account of how the Mongolian Red Cross, founded in 1939, was making substantial progress in health education through talks by experienced Red Cross workers. The nursing services and many other of the peace-time achievements of the then 70 or more National Societies were reviewed and debated in a spirit of good neighbourliness and mutual concern in furthering their common tasks.

CRUEL METHODS DON'T END CRUELTIES

Then, again, the whole assembly was uplifted by men who belonged, like Dunant, to the whole world, and not to a tiny part of it.

"*The extension of the principles of the Red Cross into international relations would replace the present world of horror and hatred by a world of happiness and love*," said Dr. Sarvapalli Radhakrishnan, Vice-President of the Republic of India, European scholar, Asian philosopher, and world statesman, addressing the Conference. Since the foundation of the Red Cross, he continued, things have greatly changed. There had been phenomenal advances in science and technology. Earth satellites were circling the globe. The world had become more unified. There could no longer be any isolation of one country from another. Yet the present world was divided into hostile groups, and that hostility was manifested in the Cold War. But cruel methods need not be used to remove cruelties. To end this state of affairs, one had to adopt an attitude of humility. The "crusading" spirit did not help. The division in the world today was only the reflection of the division in the human soul. The remaking of the individual was the first essential of the day. The cross—the emblem of the Red Cross—Radhakrishnan concluded, was the symbol of material death, but spiritual victory. It was a symbol of love and brotherhood. It was by faith in *these* qualities that we could achieve a world of happiness.

Thanks to the skill and moderation of the Indian delegation (who managed to check the exuberance of the Communist delegations far more effectively than the uncompromising attitude of some other delegates) the Conference *unanimously* passed—much to its own surprise—a resolution of the Indian Red Cross asking governments to eschew war and adopt "protective measures" against the awful consequences of the use of incendiary, chemical, bacteriological, radio-

Helping ward off famine after long months of drought in India, 1951.

217

"Man goes on playing with fire of unknown force." The auditorium of Hiroshima's Town Hall, showing the effects of atomic fire and destruction.

active, or other such agents. The resolution was passed by 115 to nil amid prolonged applause. This unexpected result opened the door at once to the really essential question before the Conference: But how *can* we protect the human race against these "awful consequences"?

This question became particularly germane to the discussion when Mr. Masutaro Inoue, the Japanese delegate (who introduced a resolution on cessation of nuclear tests), informed the Conference that several people *died every day*, even now, because of the after-effects of radiation due to the Hiroshima and Nagasaki bombings. The Japanese Red Cross had collected statistics and material on the deadly effects of atomic radiation in its hospitals and wanted to carry this research further. Yet when he urged, as a Red Cross worker, that an expert commission should be appointed to study the important material, "since only the Red Cross could *do* anything in the matter," the United Kingdom Government delegate stood up and reminded the Conference that the United Nations was at the moment discussing this very question. "Nothing must be done in this International Conference that would impede the work of the United Nations," he begged. The Japanese resolution, he said, had called for the setting up of a commission of experts to study the effects of radio-activity on this generation and the

218

future generation, but this work was being done by the U.N. Scientific Committee and their report was soon due. So the sensible Japanese request was shelved, and, presumably, the Japanese Red Cross Society will continue to count the daily toll of its Hiroshima and Nagasaki victims until the 1963 Conference. (Imagine the Red Cross "impeding the work of the United Nations"!)

The U.N. Scientific Committee's report on the effects of atomic radiation was, in fact, issued in August, 1958. Even the London *Times*, in one of those characteristic understatements which mark the British official attitude on this topic, had to confess:

> Man, in fact, goes on playing with fire of unknown force. The committee itself could not express views on national or international policies, but it does permit itself to say, with the utmost restraint, that all steps designed to minimise irradiation of human population "will act to the benefit of human health". And, among the steps, it specifies the stopping of contamination by explosions of nuclear weapons.

Throughout this impartial report the emphasis is upon the urgent need for *intensive investigation* into the problems involved. The U.N. Committee states: "Our ignorance of fundamental biology (taken in its widest possible sense) is undoubtedly the major factor limiting our understanding of radiation effects on man." The only way of meeting the challenge, it contends, is by the training of scientists in the different disciplines that biological research demands. Shall the Japanese appeal remain unanswered—while the statesmen, in their anxiety not to impede the United Nations, continue to "play with fire"?

TOTAL WAR NEVER PAYS

We therefore turn to consider the famous "draft rules" which formed the major item on the Agenda under the heading: *The Limitation of the Dangers Incurred by the Civilian Population in Time of War*.

In preparing and annotating these draft rules (in a most important document of 160 pages) and circulating them to all Governments and to the National Societies a year before the Conference met, the International Committee pointed out that, "while exerting constant endeavours to bring about peaceful relations between the nations," the Comittee recognised that "there is still a grave danger of force being used to settle disputes between States", and that the Red Cross must try continuously to ensure that, if violence is used, certain humane rules, implemented by practical measures *taken in good time*, are available to protect the people who are not taking part directly in the military activities. That is the simple proposition which gives the Committee its mandate; it is humanitarian, not "political".

But the International Committee has—fortunately for the human race—never shut its eyes to realities. However delicate its diplomacy and restrained its language, it has never tried to varnish truth to suit this or that Government's whim, when the principles of the Geneva Conventions have been at stake. (Its diplomatic correspondence files contain masterpieces of studiously inoffensive straight-talking, which must have given some government officials sleepless nights.) All Governments were reminded this time that they had already been requested by the Committee, as long ago as April, 1950, to explain, precisely, "*how* blind weapons could spare hospitals, prisoner-of-war camps, and the civil population", which it was the function of the Red Cross to protect?

In the absence of any convincing—or any other—reply, the Committee, in introducing the draft rules, gave its own answer in categorical terms:

> In view of the developments which have taken place in methods of making war, and the continual invention of new weapons, a conflict would today be a catastrophe out of all proportion to the ends it might be hoped to attain. . . . The greatest courage and devotion would be unavailing under such circumstances, and the recent Geneva Conventions would themselves be ineffective if the belligerents were unrestricted in their choice of means and methods of warfare.

It may be true (from the lawyer's angle) that the rules governing the *conduct* of hostilities belong rather to the Hague Convention—the Laws of War—than to the Geneva Conventions. In fact, some National Red Cross Societies, somewhat close to their Governments, had questioned the competence of the International Red Cross to deal with such "political" (i.e. military) matters. But the International Committee put it squarely to all the National Societies, in sending them the draft rules, that "when existing law no longer offers sufficient protection to persons not taking part in hostilities, the Red Cross is fully justified in taking up the question". It did this, as we have seen, in the case of prisoners-of-war and, more recently, in the case of civilian inhabitants of occupied territory—matters which originally came under the Hague rules of *war*. Now, the International Committee had moved right into the centre of the Great Debate on human survival and made its own position perfectly plain for the whole world to see.

To the aforementioned brand of fatalism, the Committee had a clear answer. *Military considerations must give way to the demands of humanity*, insist these 25 Swiss citizens, now speaking for the world conscience. Furthermore, "reason must be the master of scientific inventions and, although the law cannot disregard them, it must not merely recognise the effects they produce, *it must control them*".

In presenting their new rules they were most careful to underline that the preparatory work was carried out entirely within the jurisdiction of the Red Cross itself, uninfluenced by any Government, and also that the present draft instrument is not a completed legal document, containing all the technical clauses usually to be found in an inter-governmental treaty.

To strengthen their position, before committing themselves to print, the Committee had brought together in Geneva to advise them what was undoubtedly the most varied and distinguished group of highly-qualified experts on modern warfare ever assembled under one roof, covering between them a wide range of military and medical affairs, of which the following few names are indicative: Major Richard A. Baxter, Judge-Advocate General's Office, Department of the Army, Washington, D.C.; Professor Maurice Bourquin, Professor of Law at the University of Geneva; the late Dr. Costedoat, Medical Inspector-General, Technical Adviser to the Ministry of Public Health, Paris; Dr. Juji Enomoto, formerly Instructor of the Navy Staff College, Tokyo; His Excellency Y. D. Gundevia, Ambassador of India in Switzerland; Professor La Pira, Mayor of Florence and former Senator; Dr. M. W. Mouton, of the Royal Netherlands Navy; and other specialists drawn from over a dozen countries.

These acknowledged experts, who in this way cleared the ground for the New Delhi Conference, confirmed, for a start, that certain basic rules of the Laws of War, established before aviation existed—such as those prohibiting direct attacks on non-combatants—*were still in force today*. They went further and stated that total war from the air had not "paid". They agreed that indiscriminate bombing bore "no relation either to the efforts it had cost or to the expenditure, including that of human lives, which it had involved". They recognised, too, that "military necessity" must in certain cases give way to the necessities of humanity. Finally, faced with the terrifying developments in weapons of mass destruction, they put on record their firm belief that "attempts to produce a code of rules would be all the more effective if States would agree to renounce the use of such weapons".

The 1957 Conference did not, therefore, begin where the journalists imagined they found it, but where many years of careful preparation had placed it—on the firm ground of experienced investigation about which the general public (and probably the advisers of most governments) know practically nothing. The draft rules were the subject of a long debate at New Delhi, the report of which has since been circulated—with various procedural proposals—to all the world's governments, as well as to the National Societies, so that *decisions* may be taken at the next Conference in 1963. It is, therefore, imperative that, meantime, the civilian population of this precious planet of ours should be given full and unfettered opportunity to make their voice distinctly heard, above the babel of the nuclear nihilists, on the simple question of whether they are to live or die.

It is above all clear that the whole Red Cross movement, especially the National Societies—now that the International Committee has done its own work—must take the lead in instructing and mobilising public opinion and in convincing the governments that the sands are running out and that *now* is the time of decision. Just before his recent death, Prince Frederic de Mérode, President of the Belgian Red Cross, an outstanding Red Cross personality and ardent protagonist of the new rules, declared: "The 110 million members composing the Red Cross would fail to understand its silence on such a matter. But if it is to speak, it must speak as the representative of the universal conscience of the people."

"THE CHOICE OF WEAPONS"

In that setting, we can now pass in review some of the key rules on which so much depends in the years immediately ahead, and whose implications must be obvious to the most prejudiced mind.

The first of the new rules simply states that the right of the belligerents in any conflict to injure the enemy is *not unlimited*. Fighting units must "confine their operations to the destruction of his military resources, and *leave the civilian population outside the sphere of armed attacks*". That is pretty definite. But it is merely the restatement of the well-known rule of International Law concerning non-combatants, included 50 years ago in the Hague Conventions and the other later Conventions. It has now been restated because *all* combatants in the last war flagrantly ignored it. War reduces *all* nations to the lowest denominator. A "just war", once the concept of the theologians, disappeared for ever amidst the debris of Hiroshima and Dresden and Seoul, not to forget Warsaw or Rotterdam.

"Attacks directed against the civilian population, as such," continue the rules, "whether with the object of terrorising it or for any other reason, are prohibited. This prohibition applies both to attacks on individuals and to those directed against groups." As the text proceeds, it becomes more specific: "It is also forbidden to attack dwellings, installations or means of transport, which are for the exclusive use of, and occupied by, the civilian population."

Indeed, this rule goes on to emphasise that the person "responsible" for ordering or launching an attack shall, first of all "make sure that the objective, or objectives, to be attacked *are* military objectives, within the meaning of the present rules, and are duly identified". When the military advantage to be gained "leaves the choice open between several objectives", he must select the one which involves least danger for the civilian population. Moreover, he is required to refrain from an attack if, after due consideration, it is apparent that the loss and destruction "would be disproportionate to the military advantage anticipated".

In particular, towns and other places with a large civilian population, which are not in the vicinity of military or naval operations, must be spared from attack. All possible precautions must be taken, *both in the choice of weapons and methods to be used*, to ensure that "no losses or damage are caused to the civilian population in the vicinity of the objective, or to its dwellings". The prohibition of target-area bombing is absolute and unmistakable: "It is forbidden to attack without distinction, as a single objective, an area including several military objectives at a distance from one another where elements of the civilian population, or dwellings, are situated in between the said military objectives."

A brief Article at the end outlines the procedure to be followed in case of a breach of the rules. It states that "All States or Parties concerned are under the obligation to search for and bring to trial any person

Nagasaki, 1945. The complete devastation reaches as far as the hills in the background.

having committed, or ordered to commit, an infringement of the present rules, unless they prefer to hand the person over for trial to another State or Party concerned with the case." In other words, the war criminals who defy these rules—like those designated in the 1951 Genocide Convention—are to be tried and punished.

No wonder this healthy menu, prepared by the Red Cross leaders, was too strong meat for *some* participants of the New Delhi Conference to digest! But it remains to mention that the Conference had also before it the following fundamental rule—Article 14—which can leave no doubt as to its meaning or purpose:

> *The use is prohibited of weapons whose harmful effects—resulting in particular from the dissemination of incendiary, chemical, bacteriological, radio-active, or other agents—could spread to an unforeseen degree or escape, either in space or in time, from the control of those who employ them, thus endangering the civilian population.*

RED CROSS MUST SPEAK OUT!

In introducing the draft rules, Mr. Frederick Siordet, Vice-President of the International Committee of the Red Cross, told the Conference that "the protection of civilian population will be jeopardised so long as indiscriminate attacks may be made on military personnel and civilians alike with weapons of mass destruction" and he called on all delegates to unite and state their approval of the basic principle of the draft rules. That is where the International Committee stands today.

Naturally, Article 14, prohibiting the use of weapons over whose *effects* control could not be exercised, came in for most vigorous comment. Dr. F. Janouch, President of the Red Cross Society of Czechoslovakia, however, thought that this article was not formulated with sufficient clarity and that it should contain a clear prohibition of the use of nuclear and thermo-nuclear weapons; and he was supported by the delegates of the People's Republic of China, Rumania, the U.S.S.R., Bulgaria and the German Democratic Republic. On the other hand, Ambassador Melquiades Gamboa of the Philippines said that the Conference should not go into the prohibition of nuclear weapons as there were two clear schools of thought about it, and such a problem "bristles with political implications". He wanted the retention of the right of a nation to use nuclear weapons in self-defence.

The representative of the Netherlands Red Cross, referring to the dangers of indiscriminate warfare, stated that the draft rules were of such a nature that it would be almost impossible to adhere to them, *by people fighting a war*. (As we shall see at the end of this chapter, this was the very point which the incisive mind of General Gruenther carried to its logical and practical conclusion.) But the Chilean representative announced that his country approved of the draft rules in principle. Since the same problem was being discussed by the United Nations in its Disarmament Commission, approval of Article 14 should be held in abeyance for two years and, if not accepted by the U.N. during this period, should be automatically considered to be approved. He was followed by Mr. Masutaro Inoue of Japan, who suggested that the term "war criminal" should be applied not only in the case of people of a vanquished country, but also of the country which had won the war. He also argued that the abolition of war altogether would be a great deal simpler than trying to apply the rules.

The Belgian delegate, the late Prince Frederic de Mérode, said that the question of "self-defence" had been left far behind by the draft rules. Wars were matters for governments and the Red Cross should concern itself only with peaceful solution to various problems. The issue of military defence should be raised to the moral plane. The

Red Cross must speak out in its real capacity; this great issue should be voted upon and not shelved.

Dr. Ton That Tung, leader of the Red Cross delegation from the Democratic Republic of Vietnam, struck a somewhat refreshing note when he said that the issue was not a problem for the United Nations or a problem between East and West. It was simply an issue whether certain countries were going to allow massacre of civilian populations. The Red Cross was not a military organisation and the only thing it could do was to take a *moral* stand.

Justice Emil Sandström, of Sweden, pointed out that the political aspect of Article 14 was already being discussed in the U.N. Disarmament Commission. The Red Cross had already taken decisions on prohibition of nuclear bombs and even tests, but no sides had been taken in these resolutions—only the positive feeling that something should be done for the world population in general. Under these circumstances the draft rules should be submitted *without changes* to governments for their consideration.

Interestingly enough, this procedure, which the Conference then adopted, follows very closely that of the first Geneva Conference in 1863. Some months later the Committee issued a full record of the New Delhi discussions—running to nearly 200 pages—of which the above comments are merely samples.

Thus, our story of the Red Cross ends with the National Societies and, presumably, their hundred million and more members, as well as the world's Governments, "considering" barely half a dozen pages of humanitarian rules, which, as General Alfred W. Gruenther, 38 years a professional soldier and leader of the American Red Cross delegation (who reserved his own position), correctly stated—a thought that must be in everybody's mind:

" . . . *if taken together, can be considered as virtually prohibiting the use of atomic weapons in war.*"

POSTSCRIPT

On the Strategy of Peace

A Personal Interpretation

I

AT the end of the last chapter, entitled "The Future of the Red Cross", of Martin Gumpert's classic biography of Dunant, written twenty years ago—towards the end of an armaments race which gave the competitors no security and culminated in the Second World War—appears this epitome of the life and work of the founder of the Red Cross:

> The Red Cross is the work of Henri Dunant and is part of the sum of his ideas. He thought this idea through to the end, and at the end stood the word *Peace*. It was not granted him to guide his work to this same end, but it is bound up organically and insolubly with his spirit and his fate.

The primary object of the present book has been to describe the progress and achievement of the International Red Cross during its first century. But its underlying theme has been world peace—just as it was with Dunant.

Now, at the end of our own journey, it is impossible to take our leave of the Red Cross, facing so uncertain a future, without attempting to pull together, however provisionally, the elements of a positive programme based on the humanitarian necessities of the Atomic Era. The need for a new global strategy of peace has become increasingly insistent throughout these chapters, as the peril of war has darkened. We, also, must think the Red Cross idea through to the end.

The future of the Red Cross and the future of Peace are one and the same thing. That is where our programme must start. Not a single provision in all that varied humanitarian activity envisaged in the Geneva Conventions can be put into effect under the conditions of planetary annihilation which the Nuclear Powers are preparing as fast as their resources permit—in the *name* of Peace.

227

The Red Cross cannot prepare for any "next" World War, as it prepared for the World War of 1914-18 and the World War of 1939-45. (The same war, though popularly termed "First" and "Second".) Hiroshima changed all that. A single 20-megaton hydrogen bomb *carries more explosive power than all the bombs put together that were dropped during the entire "Second" World War.*

This basically new situation has been placed before the reader, right from the Introduction, quoting the brutally frank admissions of some of the world's leading "civil defence" authorities, to the final chapter, citing the draft rules as totally incompatible with the new weapons of uncontrolled destructive power which the Nuclear Governments announce are being inserted in the war-heads of the inter-continental rockets and carried in waiting planes of supersonic speed, ready to be dropped on their human targets at fifteen minutes' notice—all round the clock.

For the first time in history, even the generals are admitting that there can be no national survival and definitely no "victory" in a nuclear war. The only "defence" now left—in exchange for the colossal expenditure of dollars and pounds and roubles by the Nuclear Powers—is that practically all the inhabitants of Britain and the United States would perish, with the possible hope that some of them might spend their last few minutes of life on this earth in exterminating most of the Russians—or *vice versa.*

The Red Cross, as we have studied its principles and practice in this book, is completely irrelevant to a future war of this kind. Not even a "decent burial" (in accordance with Article 17) would be possible for the incinerated millions of victims of this cosmic Buchenwald—there would not be enough human beings left within travelling distance to bury the corpses.

Since, therefore, it is utterly impossible for the Red Cross to *prepare* for a nuclear war, it can only *prepare* for a genuine peace.

This does not mean that its proper place in the Space Age has become less important or less vital. On the contrary, in addition to all it has so far achieved, another task of great urgency, and one requiring exemplary moral courage, has now fallen on its broad shoulders. The certitude that it cannot function in a nuclear war involves a fundamental change in its public witness.

Nor does this mean that the movement, as such, ceases to be non-political. On the contrary, it means that the movement, in rejecting the politics of race-suicide, can and will stand up to any and all "political" authorities who insist on defying world humanitarian law and the universal conscience of mankind.

What is at stake, throughout the Red Cross movement today, is the democratic ideal itself. Total war threatens the life of every man, and the Red Cross, like all other democratic institutions, will be completely destroyed once the retaliators retaliate with nuclear weapons. But the most powerful defence of Democracy is still Democracy. All mankind looks now to the Red Cross to have the integrity to stand up and be counted.

Indeed, if the Red Cross—now the facts are beyond dispute—were to truckle to any political body and give its approval, tacit or expressed, to military expediencies subversive of the world humanitarian law which it has so laboriously built up and enshrined in the Geneva Conventions, which virtually *all* Governments have ratified and pledged to uphold in their dealings with one another, then the Red Cross would become "political" in the worst sense of the term. It would betray, as an ideal, a hundred years of noble tradition and play the part of an accessory to international law-breakers, whose offences are proscribed under its own Conventions. It would, as an organisation, disintegrate like the political (i.e., military) world around it. The Red Cross stands at the crisis of its history and must stand unbroken.

"The present crisis," writes Dr. Jean-G. Lossier, "is not necessarily proof of defeat, but rather of the dire effort which it costs the human being to adapt himself to any fundamentally new condition. Struggling in the wreckage of his old world, he is nevertheless striving forward towards the world in his likeness and to his measure, which he is determined to achieve."

II

This organic shift in the frame of reference within which the Red Cross has operated for a hundred years presents a still greater challenge to the individual attitude of every one of its one hundred million and more members. Personal responsibility can never be passed on to an organisation. Today, it is impossible for any sensitive individual, who puts "humanity" first, to rest his own safety, or that of his family or his nation, upon the ability of his Government to exterminate millions of human beings at the touch of a button. There can be no "humanity" whatsoever in a system of national defence which depends on the constant threat of irretrievable disaster to the whole human race.

If the Red Cross citizen were to remain silent or indifferent while such diabolical policies were being promoted on his behalf, the very stones would cry out to his shame. His own idealism, his faith in Red Cross principles and, possibly, a long record of selfless service for his fellow men, *compel* him to tear down the evil banners of fear and mistrust which are being paraded in the name of national "security", and raise aloft in their place the Red Cross standard of courage and compassion in the name of all humanity.

Until now, the Red Cross, collectively and individually, has been able, with apparent consistency, to act like the ancient Samaritan, binding up the wounds of the antagonists after a fight—even if they could then go on to attack each other again. But the frequently met objection that the Red Cross was, in practice, primarily an ancilliary war service—and on that account tolerated and sponsored by the military—no longer holds good. For the Red Cross *cannot* heal the wounds of a nuclear war. It can only mobilise to prevent them.

The charge that the Red Cross has *assisted* the war-makers has been constantly refuted throughout its history. Yet it is most instructive to observe how the answer to that allegation has moved, over the years, from the negative to the positive, from the apologetic to the assertive. In 1863, we find Gustave Moynier, opening the first Conference with the words:

> It has been said that, instead of seeking ways to render war less murderous, we should do better to attack the scourge at the root, and work for universal and lasting peace in the world. To hear our critics, it would really seem that we are as good as trying to have war accepted as a necessary evil.

Today, however, we listen to the present Director of General Affairs of the International Committee, saying: "The foundation of the Red Cross and the first Geneva Convention—bound up inseparably with it —constituted one of the most powerful onslaughts made on war since the world began." Dr. Jean S. Pictet then concludes his recent monograph on *The Red Cross and Peace*, with this moving affirmation: *"The Red Cross is the only great idea in whose name men have never slain; it remains one of the few reasons for not losing hope; its work during many years offers the certainty and proof that love is stronger than death."*

More and more Red Cross leaders, in Europe, in the Americas, in Asia and in Africa, are beginning to accept this confident and dynamic rôle of the International Red Cross in its present historical context—none less than those whose daily activities bring them into direct contact with the young. Speaking of how "modern science has so reduced the dimensions of our planet", Dr. Goetz Fehr, Chairman of the Junior Red Cross Advisory Committee, has stated:

> It is only by recognising the magnitude of the task which falls on the younger generation that we realise how much it needs the support of universal institutions within which men can work together in a common cause. The significance of the Red Cross thus appears in a new light, all the more so in that, nearly a hundred years after its foundation, it has successfully accomplished the first stage of what might be called "negative solidarity"—a common defence against the dangers of war—and can thus assert itself as a positive and united force in the world.

Now that the scientific revolution of our times has entirely transformed the physical conditions under which the Red Cross, like all other vital institutions, must function, it must act like the modern doctor—the enemy of disease, of war—who never abandons his patient, but brings him back to health and keeps him that way. The definition of "health", quoted in an earlier chapter, from the forefront of the World Health Organisation's constitution, becomes henceforth the Peace Affirmative of the Red Cross. Here are, then, the marching orders of the rank and file of the movement—especially of the young—as it crosses the Century-mark and recruits its second hundred million:

> Peace (health) is a state of complete physical, mental and social well-being, and not merely the absence of War (disease).

It will be recalled that the WHO organised its World Health Day celebrations in 1956 around the theme *Destroy Disease-carrying Insects*, and 23 National Red Cross Societies took a leading part in the campaign in their respective countries. How long will it be, we can ask, before the whole movement thinks the Red Cross idea through to the end and celebrates Red Cross Day in every country around the theme:

DESTROY WAR-CARRYING PLANES?

III

In this Postscript, therefore, something of the positive health programme of peace for which all people are looking should be put forward, even at the risk of omitting much that is essential and leaving open some debatable issues for possible second thoughts. Not that a different basis of Red Cross policy is being urged, for Red Cross policy is permanently laid down in the Geneva Conventions, the Draft Rules, and the resolutions of its International Conferences. What is needed is world-wide enforcement of that policy by public opinion, by the will of the people in every country.

But specific guidance is plainly required by the 125 million individual members who compose the Red Cross International, in shaping the attitudes and policies *of their own governments*. As good loyal citizens of the 80 or more member-countries, this ever-growing membership has a vital part to play, within the political, educational, religious, and other social organisations of their own countries, as well as internationally, through Red Cross and other democratic movements.

How, then, is the individual Red Cross citizen to think and to act when he finds himself enmeshed in a situation, like the present, when billions and billions of dollars and pounds and roubles are being poured out on an insane arms race, which can have only one termination—*his*? At the same time—as far as he can see—every proposal for disarmament, whether sincere or insincere, is bogged down by national excuses and mistrust, mutual recriminations, and worsening rivalries—of which competitive Space projects, controlled by the military, are perhaps the most alarming and ridiculous. No visible progress results and all these recurrent failures drive up the arms budgets yet higher. Where is the "joker" in this satanic pack?

Many years of attendance at international disarmament discussions—all the way from the historic World Disarmament Conference at Geneva, in 1932, to the gatherings of the Disarmament Commission in London and New York since the war—have convinced the author of certain simple clues which go a long way to explain why *nothing happens* after all the eloquent speeches are made, and the satisfied speech-makers go back to the White House, to Downing Street, or to the Kremlin—as the case may be. (This peculiar phenomenon is examined at greater length in his book on the future of the United Nations, *Revolution on East River*, especially in Chapter IV on "Blind Man's Bluff"; but a bare summary of the chief reasons for the stalemate must suffice now.)

In the first place, there is *no hope of agreement* between the Nuclear Powers, so long as each side in the Cold War insists on presenting "disarmament" proposals—even if there is frequently a large voting majority at the U.N. for the Western side—which they know in advance the other side cannot or will not accept. These successive proposals, emanating, without exception, from security-minded politicians and professional military men, are so drafted as to convince and mollify their people *at home*, not the people against whom the proposals are aimed. As Señor Salvador da Madariaga, Spanish diplomatist and historian, who was Secretary of the League of Nations Disarmament Section, put this point so wittily when writing about the failure—incidentally, it was not Russia who was blamed in those days—of the 1932 Conference: "THEY ALL CAME TO GENEVA TO DISARM—EACH OTHER!"

In the second place, watching this continuing *impasse*, and being constantly re-assured by vote-catching politicians and a bellicose Press, ordinary citizens cannot be bothered to think the issues through and so they fall back on the escape techniques of putting their own responsibility on to some other country. At the same time, they are instigated to oppose *any* reduction in the gargantuan armaments of their own country—which are, naturally, entirely peaceful. When it is explained to them that there is no hiding place any more behind modern armaments, their reply is: "But, if we disarm, THEY will walk over us!" Each government today, carried along by the gathering momentum of the enormous military, financial and business interests which batten on its war appropriations, and backed to the hilt by a pre-atomic Press, plays on this primitive fear *motif* for all it is worth.

Such is the Human Tragedy: everybody *wants* peace, everybody *talks* peace—but everybody *plans war*.

It would be just as easy, from a purely technical point of view, to run a world-wide competition in *disarmament* as in *rearmament*—and infinitely safer. In fact, Major Victor Lefebure's brilliant study on *Scientific Disarmament*, a quarter of a century ago, laid down the proposition that disarmament is basically the same process as rearmament—but in *reverse*. Yet no one will begin putting armaments into reverse and start the long overdue competition in *disarmament*, because everyone in every country is being told by their own propagandists: "THEY will walk over us!"

In the third place, because genuine disarmament would involve so comprehensive a reorganisation of a country's economic and social

233

life, the *real* problems are played down by political leaders and newspaper editors, who prefer to take the easier and safer course (for themselves) and pass the buck to the current "critical international situation", which, they insist, must "improve" before they can do anything about disarmament. Or a whole series of elaborate technical obstacles (e.g. "iron-clad inspection"), susceptible to a score of different meanings, are thought up for every occasion when international agreement seems within sight. Or is it that the real obstructionists are naïvely waiting for Russia (200 million), China (600 million), and half a dozen other Communist countries either to dismantle their internal régimes and economic systems or to dissolve into atom dust?

IV

What does all this mean in human terms?

The present writer stayed for some time in an expanding and prospering Los Angeles suburb where, five years before, there had been only desert; and he discovered that practically every family was dependent for its existence, directly or indirectly, on the "government work" which had brought them from many far-away States to the Promised Land. "Here in Los Angeles, heart of the aircraft and missile industry," writes a troubled citizen, "there is such a concentration on weaponry that one wonders if the vast and complex economic aspect of it all could ever permit a more diplomatic approach to Russia."

That is just what more and more intelligent people in the Western world are wondering. Whole communities are rapidly being built— as everybody knows—around the new centres of war industry and thousands of young scientists are being trained for the *sole* purpose of making or discharging nuclear missiles. Yet nobody cares to ask: What is going to happen to all these peace-loving and—taken individually— harmless people who are merely following their domestic and vocational interests, if a worth-while scheme of disarmament were to be accepted and put into operation tomorrow?

For such reasons as these, the blinding spotlight of national publicity is kept focused constantly on the wrong issues. Powerful military lobbies work on every war-scare, which their editorial partners do much to provide or magnify. While the common people, who have an increasing stake in the flourishing war business, are more and more ready to believe, fed daily on slanted news, that it is always the "other fellow" who stands in the way of disarmament. Disarmament depends on somebody else—not *them*. So they can rest secure—on top of a volcano. Thus, Democracy abdicates and Fear takes control.

The truth is—since disarmament is rearmament in reverse—that elaborate planning of national production, manpower, and public finance is necessary, and should be undertaken in good time, long before any international agreement can be accepted at all. It is not the *international agreement* which is today the difficulty; it is the *national intention* which is the real difficulty. The experts, after years and years of conferences, have exhausted practically all the technical problems in arriving at workable solutions between East and West—or even between North and South, if the atomic development of the Arctic and the Antarctic should eventually lead to rival military blocs. The recent joint research project in this field, *Inspection for Disarmament*, edited by Seymour Melman (Columbia University Press, New York, 1958), confirms what every politician should know, namely, that workable systems of inspection can now be designed to ensure compliance with international disarmament agreements; and the Geneva experts have clearly indicated the general lines of a plan of inspected disarmament *technically* feasible both to Russia and the West. But what the experts can never solve is the irrational and suicidal reliance of governments on weapons which can never bring their people peace. Only the people themselves can solve that problem.

If governments were genuine in their appeals to each other to disarm, they would be acting at once themselves, at least by putting in hand the preliminary stages of disarmament, involving considerable transfers of manpower, equipment and materials to peaceful purposes, and the re-allocation of part, at least, of their gigantic war appropriations to a range of public benefits, such as improved railways and roads, new and better hospitals and schools, anti-malaria and polio campaigns, and so on. A government in earnest about disarmament would joyously initiate those important changes in national taxation which might well, in a few years, transform the living conditions of millions of its own workers, whose national output is at present being blasted away in futile competition with that of millions of similar workers in some other country. Competition in disarmament would then become a fine patriotic achievement, adding greatly to the permanent wealth of mankind, the welfare of one's own land, and the economic freedom of the individual.

Peace planning on this scale—the only scale worth considering—

must obviously be scheduled over a number of years, and, of course, carried out jointly with other nations. Fortunately, men of stature are arising in all civilised countries to break the stranglehold of the men of fear over the public mind, and give the common people hope. Grenville Clark, for example, veteran American lawyer and distinguished public servant, and Professor Louis Sohn, Harvard Professor of International Law, have set out in meticulous detail in their last brilliant work, *World Peace through World Law* (1958), the various stages through which genuine disarmament could be developed over a ten-year or longer period, with alternative proposals in case of default or delay. While on the other side of the Atlantic, the Rt. Hon. P. J. Noel-Baker, former Cabinet Minister and leading British authority on disarmament, in his impressive argument in *The Arms Race* (already noticed in Chapter I), has presented similar concrete proposals on how this urgent and gigantic "switch-over" can be made.

There are but two recent examples of the competent and independent thought that has been given to the *real* problem of disarmament by men who *believe* in it, who do not draw their opinions from the newspapers or their salaries from the war-machine. The United Nations files are, in fact, crammed to overflowing with similar expert guidance freely available to political leaders who desire to profit by it. But reluctant governments prefer to listen to their own hate-merchants and missile-men—and to play for time, time which the ordinary citizens of the world no longer have.

Too often, alas, political leaders, tired in mind or body, leave these awful decisions to place-men whose responsibility to the public at large is tenuous or non-existent. Professor Rabi, for instance, who until recently was the Chief Adviser on weapons to President Eisenhower, said that "the facts about modern warfare have just not penetrated; and that goes for the heads of governments, for otherwise they would ponder these facts every day as the daily Number One problem". The Rt. Hon. P. J. Noel-Baker is even more specific when he states: "My own experience in dealing with disarmament in Parliament is that very few people in authority have found time to read the essential documents, still less the record of what has been said by British delegates in disarmament discussions. And their speeches leave me with the feeling that they do not devote more than a *few hours a year* to the practical problems involved in armament reduction, and the strengthening of the rule of law through the United Nations."

If the Red Cross citizen has to choose between the perfunctory opinions of his own ill-informed and pre-occupied national leaders and the considered judgment of the International Red Cross on the life-and-death issues which are its paramount concern, then can there be any doubt as to where his duty lies?

V

We come now to the "inarticulate major premise", as it can be termed, of the Great Debate.

Is it, in fact, *true* that the United States and the United Kingdom, plus all the rest of the 80-odd members of the United Nations—minus the 8 or 9 Communist ones—would be "walked over" if they started the great switch from a War to a Peace economy, from national disease to international health?

The answer is again to be found in what independent and dedicated minds in *all* countries are thinking today. A representative list of their names and their pronouncements in this Postscript would multiply the length of this book many times. But on two matters they are unanimously agreed: first, a negotiated accommodation between the "West" and the Communist countries is indispensable for human survival; and, second, the Communist leaders and their peoples are at one in their desire to achieve a disarmed peace with the peoples of the "West".

It is no longer a question of "trusting the Russians"; but of trusting our own common sense. It must surely be a matter of ordinary gumption that our "enemies"—which presumably includes all their children as well—want just what we want, and they know that they can never get it by atomic death.

"I cannot forecast to you the action of Russia," declared Mr. Winston Churchill in 1939; "it is a riddle wrapped in a mystery inside an enigma; but perhaps there is a key. That key is Russian national interest." This pastmaster of the telling phrase had stumbled on the most elementary —and most overlooked—rule of international conduct. Communist "peace" propaganda may be bad propaganda; but it makes good sense. Communist leaders know—as every observant visitor to Russia or China can confirm—that gigantic atomic-energy and electrification projects, huge industrial constructions and irrigation schemes, the building of new harbours and dams, schools and sanatoria, and numerous other physical requirements of a post-atomic civilisation, cannot go ahead as these vigorous nations plainly intend, so long as precious resources of men, management, and materials are continually being drained off to prepare for a war of mutual extermination with the "West" which nobody wants. More and more competent observers, who have no political axe to grind, are therefore coming to the opinion that the initiative now rests with the United States, not with Russia. *Can* the United States switch from a built-in War economy to a genuinely "free" Peace economy? That is the overriding question which only Americans can answer.

The question which has, in fact, to be answered by the political leaders, and by the people of the "West", is not what can be done, by means of uncontrollable explosives, to "stop" nations walking over each other. In earlier chapters we saw Suez, Hungary, Jordan, and Lebanon suffering from this barbarian practice only yesterday, at the hands of the Nuclear Powers themselves. Walking-over goes on, *in spite* of the massing of nuclear armaments. Armaments, however terrifying, will never stop the walking-over of small nations. But for the United Nations' increasing ability to throw back the invaders, as it grows in strength and experience, aggression will continue to flourish and no amount of armed force will ever be able to check it.

The question which matters for the citizen, therefore, is: *In what direction are armaments moving?* If they are moving towards greater destructiveness, to greater violence, there can be no salvation for anybody. Free Worlders and Communists will die in a common grave. We shall *all* be walked over.

VI

We come, then, to the crux of the menace which threatens the so-called "West", as it equally confronts every nation. It can be simply stated, though it may shock some readers to see it put so baldly. Our real peril is not in our stars, but in ourselves. It lies in our blind belief in and constant practice of violence in international affairs. Organised violence—Militarism—is our enemy, the common enemy of the human race.

Lester Pearson, former Canadian Foreign Minister, pointed out in his *Democracy in World Politics* (Princeton, 1956), that, although no nation wants to be "walked over" and although non-violence cannot descend on the earth in a day, that is no reason for not trying to move *at once* "towards less reliance on violence, rather than more".

Violence in personal, community, and national affairs has, over the centuries, been gradually eliminated from civilised living, or, at least, reduced to effective judicial or social control. Law has steadily replaced War—law directed against the individual, *not the nation*. As we noted in reviewing the Geneva and Genocide Conventions (Chapter III), it is the individual, not the nation, who is made responsible to the law. Where violence remains in social life, it is *marginal*; the police or the courts can normally handle it. Where it ceases to be marginal it becomes WAR—or, sometimes, revolution.

This brings us back to the United Nations, and its fast-growing apparatus of peace-making, or law-making in the truest sense. As the world's modern substitute for the outworn methods of international violence, the U.N. now becomes the moral equivalent of war and the instrument of peaceful change.

Communism, doubtless, is—at least, in its recent stages of growth—an "evil" which cannot be accepted as a working philosophy or as a form of government by peoples belonging to what we call the "Western" tradition. (Though our finest "traditions"—Christianity, for example—are actually from the *East*.) There is no need to belabour this obvious truth. Nevertheless, the universal "enemy" which is certain to destroy our Western way of life altogether, from within and from without, is not something called Communism—or the Russians, the Chinese, the Czechs, and the rest of the struggling Popular Democracies—but this universal disease of *Militarism*. It threatens the Communists as much as it threatens the "West"; and it threatens all the Neutrals as well. The H-Bomb is its apotheosis.

Dr. Jean S. Pictet, in his *The Red Cross and Peace*, reminds us that "in 3,400 years of recorded history, there have been some 3,150 years of war, local or general, and only 250 of peace; while more than 8,000 peace treaties have been signed". The depressing aspect of this appalling record of man's credulity and gullibility, is that Militarism has waxed on it and expanded until it has become so respectable that it threatens to abolish the Earth, without evoking effective protest from platform, Press, or pulpit. The "peace treaties" have been, for the most part, vindictive and fraudulent, and based on force and not on consent. The years of so-called "peace" in between have, in consequence, been given over to preparation for the next war—just as we are preparing today.

Communism only comes in at the tail-end of this age-long vicious spiral. It is sufficiently amoral, or "realistic", to accept things as they are and to prepare for the *worst*—just as the "West" is now doing. It is the *war system* itself that we must eradicate; not the "isms" that thrive on it. And that can be done only by erecting a new order of world relationships in its place.

Can it be done—in time?

VII

Happily, new forces are arising to break the vicious spiral of fear. The civilised man of the West is everywhere searching in his heart and mind for a different kind of self-defence—a self-defence which will not destroy him in the process. He is slowly discovering that his official "enemies" (Russians, *ad lib.*) have precisely the same interest as *he* has in staying alive. He is beginning to see, too, that he can only survive if he is as concerned over making his "enemies" (Russians, *ad lib.*) feel as secure as he does over his own safety. Indeed, instead of seeing the surrounding world split—as all the radio-stations and editorials are telling him it is—between a "Free World" and "Communists", with a few annoying "Neutrals" who won't see the light, he discovers that the real world about him is split between the "massive retaliation" people, who imagine that peace can be maintained by the most terrible violence the earth has ever known, and the normal people, who are quite certain that it cannot be done that way and are prepared to stand up and say so.

In making this tremendous advance in his thinking, the civilised man of the West is gaining in self-confidence and joining hands with the civilised men of the East—whom he now sees are neither fools, for not joining the Nuclear Club, nor the dupes of Communism. One of the surprises which awaits many a Western visitor to India, for example, is that the Western concept of the Iron Curtain is strangely absent. A glance at the map alone should have made it clear that "behind the Iron Curtain" is a geographically meaningless phrase for Eastern peoples, who compose more than half the human race. In fact, the coming of the East—so rapidly—into the Western orbit, is beginning to make nonsense of many of the shibboleths on which yesterday's "military necessity" still stakes its outmoded claim to unquestioning obedience as the most autocratic power on earth.

Finally, the civilised man of the West finds that, in defending Western values and Democratic ideals against the assaults of the missile-men, it is not Communists who become his true allies, but the untapped moral forces of the re-awakening Asia and Africa. These are now his partners in ultimate victory over those same powers of violence which have distorted and corrupted *both* the Western and the Communist forms of government alike.

Typical of this stimulating and health-giving partnership with the fast-expanding "neutral" world, heed might be given to one such Eastern leader, engaged on the superhuman task of rebuilding a vigorous multi-racial nation from scratch, who plainly tells the West: "As a man, a father, an Asian, and a human being made in the image of God, I am appalled at the cynicism of those who wield atomic weapons." President Sukarno of Indonesia, a hard-headed champion of human freedom, addressed an open letter to the leaders of the Nuclear Powers in June, 1958, and concluded his appeal to them thus:

> *There can be no question now of the West giving moral leadership to Asia.* Your moral leadership has, for us, meant first colonialism and now the philosophical, moral, political and social bankruptcy of a nuclear arms-race. . . . You are losing the battle for the hearts and minds of men.

VIII

Here, then, in the last few pages of this book, we are back with Dunant, thinking the Red Cross idea through to the end, when he tells us that although, for the time being, the Red Cross had necessarily to act the Samaritan in war, ultimately it had to become the doctor in peace. That time has now arrived.

The New Delhi Conference demonstrated that the East had, for the most part, already made that transition, and were waiting for the West to catch up. For the East, the Free World *versus* Communist parody had broken down—or never existed—under the human necessities of our united world. Once again, the Red Cross had reached through the temporary man-made barriers and called on its defenders to fight their common enemy, WAR, instead of each other.

The counsels of the Eastern leaders, as we have noted, reflected not only the thinking of Dunant—one of the first true Europeans—but also that of the great philosophers and religious teachers who have preached the universality of peace down the centuries. This ageless "new approach" to the conduct of each country's foreign relations had thus become the paramount mission of the Red Cross as a universal movement, knowing no frontiers. The next step was clear to everyone—difficult though it might be for some to take, especially for the unimaginative West—and this was to win the response of the recalcitrant governments before the 1963 Conference in Geneva.

In two ways, specifically, this powerful and dedicated hundred-and-a-quarter-million strong membership—linking all nationalities and all faiths and all ideologies—might well become the irresistible shock-troops in the fight on a world-wide front to translate the Red Cross ideal into the substance of the reluctant governments' policies. The means of achieving this might indeed be "political"; but its incentives, like its practical results, are unquestionably humanitarian.

First, then, the original concept of *neutrality* in the midst of rival militarisms, on which the Red Cross founded its triumphant work on the battlefield, has now taken on a wider application, and its political implications have to be honestly faced. Non-involvement, as a positive attitude, has already spread in less than a decade over most of the peoples of the Far East—except where Western or Communist strategists had already staked out their rival positions—and has given our own divided Europe a new hope and a new perspective. It is futile to close one's eyes to these dynamic innovations for the sake of preserving outworn labels. Neutralisation—or "phased disengagement", as some authorities call this unmistakable trend in European policy—is in essence an extension of the security or "safety" zones which Dunant first devised on the spot during the Franco-German War. It means, for example, that the withdrawal of the Russian occupation forces in Central Europe is phased with the dismantling of the West's military bases, alongside the "neutralisation" of Formosa, and similar dangerous cross-roads, where the rival power blocs are striving for an illusive supremacy. The details of World Peace Operation cannot be pursued here; but its outlines are emerging every day.

History has, of course, provided many earlier examples of zones of successful disengagement, and the Geneva Conventions have since given them the authority of International Law. The long-awaited recent Austrian Peace Treaty, for instance, is based firmly on this essential Red Cross principle. For nearly ten years, years of despair and unsettlement and the increasing danger of dismemberment—such as fell to the lot of less fortunate Korea—Austria remained torn between the rival antagonisms of the "victors" of the war, each manoeuvring to keep

Austria on its side. But, at last, Austria has been neutralised by mutual consent, and its neutrality guaranteed by International Law. Its people can breathe again. What can be done for a single country can be done for a whole continent.

This same basically Red Cross concept of disengagement or non-involvement—already put into practice long ago by democratic Finland and, largely, by Sweden, both neighbours of Russia, and even more so by permanently neutral Switzerland—is winning wider support in every country as the most workable policy for a united Germany and a peaceful Europe. How Dunant would have rejoiced to see the principle he fought for so hard and so consistently, all through his life, now adopted by nation after nation!

As we have seen, too, non-involvement grows in strength throughout the Middle East, where determined leaders, who have been trained for the most part in Western political thought and democratic practices, also find their countries menaced by the rival imperialisms on both sides of them. They are rejecting *both* Communism *and* Militarism, simply because they want to be left alone under their own imperfect, but rapidly evolving, forms of government, rather than disappear as pulverised pawns in the mortal game of military prestige played by the Nuclear Giants.

It should be obvious that, for some years ahead, the Middle East will remain disturbed and uncertain; leaders and governments are bound to change—violently or otherwise. Frontiers also may change in a vast region notorious for artificial boundary-lines drawn, for the most part, to suit the defence strategy of the Great Powers, not for the benefit of the people most concerned. But gunboat diplomacy will not elect stable governments nor foreign troops guarantee the flow of oil to Western markets. Whatever political, economic or social changes are inevitable, in this fast-growing area of the earth, the one thing which is *certain* to fail is outside intervention by military force. The United Nations is both the forum and the instrument of peaceful adjustment; and its Charter is the only valid authority for necessary aid from foreign governments, co-operating to ensure that its principles are upheld.

It is, therefore, foolhardy of the Western Powers to pretend that they can continue to "protect" the expanding destinies of Europe, the whole Far East and, especially, the Middle East, by military methods. The cracking of the Cold War alliances and the failure of conference after conference to mend the widening cracks, is proof of the futility of trying to run a Copernican system in an Einsteinian universe.

There is no longer excuse for any Red Cross citizen to ignore these elemental realities. His whole creed is based on the concept and practice of neutralisation, and a hundred years of experience convinces him that it works. He wants to see safety zones progressively extended —and acknowledged as such by both sides of the Cold War—not merely across Central Europe, pushing the nuclear threat farther and farther back, but he wants even more the neutralisation of the whole wide earth. Then, and only then, Man can enter into his rightful heritage and plan for LIFE!

IX

The second way in which the whole Red Cross membership can help build the permanent defences of peace is to insist all the time that the United Nations economic and social organisations—which are *acting* on the Red Cross ideal of "Above all Nations is Humanity"—are provided by their Governments with the sinews of peace that are so badly needed. Manifold experiments in world co-operation are at present starved of adequate finance and personnel and are refusing urgent demands every day, simply because of their limited resources. The Special U.N. Fund for Economic Development (SUNFED), for example, has been postponed year after year because of lack of finance from the Nuclear Powers. It could be put magnificently on its feet by a contribution of *less than one per cent* from the world's present arms budgets.

Intimately linked with the Red Cross movement, as this book has stressed, all the humanitarian agencies of the U.N. must receive financial and material aid in order to transform them into the permanent institutions of peace which this planet can no longer do without. Bringing together different systems of government and varying economic outlooks into a workable—even if as yet ill-defined—form of *international* democracy, the Specialised Agencies, based on the U.N. Charter, provide the most effective answer to the threat of the totalitarian philosophies, on the one hand, and to the moral bankruptcy of the West's foreign policies, on the other hand.

This approach also naturally carries with it the recognition that a re-vitalised United Nations could never shut out, on ideological or political grounds, large areas of mankind, because their form of

244

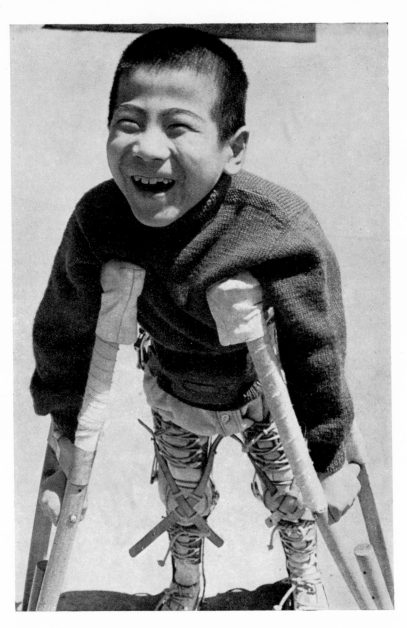

Target for Today.

The boy Shigenori—see pages 145–6.

government is disliked by some elements in the Western world. The Red Cross has never been interested in a man's politics. Humanity knows no favourites. The foundations of World Government, which mankind would now seem to be trying to lay down, can rest secure only on the Red Cross ideal of UNIVERSALITY.

X

It has been said that never before had any Utopia been realised with such astonishing rapidity as the dream of Henri Dunant. Utopia has become the only practical politics for today. Either the Great Society lives by the ideals and practices of the Red Cross, or it disintegrates along with them.

Coming back, therefore, to the heart of the Red Cross idea, no other way is now left to meet the challenge of the present hour than the course indicated by Leopold Boissier, President of the International Committee, in these simple words: "We must have faith in man's repentance, we must believe in the power of Right."

This means that there must be forgiveness—forgiveness for anyone whom "we" imagine has so injured "us" that he or his system has to be broken by physical violence or utterly destroyed by military strength.

For our world community cannot start all over again. We cannot have a clean slate given to us, with all the wicked Communists or Capitalists or Imperialists eliminated and only the "good ones" (us) left, to—

Take this sorry Scheme of Things entire
And shape it nearer to the Heart's Desire!

We have to start where we are *now*. Unless there is forgiveness, there can be no hope. Unless there is faith, there can be no survival. Without love, we perish.

Bending over the aggressor, and would-be conqueror, Dunant gently reminded the fear-ridden peasant woman: "The enemy is—A MAN."

That is where the Red Cross began. That is where War will end.

APPENDIX A

GENEVA CONVENTION OF AUGUST 22, 1864

FOR THE AMELIORATION OF THE CONDITION OF THE WOUNDED IN ARMIES IN THE FIELD
(*Official Text*)

ARTICLE I

Ambulances and military hospitals shall be recognised as neutral and, as such, protected and respected by the belligerents as long as they accommodate wounded and sick.

Neutrality shall end if the said ambulances or hospitals should be held by a military force.

ARTICLE 2

Hospital and ambulance personnel, including the quarter-master's staff, the medical, administrative and transport services, and the chaplains, shall have the benefit of the same neutrality when on duty, and while there remain any wounded to be brought in or assisted.

ARTICLE 3

The persons designated in the preceding Article may, even after enemy occupation, continue to discharge their functions in the hospital or ambulance with which they serve, or may withdraw to rejoin the units to which they belong.

When in these circumstances they cease from their functions, such persons shall be delivered to the enemy outposts by the occupying forces.

ARTICLE 4

The material of military hospitals being subject to the laws of war, the persons attached to such hospitals may take with them, on withdrawing, only the articles which are their own personal property.

Ambulances, on the contrary, under similar circumstances, shall retain their equipment.

ARTICLE 5

Inhabitants of the country who bring help to the wounded shall be respected and shall remain free. Generals of the belligerent Powers shall make it their duty to notify the inhabitants of the appeal made to their humanity, and of the neutrality which humane conduct will confer.

The presence of any wounded combatant receiving shelter and care in a house shall ensure its protection. An inhabitant who has given shelter to the wounded shall be exempted from billeting and from a portion of such war contributions as may be levied.

ARTICLE 6

Wounded or sick combatants, to whatever nation they may belong, shall be collected and cared for.

Commanders-in-Chief may hand over immediately to the enemy outposts enemy combatants wounded during an engagement, when circumstances allow and subject to the agreement of both parties.

Those who, after their recovery, are recognised as being unfit for further service, shall be repatriated.

The others may likewise be sent back, on condition that they shall not again, for the duration of hostilities, take up arms.

Evacuation parties, and the personnel conducting them, shall be considered as being absolutely neutral.

ARTICLE 7

A distinctive and uniform flag shall be adopted for hospitals, ambulances and evacuation parties. It should in all circumstances be accompanied by the national flag.

An armlet may also be worn by personnel enjoying neutrality but its issue shall be left to the military authorities.

Both flag and armlet shall bear a red cross on a white ground.

ARTICLE 8

The implementing of the present Convention shall be arranged by the Commanders-in-Chief of the belligerent armies following the instructions of their respective Governments and in accordance with the general principles set forth in this Convention.

ARTICLE 9

The High Contracting Parties have agreed to communicate the present Convention with an invitation to accede thereto to Governments unable to appoint Plenipotentiaries to the International Conference at Geneva. The Protocol has accordingly been left open.

ARTICLE 10

The present Convention shall be ratified and the ratifications exchanged at Berne, within the next four months, or sooner if possible.

In faith whereof, the respective Plenipotentiaries have signed the Convention and thereto affixed their seals.

Done at Geneva, this twenty-second day of August, in the year one thousand eight hundred and sixty-four.

Argentina	. . . 1879	Mecklenburg-Schwerin .	1865
Austria	1866	Mexico	1905
Baden	1864	Montenegro . . .	1875
Bavaria	1866	Netherlands . . .	1864
Belgium	1864	Orange Free State . .	1897
Bolivia	1879	Panama	1907
Brazil	1906	Papal States . . .	1868
Bulgaria	1884	Paraguay	1907
Chile · . . .	1879	Persia	1874
China	1904	Peru	1880
Colombia . . .	1906	Portugal	1866
Congo	1888	Prussia	1865
Cuba	1907	Rumania . . .	1874
Denmark . . .	1864	Russia	1867
Dominican Republic .	1907	Salvador	1874
Ecuador	1907	Saxony (Kingdom of) .	1866
France	1864	Serbia	1876
German Empire . .	1906	Siam	1895
Great Britain . . .	1865	South African Republic	1896
Greece	1865	Spain	1864
Guatemala . . .	1903	Sweden and Norway .	1864
Haiti	1907	Switzerland . . .	1864
Hesse	1866	Turkey	1865
Honduras and Nicaragua	1898	United States of America	1882
Italy	1864	Uruguay	1900
Japan	1886	Venezuela . . .	1894
Korea	1903	Wurtemberg . . .	1866
Luxemburg . . .	1888		

APPENDIX B

GENEVA CONVENTIONS OF AUGUST 12, 1949

A brief Summary, and List of Ratifications, prepared by the
INTERNATIONAL COMMITTEE OF THE RED CROSS, GENEVA

(The Roman figures in brackets refer to the Number of the Convention;
the Arabic figures indicate Articles.)

GENERAL RULES COMMON TO THE FOUR CONVENTIONS

Once armed conflict breaks out, the Conventions shall be applicable in all circumstances (2).

In case of civil war or internal strife, certain essential principles at least must be observed (3).

The following are prohibited at all times and in all places: the taking of hostages, execution without regular trial, torture, and all cruel and degrading treatment (I–IV, 3; I, II, 12; III, 13; IV, 32, 33).

Reprisals on persons protected by the Conventions are forbidden (I, 46; II, 47; III, 13; IV, 34).

No one may renounce or be forced to renounce the protection accorded him by the Conventions (I–III, 7; IV, 8).

Protected persons must at all times be able to have resort to a Protecting Power (the neutral State responsible for safeguarding their interests), and to the International Committee of the Red Cross, or any other qualified humanitarian agency (I–III, 8, 9, 10; IV, 9, 10, 11).

I. Geneva Convention for the Amelioration of the Condition of the Wounded and Sick in Armed Forces in the Field.

II. Geneva Convention for the Amelioration of the Condition of Wounded, Sick and Shipwrecked Members of Armed Forces at Sea.

The *wounded and sick* of armed forces must be respected and protected in all circumstances. There must be no attempt on their lives or violence on their persons. They must be aided and cared for (I, 12, 15).

251

The *shipwrecked* shall be similarly treated (II, 12, 18).

Belligerents must treat the wounded, sick or shipwrecked members of enemy forces taken prisoner as they do their own (I, 12, 14; II, 12, 16).

The dead must be collected and their bodies protected against robbery (I, 15; II, 18).

Bodies must be identified before burial and death confirmed, if possible by medical examination (I, 16, 17; II, 19, 20).

Everything which serves for the care of the wounded and sick shall, in their interest, be respected and protected—namely: personnel, establishments, vehicles, and medical supplies belonging to the military Medical Services, the National Red Cross or other Relief Societies—and shall be indicated by the emblem of the red cross on a white ground.

Medical and religious personnel includes: (a) persons responsible for the care and transport of the wounded and sick, and for the prevention of disease (doctors, orderlies, nurses and stretcher-bearers); (b) the administrative staff of medical establishments and units; (c) chaplains (I, 24–27; II, 36, 37).

Such personnel shall wear an armlet with a red cross, and carry an identity card (I, 40; II, 42). They may bear arms for their own defence and that of the wounded (I, 22; II, 35).

If medical and religious personnel fall into enemy hands, they shall be allowed to continue their duties towards the wounded and sick (I, 19). Personnel whose retention is not indispensable to the care of prisoners shall be repatriated (I, 30, 31; II, 36, 37). Those retained shall not be considered as prisoners of war and shall have wide facilities for their work (I, 28).

Civilians may not be prevented from giving care and shelter to the wounded and sick, whoever they may be, and shall not be penalised for doing so; they must on the contrary be aided in this work (I, 18).

Medical units and establishments shall include all buildings or permanent installations (hospitals, stores, etc.), or mobile units (ambulances, field hospitals, tents, open-air installations, etc.) used exclusively in collecting and caring for the wounded and the sick (I, 19).

They may not be attacked or damaged, or prevented from operating even if, for the moment, they do not contain either wounded or sick (I, 19).

The same shall apply to medical vehicles: ambulances, lorries and trucks, hospital ships, lifeboats, medical aircraft, etc. (I, 35, 36; II, 22–27, 38, 39).

Medical equipment (stretchers, medical and surgical appliances and instruments, medical supplies, dressings, etc.) must never be destroyed, but must be left at the disposal of the medical personnel, wherever they may be (I, 33, 34; II, 28, 38).

The *emblem of the red cross** on a white ground, symbol of aid to the wounded and sick, shall be used to designate buildings, staff, and material entitled to protection. It may not be otherwise employed and must at all times be scrupulously respected (I, 38–44; II, 41–43).

III. Geneva Convention relative to the Treatment of Prisoners of War.

Members of the armed forces and assimilated personnel who fall into enemy hands shall become prisoners of war (4). They shall then be in the power of the enemy State, but not of the individuals or troops who have captured them (12).

Prisoners of war are entitled in all circumstances to humane treatment and to respect for their persons and their honour (13, 14).

They shall all be treated alike; privileged treatment may be accorded only on grounds of health, sex, age, military rank or professional qualifications (16).

Prisoners of war, if questioned, are bound to give their name, first names and age, rank and army number. They may not be compelled to give other information (17).

They shall be entitled to retain their effects and articles of personal use. The enemy may impound their military equipment, except articles of clothing and feeding utensils. Sums of money and valuables may not be taken from them except against receipt, and must be handed back at the time of release (18).

Prisoners of war shall in general be subject to the discipline and the military code of the capturing State (called the Detaining Power) (39, 82–88). For security reasons, their liberty may be restricted, but they may not be imprisoned unless for breaches of the law (21). Before sentence, they must have the possibility of stating their case (96, 99, 105, 106).

The Detaining Power shall supply prisoners of war free of charge with adequate food and clothing, provide them with quarters not inferior to those of its own troops, and give them the medical care their state of health demands (15, 25, 26, 27, 30).

---

* Some Middle East countries use the red crescent in place of the red cross; in Iran (Persia) the red lion and sun is used.

Prisoners of war, with the exception of officers, may be obliged to work. They shall receive pay; working conditions shall be equal to those of nationals of the Detaining Power. They may not be compelled to do military work, nor work which is dangerous, unhealthy, or degrading (49–54).

When taken prisoner, they shall be enabled to advise their next of kin and the Central Prisoners of War Agency (International Committee of the Red Cross). Afterwards, they may correspond regularly with their relatives, receive relief and be attended by clergymen of their own religion (33, 70, 71, 72).

They shall be entitled to elect a spokesman (prisoners' representative), who shall act for them with the authorities of the Detaining Power and with welfare organisations assisting them (79).

They shall have the right to address complaints and requests to representatives of the Protecting Power who are authorised, as are Delegates of the International Committee of the Red Cross, to visit the camps, and talk with them either directly or through their representative (78, 126).

The text of the Convention must be posted up in each camp, so that prisoners may at all times ascertain their rights and duties (41).

Prisoners of war certified seriously ill or wounded shall be repatriated, but may not afterwards take up active military duties (109, 117).

At the end of active hostilities, prisoners must be released and repatriated without delay (118).

IV. Geneva Convention relative to the Protection of Civilian Persons in Time of War.

A civilian is defined as a person who does not belong to the armed forces and takes no part in hostilities. Civilians may never be attacked; they shall be respected, protected, and at all times humanely treated (3, 27). They shall be entitled at all times to correspond with their relatives (25).

Civilian wounded and sick, civilian hospitals and staff, and civilian ambulances shall be the object of particular respect and may be placed under protection of the Red Cross emblem (16–22).

Unless security reasons forbid, civilians in enemy territory must be allowed to leave (35). If they do not leave or are retained, they shall be treated in the same way as aliens in general (38). If security reasons make their internment imperative, they shall have the right to appeal, and to have their case impartially reviewed (41–43).

The civilian population shall, so far as possible, be enabled to continue as usual (47). The Occupying Power shall be responsible for the maintenance of public order (64).

Deportations and transfers of population shall in general be prohibited (49). Every compulsory enlisting of manpower shall be subject to strict regulation. Persons under eighteen years of age are entirely excepted, and enlisted workers may not be forced to do labour which would make them participate in military operations (51). Pillage and unnecessary destruction of property are forbidden (33, 53).

The Occupying Power shall be responsible for the welfare of the children (50), the maintenance of the medical and health services (56), and the feeding of the population (55). It shall allow the entry of relief consignments, and facilitate their transport (59–62). In general, the authorities, administration, and public and private institutions shall continue to function (54, 63, 64).

The Occupying Power has the right to defend itself against acts hostile to its administration and the members of its armed forces (64). It may introduce special laws in this connection (64). It may try accused persons before its own tribunals, but no sentence may be pronounced without regular trial (66). It may, for imperative security reasons, intern certain persons (78). All these measures are, however, governed by explicit provisions and subject to the supervision of the Protecting Power (65–77, 78, 136, 137, 143).

Civilians in enemy territory and the inhabitants of occupied territories have certain rights in common.

They are in all circumstances entitled to respect for their persons, their honour, family rights, religious convictions and practices, and their manners and customs. They shall at all times be humanely treated (27); no coercion shall be exercised against them (31). Women shall be especially protected against any attack on their honour, and, in particular, against rape and any form of indecent assault (27).

These civilians shall have the right of free resort to the Protecting Power, the International Committee of the Red Cross and the National Red Cross of the country where they may be (30). The representatives of the Protecting Power and of the International Committee shall be able to visit them freely (30, 143).

The enemy Government shall be responsible for the treatment given them by its officials or military personnel (29).

Finally, should they be interned—a measure which cannot be taken as a form of punishment—they shall be entitled to treatment which shall in general, and taking into account the fact that they are civilians, be analogous to that of prisoners of war (79-135).

FOUR GENEVA CONVENTIONS OF AUGUST 12, 1949

List of Ratifications and Accessions (in chronological order)
(In some cases with Reservations)

No.	Country	Date of ratification	No.	Country	Date of ratification
		1950			**1953**
1	Switzerland	31 March	24	Japan	21 April
2	Yugoslavia	21 April	25	Salvador	17 June
3	Monaco	5 July	26	Luxemburg	1 July
4	Liechtenstein	21 September	27	Austria	27 August
5	Chile	12 October	28	San Marino	29 August
6	India	9 November	29	Syria	2 November
7	Czechoslovakia	19 December	30	Vietnam	14 November
			31	Nicaragua	17 December
		1951	32	Sweden	28 December
8	The Holy See	22 February			
9	Philippine Islands	7 March			**1954**
	(1st Conv. only)		33	Turkey	10 February
10	Lebanon	10 April	34	Liberia	29 March
11	Jordan	29 May	35	Cuba	15 April
12	Pakistan	12 June	36	Union of Soviet	10 May
13	Denmark	27 June		Socialist Republics	
14	France	28 June	37	Rumania	1 June
15	Israel	6 July	38	Bulgaria	22 July
16	Norway	3 August	39	Ukrainian Soviet	3 August
17	Italy	17 December		Socialist Republic	
			40	Byelorussian Soviet	3 August
		1952		Socialist Republic	
18	Union of South Africa	31 March	41	Netherlands	3 August
19	Guatemala	14 May	42	Hungary	3 August
20	Spain	4 August	43	Ecuador	11 August
21	Belgium	3 September	44	German Federal	3 September
	Philippine Islands	6 October		Republic	
	(2nd, 3rd and 4th		45	Poland	26 November
	Conventions)		46	Thailand	29 December
22	Mexico	29 October			
23	Egypt	10 November			

No.	Country	Date of ratification	No.	Country	Date of ratification
		1955			1957
47	Finland	22 February	61	Iran	20 February
48	United States of America	2 August	62	Haiti	11 April
			63	Tunisia	4 May
		1956	64	Albania	27 May
49	Panama	10 February	65	Democratic People's Republic of Vietnam	28 June
50	Venezuela	13 February			
51	Iraq	14 February	66	Brazil	29 June
52	Peru	15 February	67	(North) Korea	27 August
53	Libya	22 May	68	Great Britain and Northern Ireland	23 September
54	Greece	5 June			
55	Morocco	26 July	69	Sudan	23 September
56	Argentine Republic	18 September			
57	Afghanistan	26 September			1958
58	Laos	29 October	70	Dominican Republic	22 January
59	Democratic Republic of Germany	30 November			
60	People's Republic of China	28 December			

A SHORT READING LIST

BARTON, Clara	A Story of the Red Cross	Appleton & Co (New York) 1904
DAVISON, Henry P.	The American Red Cross in the Great War	Macmillan (New York) 1919
DULLES, Foster Rhea	The American Red Cross: A History*	Harper & Bros. (New York) 1950
DUNANT, Henri	A Memory of Solferino	Cassell (London) 1947
GUMPERT, Martin	Dunant—The Story of the Red Cross	Oxford University Press (New York) 1938
HART, Ellen	A Man Born to Live*	Gollancz (London) 1954
HUBER, Max	The Red Cross: Principles & Problems	Kundig (Geneva) 1942
HUBER, Max	The Good Samaritan	Gollancz (London) 1945
HURD, Charles	The Compact History of the American Red Cross*	Hawthorn Books (New York) 1959
JORDAN, Ella	Operation Mercy	Frederick Muller (London) 1957
LOSSIER, Jean-G.	Fellowship: The Moral Significance of the Red Cross	ICRC (Geneva) 1958
PEACEY, Belinda	The True Book About the Red Cross*	Frederick Muller (London) 1958
PICTET, Jean S.	Red Cross Principles	ICRC (Geneva) 1956
PICTET, Jean S.	The Red Cross & Peace (Pamphlet)	ICRC (Geneva) 1951

BRITISH RED CROSS SOCIETY:
  The Proudest Badge* (Pamphlet, revised by Belinda Peacey)
  Handbook for Branches (Pamphlet)
  Quarterly Review

AMERICAN RED CROSS SOCIETY:
  American National Red Cross—Its Origin, Purposes, and Services
  The American Red Cross—A Brief Story (beginnings to the War in
    Korea) (Pamphlet)
  This is the Red Cross (Pamphlet)
  For the Common Weal (Report on international activities (Pamphlet))

INTERNATIONAL COMMITTEE OF THE RED CROSS:
  Geneva Conventions (Illustrated Pamphlet)
  The International Committee of the Red Cross (Pamphlet)
  Report on the Relief Action in Hungary (1957)
  International Review of the Red Cross* (Quarterly)

LEAGUE OF RED CROSS SOCIETIES:
  The League of Red Cross Societies, Its Foundation, Organisation,
    Programme (1958 Edition)
  The Red Cross in Pictures (1958)
  Handbook of the International Red Cross (Texts of the Geneva Con-
    ventions, resolutions of the International Conference, Statutes, etc.)
    (1954 edition)
  Universality in Action (1952-1956 Report)
  Hungarian Refugee Relief (1958)
  The Red Cross World* (Quarterly) Official organ of the League
  Junior Red Cross Newsletter* (Quarterly)

----

*The above list consists of publications in the
English language only*

Especially recommended for general reader (see page 9)

Index

Rebellion, *see* Civil war
Rebirth of the Near East, 28
Red Cross and Peace, The, 104, 230, 239
"Red Cross and the Prevention of War, The" (article), 4
Red Cross Principles, 116
Red Cross World, The, 124
Refugees, *see also* Civilians
  Austria, in, 147, 175
  Hungarian Revolt, in, 171, 175
  Jordan, in, 147
  Lebanon, in, 147
  Syria, in, 147
  UN High Commissioner for, 120, 125, 147, 175, 214
Religious personnel,
  armlets of, 65, 248, 252
  arms, bearing of, 65, 252
  Conventions of 1949 and, 65–77, 252
  identity card, 65, 69, 252
  neutrality, of, 65, 247
Repatriation Commission, Neutral Nations, 205
"Report on the Study of Non-Military Defence", 5
Research Development Corporation, 5
Revolution on East River, 214, 232, 271
Riggs, Professor Robert E., 198–200
Rougé, B. de, 120
Rousseau, Jean-Jacques, 2, 33, 142
Roux, Professor Emile, 120
Ruegger, Paul, 112
Russia,
  Brest-Litovsk, Treaty of, and 105
  Convention of 1929, and, 137
  Genocide Convention and, 76
  "germ warfare" allegations, 7
  Human Rights, Declaration of, and, 76
  Hungarian Revolt and, 168–76
  International Committee and, 137
  Junior Red Cross in, 165
  Korea and, 198
  New Delhi Conference, and, 214–5
  prisoners-of-war, and, 73, 137
Russo-Turkish War, 54

ST. ANDREW'S UNIVERSITY, 109
St. John of Jerusalem, Order of, 71, 91
Salenick, Emilia, 165
Salle de la Réformation, Geneva, 35
Sandström, Justice Emil, v, 212–3, 226

Saxony, Prince of, 50
Scantlebury, Mrs. G. C., 216
Schweitzer, Dr. Albert, 30–2
Scientific Disarmament, 233
Seishi Ryogo En (Tokyo hospital), 145
Shigenori (Japanese boy), 145–6, 245
Shipwrecked, the,
  care of, 252–3
  Conventions of 1949 and, 65–77, 251–3
  treatment of, 65
Sick, the, *see* Wounded and sick
Siordet, Frederick, 224
Smuts, General Jan, 105
Social Contract, 142
Sohn, Professor Louis, 236
Solferino, Battle of, 13–18
Souvenir de Solférino, 19–20, 40, 88
Spanish Civil War, 115
Special Relief Committees, 39
Story of the Red Cross, A, 94
Stowe, Harriet Beecher, 24
Study of War, A, 76
Sudan Red Crescent, 156
Suez conflict,
  Britain and, 74
  Conventions of 1949, and, 177–9
  Danish Red Cross and, 180
  Egyptian Red Crescent and, 178–83
  prisoners-of-war in, 178–9, 181–2
  refugees during, 177, 181, 183
  relief supplies, 180
  UNEF and, 177, 182
  wounded and sick in, 182–3
Sukarno, President, 241
SUNFED, 28, 244
Swiss Red Cross, 215
Syria, refugees in, 147

TAIWAN, *see* Formosa
Telecommunications Union, International, 36
Thudichum, Mr. M., 179
Times, The, 5, 90, 219
Ton That Tung, Dr., 226
Tour, Mrs. Maria, 216
Tracing Service, International, 139
Transports, Foundation for the Organisation of Red Cross, 139
Traz, Mr. de, 189–93
True Book About the Red Cross, The, 51, 115
Tumendelger, Mrs. Damdin, 216

Biographical Note on

JAMES AVERY JOYCE

The Author of *Red Cross International* is an international lawyer, economist, and educator. A graduate of the University of London, he has frequently worked in Geneva on international projects close to the Red Cross. One time on the staff of the International Labour Office in Geneva and a Consultant at the Economic and Social Council of the United Nations in New York, he has also lectured on international relations at leading Universities and colleges across three Continents. He is author of a number of popularly-written books, including *Justice at Work*, on the human side of the law in England, *World in the Making*, being the story of international co-operation told for teenagers, and *Revolution on East River*, on the future of the United Nations.